The Political Economy of Public Sector Governance

This book provides a general, nontechnical introduction to core ideas in positive political theory as they apply to public management and policy. Anthony Michael Bertelli helps readers to understand public sector governance arrangements and their implications for public management practice outcomes. By offering a framework that applies to specific administrative tasks, *The Political Economy of Public Sector Governance* allows readers to think clearly about many aspects of the modern administrative state and how they fit into a larger project of governance.

Anthony Michael Bertelli holds the C. C. Crawford Chair in Management and Performance in the USC Price School of Public Policy and the USC Gould School of Law at the University of Southern California. He is the author of *Madison's Managers: Public Administration and the Constitution* (with Laurence E. Lynn, Jr.) as well as more than thirty scholarly articles and serves as co-editor of the *Journal of Public Policy*.

The Political Economy of Public Sector Governance

ANTHONY MICHAEL BERTELLI

University of Southern California

CAMBRIDGE UNIVERSITY PRESS
Cambridge, New York, Melbourne, Madrid, Cape Town,
Singapore, São Paulo, Delhi, Mexico City

Cambridge University Press
32 Avenue of the Americas, New York, NY 10013-2473, USA

www.cambridge.org
Information on this title: www.cambridge.org/9780521736640

First published 2012

Printed in the United States of America

A catalog record for this publication is available from the British Library

Library of Congress Cataloging in Publication data
Bertelli, Anthony Michael.
The political economy of public sector governance / Anthony Michael Bertelli.
p.   cm.
Includes bibliographical references and index.
ISBN 978-0-521-51782-9
1. Public administration.   2. Government accountability.   I. Title.
JF1351.B478   2012
351–dc23   2011048918

ISBN 978-0-521-51782-9 Hardback
ISBN 978-0-521-73664-0 Paperback

For Dad and Aunt Nora

Contents

Preface

Public administration does not fit neatly within a democratic setting. Madison argued that government would not be necessary "if men were angels." Likewise, there would be no problem with public management in a constitutional democracy if bureaucrats, contractors, and all others were faithful agents of positive authority. That this is not the case leads directly to the political creation of multifarious institutions that shape, restrict, enable, and motivate the way in which public management is practiced in democracies. This book is about that shaping, restriction, enabling, and motivation. It aims to introduce a political–economic approach to public administration to students at the advanced undergraduate, master's, and doctoral levels. My hope is that it will also serve applied researchers in public management and allied fields who would like to get an accessible overview of core ideas driving this type of research.

I have thought about writing this book for a very long time. Many conversations over the years have made it possible. Many discussions occurred in the halls and offices of places at which I have studied and worked and at a wide variety of conferences and events. This book profited over time from the comments of Evelyn Brodkin, Duncan Snidal, Carolyn Heinrich, Ed Jennings, B. Dan Wood, Ken Meier, Eric Gonzalez Juenke, Jeff Lax, Randy Calvert, Steve Kelman, Matt Flinders, Perri 6, Alan Hamlin, Chuck Shipan, Francesca Gains, Larry O'Toole, Ed Kellough, Tony Bovaird, Stu Brettschneider, Charlie Wise, Chris Skelcher, Jamie Carson, Beth Garrett, Dan Carpenter, Shui Yan Tang, Chris Redfearn, Nicole Esparza, Lisa Schweitzer, Elizabeth Graddy, David Suarez, Forrest Maltzman, Michael Bailey, Kevin Quinn, Matthew

Stephenson, Brint Milward, David Leal, Don Moinyhan, M. Jae Moon, Bert Rockman, Steve Page, Chuck Cameron, Chris Berry, Jeff Yates, and Tonja Jacobi. I absorbed your insights while standing in office doorways and the Palmer House lobby; sharing meals and many, many cups of coffee; writing down your discussant comments; and reading your e-mails. I regret forgetting anyone, though doing so is inevitable.

The ideas in this book were the focus of more involved discussions with Chris Kam, Tom Hammond, Sean Gailmard, Gary Miller, Christian Grose, Dave Lewis, George Krause, Steve Balla, Peter John, Jack Knott, Larry Lynn, Sven Feldmann, Dan Mazmanian, Hal Rainey, Hank Jenkins-Smith, Bill West, and Jim Rogers. Your time and energy on these topics were precious to me. The Georgia Political Economy Group – especially its core members, Bob Grafstein, Keith Dougherty, and Scott Ainsworth – provided a wonderful forum for discussion of and important thoughts on the approach in this book. I owe a special debt of gratitude to my dear friend and colleague Andy Whitford, who has helped my thinking about the material in this book more than anyone.

Thanks are due to Christian Grose, Stephane Lavertu, Larry Lynn, David Suarez, George Krause, Lilliard Richardson, Craig Smith, Shui Yan Tang, and Patrick Warren for comments, data, and assistance on various parts of the manuscript. Dyana Mason and Jennifer Connolly provided invaluable research assistance, particularly in relation to Chapters 5 and 6. Jessica Bull, Rachel Dolan, Philip Marcin, and Mary Ellen Wiggins also provided valuable research assistance. Aubrey Hicks, assistant director of the Bedrosian Center for Governance and the Public Enterprise, provided excellent administrative assistance as the book project came to a close.

Several courses have used some part of the material presented in this book. I thank master's students in several public administration and democracy courses at the University of Georgia, business and public policy courses at the University of Southern California, and democracy and administration courses at the University of Manchester for their engagement of this material.

My editors at Cambridge University Press, Ed Parsons and Robert Dreesen, were fantastic. Robert deserves a special note of thanks for his encouragement to write the book I imagined and his support for my project through each stage.

Finally, I am thankful to Tamaron Jang, whose love for churros left an indelible mark on Chapter 4. Her support and caring have helped me through much more than this project. The holidays were wonderful this year.

You have all made this book better. Thank you.

I

Introduction

Democracy means rule by the people. In a democracy, administration must be constructed in such a way that it serves the people through their elected representatives. The connection between the public and any given administrative action may be quite distant, but it must be in place. Accountability of public management to the popular will may be weak or attenuated, but the arrangements might be justified on other grounds. In any event, the problem of connecting the public with administration must be confronted. It is quite possible that some members of the polity, fully believing in the democratic process, disagree with an administered decision that is without democratic defect. In other words, even with democratic accountability, what government produces may not be the policy you want.

Such conflict creates a problem of governance. Consider an administrative decision to require a ten-day advance notice for the purchase or renewal of a fishing license. The casual fisherman may well disagree with such a rule as it reduces the possibility of a spontaneous outing. However, the administrator who makes the rule does so under formal authority granted by the elected representatives of the people, including the fisherman. If economic or environmental considerations such as overfishing prevail in justifying the ten-day rule, the opposing interest of the fisherman may not serve the people in a more general sense. Yet the complete absence of popular accountability, as through abdication of the responsibility of elected officials for environmental policy, presents a trade-off between some socially beneficial or efficient use of resources and direct accountability. Introducing a theoretical framework for resolving such problems is the subject of this book.

Our study of the political economy of public sector governance has two primary purposes. The first is explanation: it provides readers with a means for understanding public sector governance arrangements and the implications they have for policy outcomes. The apparatus of the administrative state is vast and complex in modern democratic societies. There are many reasons for this, from the expansion of federal administrative powers in the New Deal to the creation and expansion of welfare states by postwar governments in Europe to the technological sophistication of modern regulation and public service provision. An outdated view of the administrative state is one of large, centrally controlled bureaucracies whose formal and informal structures promote accountability to the people and technocratic rationality. The theories we engage help us understand the way in which administration shapes public policy without overreliance on bureaucratic principles. Our second purpose is design. The book offers a coherent way of thinking about how best to organize governance. A complex web of private contractors, nonprofit organizations, and public officials provide the public services as well as making and enforcing the regulations on which we have all come to rely. Any valuable conception of public sector governance must be rooted both in the vast array of tasks undertaken by the modern state and the means by which these tasks are connected to the people through their elected representatives. By offering a framework that can be task specific, this book allows readers – scholars and public managers alike – to think clearly about elements of the administrative state and how they fit into a larger project of governance. In short, this is a public policy book that treats administration seriously.

1.1. SOME BUILDING BLOCKS

To evoke complex realities in a tractable way, the theories synthesized in this book rely on a specialized language. It begins with *institutions* – rules or norms that shape and constrain human behavior – as its basic element. A stop sign, priority seating for the elderly on a bus or train, the means of renewing passports online, and our hypothetical ten-day rule for fishing licenses are all institutions. They affect behavior not through force but by inducement or incentive. A sign indicating priority seating informs transit passengers of the nature of the regulation. When a young person stays in such a seat while elderly passengers stand, informal social pressures, sneers of disgust from other passengers, and the threat of enforcement by the driver or conductor make that experience risky. These inducements may be insufficient to make the seat available for the elderly passenger. The theories we discuss seek to find the right balance of information and enforcement to compel the youth from the priority seat.

Large government bureaucracies, nonprofit organizations, and private firms contracted to perform public services are all organizations. *Organizations* are collections of institutions that permit collective action; namely, they allow many individuals to act with one purpose. This is central to a rational connection between the means and ends of *public policy*, which can be defined in general terms as efforts to change or maintain the status quo in society. Congress, the Executive Office of the President, the courts, state legislatures, and international bodies such as the United Nations and the European Union are likewise organizations. We claim that organizations do this by creating institutions to incentivize individual behavior. By viewing the problem of governance in these basic terms, we can think of bureaucratic structures as well as modern networks of regulators, service providers, and stakeholders both within and beyond the formal boundaries of the state in the same way. Incentives commit individuals in these organizations to a common purpose that is democratically connected to the polity. Elected officials define the ends of policy, while administration attends to the means. Both shape public policy.

Postwar public administration scholars in the United States have decried this politics–administration dichotomy as unrealistic, and it is now accepted that administrators engage in a politics of their own, shaping the ends as well as the means. The theories we review accept that politics and administration are interrelated, uncovering incentives for democratic control over policy in the presence of administrative politics – when administrators and politicians alike seek to determine who gets what, when, and how. Politics is a process for achieving policies. Responsibility to the public in this environment is achieved through a mixture of formal rules and informal norms inside and outside the state. We shall refer to these mixtures of institutions as *mechanisms*, or incentive mechanisms. Institutions, organizations, and mechanisms are featured on every page of this book.

Institutions do not define behavior in an absolute sense but rather shape that behavior by creating incentives. People and organizations need not respond to them. For one particular youth on our hypothetical train, sneering provides insufficient inducement to get him out of the priority seat, and enforcement action from the driver may be required. Another young person might rise while offering profuse apologies. The more complex an organization becomes, the more variety there is in the individual characteristics of its membership. Complex organizations in the context of governance, such as bureaucracies, are enticing to study precisely because of this diversity and the impact they have on governance.

New institutions are not fashioned from whole cloth but depend on other institutions that predate them. This means that the history of institutions is always important. When key actors believe that organizations and institutions are underperforming, institutional change results. Interest in reform is generated because institutions impose costs on individuals governed by them. The priority seating rule comes not without its costs; younger people who are very tired may stand, or the seats may remain empty on a crowded bus, reducing passenger safety by forcing too many people to stand. Organizations create institutions to surmount collective action problems and to achieve collective decisions. Costs are imposed by institutions within an organization like Congress – senators can place holds on nominations that can stall or effectively end the process through an internal congressional rule, for instance – and the laws that organization creates impose costs on citizens like us. These costs, often related to the dissemination of information, will be important throughout the book.

Modern governance can be defined in a simple but powerful way. Governance is constituted by the tasks the state performs for its citizens and the institutions that incentivize the performance of those tasks. The public's desire for clean water, the democratic acceptance of that task by the state, and the incentive mechanisms – statutes, administrative rules, contracts, adjudicatory processes – by which the water is made, more or less, cleaner are all a part of contemporary public management. A mechanism is neither good nor bad from a political–economic perspective. Polluting firms may refuse to respond to incentives in the Clean Water Act, allowing water in a specific lake to remain toxic, or they may dramatically curtail their behavior in a way that dramatically improves water purity measures. In this book, we will ask why that mechanism provided incentives that led to one outcome or another. With the exception of Section 6.1, we avoid normative statements, but rather focus on developing positive theories or descriptions of the processes by which budgets are allocated, powers are delegated, administrative rules are made, that invite empirical testing. Doing so provides readers with a lens through which to examine governance problems they encounter and study.

We begin our study by looking at an example of an institutional arrangement that affects the manner in which corporate accounting is conducted in the United States. This provides a context in which to develop a concise definition of what we mean by governance. We will develop many theoretical ideas in this book in context, that is, by working through examples. Educational psychologists recognize that providing information in this way helps readers devote their attention to relevant considerations rather than to irrelevant ones that tax the memory and weaken understandings of the ideas being conveyed (e.g., Wittwer and Renkl, 2010). This is particularly important for the professional students who are the core audience for this book. These readers bring substantial contextual expertise to our present study but are interested in how the material helps to explain and design governance in practice. The presentation of theoretical ideas is carefully designed to move them toward this goal. It allows readers to consider the ways in which these ideas complement other frameworks for the study of governance toward the goal of a broader understanding of the topic.

We also consider public management reform movements in this chapter. These movements have at their roots a desire to change public regulatory and service provision mechanisms. In them, we find the spirit of many of the ideas in this book as well as a measure of the practical importance of understanding positive theories of governance. This is certainly not to say that these reforms have been successful in producing the policies that the public wants most; rather, it suggests that reformers, and individual public managers on smaller scales throughout public service, are interested in creating and adapting mechanisms to produce policies that change the status quo in one way or another.

The chapters that follow provide public managers with a framework for thinking about such problems. It is far from monolithic. In fact, traditional public administration scholarship shares questions and logic with our framework. We will make explicit comparisons at various points in the book, such as the beginning of Chapter 3 and in Chapter 6, but the connections between the people and public administration should always be in the reader's mind as she engages the ideas we discuss. We also make comparisons between the political economy of public sector governance and other schools of public management thought in Section 1.4. Political–economic reasoning can uncover aspects of governance arrangements left hidden by competing theories. As such, it is an essential implement in the toolkit of modern students and practitioners of public management. Nonetheless, we must not forget that the apparatus that modern public management scholars and practitioners employ when confronting governance problems is broader. Other ways of thinking about governance cannot be neglected.

1.2. DEFINING GOVERNANCE

The complex piece of legislation known as the Sarbanes–Oxley Act of 2002 (SOX) was directed at "improving the accuracy and reliability of corporate disclosures made pursuant to the securities laws" (116 Stat. 745). The origins of this legislation lie in one of the most shocking scandals in American corporate history, the fall of Enron. One of the central problems that emerged in the collapse of Enron was the nature of the relationship between auditors, such as then accounting giant Arthur Andersen, and their clients. Auditors had been endorsing questionable claims of earnings and assets made by Enron that in the end proved disastrous to shareholders. For example, Enron would create what appeared to be an independent company, call it A, into which banks and investors placed money. Enron would then sell some of its own assets to A, collecting the money invested in A. On its balance sheet, Enron would call this money income (debt to A, however). Because Enron executives made decisions for both A and Enron itself, they were in a position to guarantee investors' returns while inflating Enron's financial health in public reports endorsed by auditors and government regulators (McLean and Elkind, 2003).

Addressing this kind of regulatory problem requires solutions to a series of *collective action* problems. Collective action problems arise when uncoordinated actions of individuals and organizations result in outcomes that could be improved for all involved. First, legislation aimed at policy change must get auditors, business executives, commodities and securities traders, and various other actors to set aside the conflicts of interest arising from their different roles – and the rewards they receive from performing those roles – in the financial sector and provide information that will alert regulators to Enron-style problems. Regulators must have the capacity to enforce rules designed to stop these problems when detected. Thus SOX is a mechanism designed to elicit accurate information from these actors and enforce a set of rules that implement a policy, namely, to save the public from the dramatic losses due to corporate corruption.

The idea behind SOX was to revitalize the investing public's confidence in corporate performance reports by enhancing the role of government regulators in ensuring that such reports provided accurate, fair *information* about true performance that is independent of the interests of the corporations themselves. Information is knowledge achieved through communication. SOX provided for the creation of the Public Company Accounting Oversight Board (PCAOB), a quasi-governmental organization charged with overseeing the auditor–corporation relationship.[1] PCAOB has broad authority to officially register corporate auditors; to set rules (institutions) for auditing standards and ethics; to inspect auditors; to investigate auditors for potential violations of its rules, securities laws, or both; and to impose fines on, suspend, or bar auditors from practice (Nagy, 2005, 2). In its attempts to ensure the quality of information that investors have about the companies in which they place their money, the PCAOB is given *enforcement* power, or authority to compel the adoption of its standards and the securities laws.

From a mainstream public management perspective, PCAOB may seem like a remedy for failed public management in the Securities and Exchange Commission (SEC) and other administrative agencies. Lawyers may see it as a regulatory scheme that displaces some judicial authority over regulating accounting practices. Political economists see PCAOB as an institutional solution to a collective action problem. Its coordination of accounting practices may improve the situation of investors and corporations. The availability of information and the threat of enforcement create incentives that advocates of SOX hope will prevent another Enron from emerging. Political–economic tools allow us to determine whether the legislation really incorporated an incentive design capable of preventing such behavior on the part of corporations. Although multiple perspectives are important to understanding such problems, the consequence of viewing modern public sector problems from multiple perspectives has been confusion about the very subject of their study: governance.[2]

---

[1] http://pcaobus.org/. The insulation of the audit activities from the president was the subject of constitutional litigation in *Free Enterprise Fund v. Public Company Accounting Oversight Board*, 130 S. Ct. 3138 (2010). The initial structure of PCAOB was designed to make a credible commitment to accounting oversight in the wake of the aforementioned scandals. To facilitate this, Congress set up a structure in which the board was under the oversight of the Securities and Exchange Commission (SEC). Because the president could not remove from office the head of the independent SEC, and because SOX did not grant the SEC head the ability to remove PCAOB members, the Supreme Court determined that the president could not exercise his constitutional obligation to execute the laws. PCAOB members can now be removed at will. This case deals with the difference between independent and executive agencies, which we discuss in Chapter 4.

[2] Rhodes (1997, 47) alone notes six different definitions of the concept. Lynn (2010, 3) categorizes definitions in the governance literature into three classes: "(1) governance as synonymous with government and its role in societal steering; (2) governance as synonymous with 'good government' or 'effective governing' in the public sphere; and (3) governance as an emerging model of societal steering 'beyond government' which involves both an expanding role for civil society institutions in directing and regulating the uses of

We claim throughout this book that each *governance task* – some function that government chooses to perform, for example, enhancing the accuracy and fairness of corporate information – has information and enforcement components (see, generally, Dixit 2004). These elements form the basis of the incentives that flow to all actors involved in a substantive policy area such as financial regulation. Would-be corporate malfeasants find that SOX has made sham transactions like those described earlier more risky and potentially costly. At the same time, more innovative means of presenting corporate performance in falsely positive light may go undetected. But honest business actors face increased costs of complying with laws they have no intention of violating. Concentrating informational (regarding both transmission and acquisition) and enforcement authority in the PCAOB makes that organization powerful as well as open to corruptibility from the companies and auditors it regulates. Public money must be spent in increasing amounts to fund the PCAOB's operations, bringing that body under the watchful eyes of legislators, organized interest groups, and citizens. Reductions in public funding might make PCAOB members think differently about enforcement, possibly increasing fine collection to offset decreases in operational funding. These and other temptations are among the incentives created by SOX that must be understood to evaluate its design. They are capable of inducing further institutional change and organizational restructuring. For instance, the PCAOB itself created an Office of Internal Oversight and Performance Assurance to monitor its own information and enforcement activities. Creating one institution or set of institutions – such as those associated with the PCAOB – may generate incentives sufficient to solve one problem while exacerbating or creating others.

As a single governance task is undertaken, the institutional environment in which it operates changes and becomes more complex. If we begin with a single governance task and consider the implications of the larger structure in which it is undertaken, for example, the U.S. separation-of-powers system, the elements of our conception of governance become clear. The distribution of governance tasks includes all things in which the modern state is involved, from corporate financial regulation to

public resources and greater reliance on deliberative, as opposed to representative, forms of democracy." The political economy of public sector governance requires a definition in the first category. Treatments in the second and third categories make it difficult to differentiate the normative from the positive and are, in my view, unconvincing as a consequence.

foster care to trash collection. Thus we focus on the tasks themselves but also on the processes and consequences of aggregating these tasks into administrative agencies and broader governmental operations.

The logic of governance in this book is straightforward. A governance task is any activity that a society directly entrusts to a state or that the state takes on after congealing clues about public preferences regarding a policy. The substantive domain of the state, in a broader sense, contains an aggregate of governance tasks. This captures the notion that no clearly identifiable person or group is the sovereign authority in a modern democratic state (Skinner, 1989). We define *governance*, then, as the sum of governance tasks in the domain of the state. The summation of governance tasks has implications, as does their grouping in a single society. It implies trade-offs – regulated markets for, state provision of, or no state involvement with an important public service, for example – for policy makers. Understanding governance means understanding the incentives policy makers face when making those trade-offs. Mainstream public management scholars focus on what are termed *structures of governance*, or institutional arrangements that are generated when policy makers respond to incentives and make trade-offs. For instance, Lynn et al. (2001, 7) define structures of governance as "regimes of laws, rules, judicial decisions, and administrative practices that constrain, prescribe, and enable the provision of publicly supported goods and services." Structures represent the myriad mechanisms created and implemented to incentivize collective action around a governance task and require no separate treatment in our approach. This has obvious implications for policy and administrative design. Consider the observation in a leading treatment of the topic that "if you want to get governance 'right' you need to manipulate the structures within which it is presumed to be generated" (Pierre and Peters, 2000, 22). In our synthesis, structures of governance are means toward an end; the end is the performance of the state's governance tasks, and that is governance itself.

The work of governance lies in designing and implementing the incentives necessary to coordinate individuals to act to further democratic policy goals. Because these incentives determine who gets what, when, and how, they are the subject of considerable debate among practitioners, scholars, politicians, and organized interest groups. They are also the foundation for a politics of public management. The tools we develop can help us understand and evaluate a broad range of proposals to change the way government does business. Because informing the design of governance is a goal of this book, it is important to consider the way in which our approach helps in understanding reform proposals. Such proposals are fundamentally about designing institutions and incentive mechanisms.

1.3. POLITICAL ECONOMY AND REFORM MOVEMENTS

As a graduate student at the University of Chicago in the late 1990s, I was introduced to reform movements in the United States and abroad that changed the intellectual agenda of public administration. These reforms provoked sometimes fiery commentary from those who claimed, among a great many other things, that the movements had neither solid theoretical foundations nor empirical support nor a recognition of the value of the administrative process to democracy. Nonetheless, public management scholarship has been profoundly changed because of the intellectual challenges that these movements presented. The reforms were undergirded by the core ideas presented in this book, and the theoretical foundations for modern public management research owe a great deal to the intellectual pulling and hauling that occurred in response to the challenges of political and managerial reform throughout the years.

An essential element in these public management reforms has been *administrative efficiency*, or a general desire for the public sector to manage its resources well. In *Reinventing Government*, Osborne and Gaebler (1992) argued that the systems of government – from budgeting to personnel – were flawed. Existing government mechanisms provided little incentive for cost-effective solutions to public service problems. The hierarchical organizations that emerged from the New Deal and Great Society eras and postwar European social welfare states were overburdened with procedures to the point of dramatic inefficiency. "To be effective today, an organization must be lean, fast on its feet, responsive to its customers, capable of adjusting to constant change, [and] able to improve productivity continually," wrote Osborne (1993, 351). Government should be entrepreneurial; public managers should find the best uses for the public funds with which they are entrusted. Government should "steer rather than row." This meant that public managers would be given performance targets and resources by policy makers and would face strong incentives to efficiently marshal those resources to attain their objectives. This proposal – goals coupled with flexibility for managers to meet them – is an incentive mechanism, and it has led to a profound reshaping of institutional and organizational arrangements worldwide.

Advocates of what came to be called the new public management (NPM) sought to design incentives to reform public administration into an efficient and responsive system. Boston et al. (1996, 26) list the key features of NPM:

1. Public management should change the notion of accountability from adherence to a process to the achievement of objectives.
2. This notion of accountability means that public policy goals should be delegated to public managers who have flexibility to manage as they see best but who must provide information to political superiors on their progress through enhanced monitoring and reporting mechanisms.
3. These changes will move governance from "large bureaucratic structures into quasi-autonomous agencies" given appropriate incentives to use resources efficiently and creatively to meet policy objectives.
4. When providing public services, contract-based incentives as well as those arising from competitive markets or bidding are preferred to bureaucratic processes.
5. Incentives for providing public services should be as explicit and strong as possible. If long-term relationships with providers generate weak incentives for meeting policy goals, they should be changed.

These principles begin to suggest a way to approach thinking about governance, namely, the substance of what the state does. We touch on each of them in the chapters that follow because they are informed by the political economy of public sector governance. Reform movements create a great many proposals for governance design, some of which exemplify just how radically the kinds of theories we discuss can influence thinking. Consider, for example, proposals for the improvement of analytic advice – policy analysis – to policy makers in the New Zealand national government. The internalization of policy advisers into bureaucratic agencies, a hallmark of the New Deal era in the United States, was challenged as "insufficiently contestable and placing public providers (especially departmental policy analysts) in a relatively privileged position" (Boston et al., 1996, 137). In other words, reformers claimed that the quality of policy advice could be improved by establishing a competitive marketplace of ideas. Boston et al. (1996, 137) note that "a number of radical proposals have been suggested [whereby] government agencies would be required to compete for contracts to supply policy outputs (or output classes)...creating an open market in which public and private organizations would compete, on more or less equal terms, for contracts to supply policy outputs." If successful, such efforts might ultimately displace policy-analytic staff within existing government agencies. The key to the politics of this proposal lies in who provides advice to inform public policy. Because expertise is associated with a limited set of people, it may be that a similar cast of advisors provides similar information from different organizations. The question for governance is thus not simply one of efficiency but rather how the new institutional arrangements change the character of information that underlies public policies. We pay close attention to such issues in this book.

The tides of reform reshaped the provision of services that had been the province of bureaucratic discretion for many years. The uninitiated reader should now be gaining perspective on the extent of administrative overhaul that NPM-style reforms inspired. Like all reforms, such changes will be measured by the outcomes they produce. It is nonetheless important to understand whether changes in public sector institutions proposed by reformers are even possible from a design perspective and, if so, whether the performance gains they advocate are realistic. Such is the need for the analytic tools we review in the chapters that follow. As we progress through the material in this book, we shall develop theoretical tools that permit a thorough understanding of the design and implications of reform proposals. These tools can help practicing public managers to think through efforts to reform their own workplaces.

The public management literature is infused with strong normative judgments about NPM because of how it changes prevailing practices. Readers will see that some NPM reforms represent an extreme position that is inconsistent with the implications of various theories we review. Because NPM encourages public administration to be designed to promote efficiency and innovation in performing governance tasks while preserving the core values that a democratic public requires of it, the political economy perspective is essential to evaluating the designs it inspires. This perspective sometimes shares and at other times challenges alternative approaches to governance in the public management literature. The next section compares and contrasts the political–economic approach with a few competing frameworks for analyzing governance problems. It is not meant to be a comprehensive review but rather to provide a taste of these literatures and how they work together with the political–economic approach to inform governance design and explanation.

1.4. POLITICAL ECONOMY AND PUBLIC MANAGEMENT

The claims we have made in this chapter, as simple as they are, form the building blocks of a political–economic approach to the study of governance that has implications far beyond the public sector (e.g., North, 1990; Williamson, 1985, 1996). Before comparing this perspective with alternative approaches, it is useful to review key elements in the logic of the political economy of public sector governance that we have been building to this point:

1. The state commits to performing certain tasks for the benefit of the public.
2. These governance tasks present certain incentives to and impose certain costs on the state, beneficiaries in the polity, and constituent groups.
3. When these tasks are aggregated, we have a portrait of governance itself.
4. The design of each governance task involves the design of incentive mechanisms and depends on a history of institutions and organizations. It is the central problem of public sector governance.
5. Efficient and effective institutional design is an essential role for public managers.

The public management literature overflows with conceptual frameworks meant to aid researchers and practitioners. This is to be expected and is valuable given the need for scholars to communicate with practitioners. That said, I find some of these frameworks difficult to employ and others unduly limiting in providing options for policy makers. The remainder of this section compares and contrasts the approach of this book to three of these alternative frameworks. This section is not a comprehensive review, but it does provide the flavor of competing views of governance.

The *tools of governance* approach addresses the question of why the state arranges governance as it does (Hood, 1983; Salamon and Elliott, 2002). Write Pierre and Peters (2000, 41), "the basic argument of the tools approach is that the means through which governments choose to govern will not only affect the outcome of the policy area, but will also have a number of secondary effects on the economy and society." No institution can be created entirely anew (see Riker, 1993). The effects of a given institution on other institutions and organizations are of paramount concern; governance works like a system, with changes in one institution inducing ripple effects across tasks (North, 1990). In this respect, our framework shares fundamental ground with the tools approach.

A second important design question is whether the state can improve on its governance arrangements. The primary task of the tools approach is to classify institutional choices available to the state and its decision makers. For example, Hood (1983) maintains four metacategories of policy tools.[3] The first category, authority instruments, encompasses the kinds of institutions we associate with regulation and the regulatory state – a set of quasi-legislative tasks in which rules (institutions) are made that impact classes of individuals and organizations. Second, treasure instruments are institutions that provide financial incentives to individuals and organizations and, in some cases, direct transfers of resources. The third group of tools, nodality instruments, includes institutions that impart nonpecuniary incentives on individuals and organizations. Government information campaigns – "Just say no to drugs" to steer youth away from addictive behavior or "Click-it-or-ticket" to encourage compliance with seatbelt laws – are examples of such tools. Finally, organization instruments involve direct action by the state in the provision of services, law enforcement, and so forth.

Our approach accepts the availability of all these tools but also attends to the design of new tools appropriate to specific governance tasks. Each of the theories we discuss provides some insight into the propriety of one tool as against another given the objective of the public sector decision maker. Rather than categorizing the tools available to perform governance tasks, we ask which tool, existing or possible, is optimal given that task. We describe the incentives flowing from extant tools and provide a structured way to think about innovating new ones.

Another class of claims in contemporary public management thought deals with the role of managers once they are charged with performing governance tasks, for instance, after they accept a contract. To contextualize the work that they do, public managers must consider the ways in which the governance tasks affect the social order and help achieve collective benefits. In other words, public managers have a role in enhancing *civil society*, defined by Putnam (1995, 664–665) as "features of social life that enable participants to act together more effectively to pursue shared objectives." He continues; "To the extent that . . . norms, networks, and

---

[3] Weimer and Vining (2005) provide a perhaps more comprehensive list of policy instruments.

trust link substantial sectors of the community and span underlying social cleavages . . . the enhanced cooperation is likely to serve broader interests and to be widely welcomed."

On this view, public managers play an important intermediary role between government and the civil society. They both "transmit information and resources from the state to civil society [and deliver] demands from actors in civil society back to the state" (Pollitt and Bouckaert, 2004, 12). Such a role for public management expands the tools available for the performance of governance tasks because "strong organizations can be used to develop partnerships and to provide an infrastructure through which government can operate . . . rather than being competitive with government the structures in civil society are seen to be complementary and cooperative" (Pierre and Peters, 2000, 38). Incentive design is essential to this role, and Chapter 5 takes on such issues directly.

If doing the best possible job of designing institutions is our goal, then the institutions generated by the state to undertake governance tasks should respect and engage existing nongovernmental institutions to the extent that they permit better policy design. Whatever one makes of the proposal, this was the motivation for the New Zealand policy analysis reforms. Good agents, as we shall see in Chapter 4, can lead to better policies. As a consequence, the theories we explore in this book are quite conscious of the concerns of the civil society literature. Political economists have more recently developed a body of theory that addresses a central gap in neoclassical theories that view the state as the primary, but benevolent, coercive force in society. In those theories, government constructs institutions to improve social welfare. From the political economy perspective, Dixit (2004, 3) asserts that "economic activity does not grind to a halt because the government cannot or does not provide an adequate underpinning of law. Too much potential value would go unrealized; therefore groups and societies have much to gain if they can create alternative institutions to provide the necessary economic governance." In other words, the institutions in civil society – whether good or corrupt or somewhere between – may complement or even substitute for institutions in the state. The many accrediting bodies of U.S. colleges, universities, and their programs, for instance, act as nonstate regulatory schemes for the quality of higher education. We address the question of whether it is appropriate to rely on or induce change in societal institutions at the task level.

A third theme in modern public administration scholarship related to the problem of incentive design has been named the *new governance*.

Essentially, the new governance refers to a set of claims that reject top-down control and influence patterns associated with the bureaucratic state and focus precisely on the kinds of strategic interactions that we address in this book. The notion of hierarchical government comprising agencies that perform narrowly circumscribed tasks in isolation from political influence is neither illustrative of nor a constructive way of thinking about the contemporary public sector.

A leading advocate of the approach argues that modern governance is essentially an amalgamation of social and political responses to a more complex world. Governance, on this view, is a complex set of interactions in which the state is not ultimately the source of authority but "facilitator and ... cooperating partner" with other organizations in society (Kooiman, 1993, 3). In this book, facilitation and cooperation are examined through choices that state and nonstate actors make when implementing a governance task. We devote attention, first, to the incentives that these choice scenarios present and, second, to simplifying the complex environment that new governance scholars observe. The principal tension between our approach and that of the new governance is the extent to which the essential features of this complex environment can be abstracted to gain analytic traction. We shall see that the benefit of abstraction is the clarity of the incentives that can be illuminated and the breadth in mechanisms and governance tasks that can be examined. As a result, our theories can appear simplistic against the richer, but narrower, institutional portraits in the new governance literature. This does not make them flat-footed. The virtues of parsimony lie in our ability to assess a wide variety of institutional arrangements in a unified way. It is not elegant explanation for its own sake.

As with the tools and civil society approaches, and many other approaches not discussed in this brief review, our claims will be both complimentary and challenging. The broader goal of all study in public sector governance is to understand the way in which the state serves the people. The political–economic perspective we enlist is often dismissed by other schools of thought as unduly reductionist and overwrought with difficult assumptions. At times, it is also challenged as ideological. An important goal of this book is to make the political–economic approach available to doctoral students, scholars, and practitioners unfamiliar with or confused about what it brings to the project of understanding contemporary governance. Questions of designing and understanding governance are global, timely, and important. I hope in some small way to encourage readers into debate about this important set of issues.

1.5. PLAN OF THE BOOK

This introductory chapter developed a language and framework that is used in the rich literature we engage. In each of the substantive chapters that follow, a variety of institutions, organizations, and mechanisms in public sector governance are presented. The level of discussion throughout the book is meant to be intuitive but not simplistic. Along the way, we address classic problems in public management by situating them within a political–economic framework. The book proceeds from the basic structure of government to some important issues faced by contemporary public managers and then to normative questions regarding the right kind of administrative state.

Political economy allows us to look at incentives, institutions, and organizations to describe what is going on and to anticipate what incentive mechanisms will do to change policy. Because of its implications for both explaining and designing governance, this is one of the most practical courses of study that a contemporary student of public management can take. However, the theories discussed in this book are largely born from formal, mathematical models of governance problems and have been inaccessible to many students and practitioners. To ease the nontechnical reader into the style of argument used in political–economic theorizing, the next chapter presents more foundational terminology and a logic that will be at work throughout the book. It begins with the principal–agent model, the central tool in political–economic modeling of governance problems. Two related categories of models, signaling and screening, are then discussed. Taken together, these more generic frameworks provide the mechanics behind the substantive claims in the rest of the book.

Part I of the book synthetically reviews a theoretical framework. The relevant literature is vast, and this book does not intend to review it synoptically. My intent, rather, is a presentation that evokes major themes. This inevitably involves choices, and many interesting and evocative works are not considered. As a guide to the broader literature, Appendix B offers a variety of recommended readings. Evocative contributions to the literature are explained in Chapters 3 and 4. In the context of the budgetary process, we develop a political–economic view of the use of resources as incentives to maintain democratic accountability. This chapter introduces a variety of auditing models that have been useful in examining a host of public sector governance arrangements. Chapter 4 turns to questions of the delegation of powers and the creation of organizations that perform governance tasks. In so doing, the chapter introduces a class of delegation models that have also been useful in understanding modern public management in a democratic setting.

Part II illustrates the value of the theoretical framework we have developed for examining questions of collaborating to perform governance tasks and for enhancing the responsibility of public managers charged with their performance. Chapter 5 examines relationships between the government and service providers in an environment of increased public sector contracting and cross-sectoral partnerships. Chapter 6 makes the normative claim that responsible public management entails a balancing of competing interests, good judgment, accountability of decisions through an ultimate electoral connection, and a rational direction of means toward ends. We also examine two mechanisms that governments have designed to assess responsibility in the performance of governance tasks. We thus close by connecting the theories we have engaged to the role of public management in democratic societies. The conclusion synthesizes our discussion and calls for the political economy of public sector governance to become part of a broader scholarly dialogue among public managers and those who study them.

2

Methodological Foundations

When we make assumptions about the behavior of individuals and institutions, we can make predictions about their behavior in a variety of situations. These situations may even include counterfactuals – what-if scenarios that did not occur in practice – allowing us to understand why particular actions were not taken. It is certainly appealing to be able to do this, but our assumptions must be tenable to make our claims reasonable. We will come to understand that all good theories capture the processes by which the phenomena we observe are generated. Good theories are not simply explanations of one event at one time.

The type of theorizing we discuss in this book is known as *rational choice theory*. Because this type of thinking about social phenomena may be new to some readers, it is worthwhile to very briefly review some basic concepts of rational choice before moving on to the types of models used to describe governance arrangements.[1]

Individuals are the basic units of all the theories described in this book. These basic units might also be *organizations*, which, for reasons that we shall describe in connection with theories presented in later chapters, are considered to act in the same way as would individuals. Individuals have *preferences*. This means that an individual values, or prefers, one legislative proposal, political candidate, or project over another. Each proposal, candidate, or project is called an *alternative*. Some sets of alternatives are more or less continuous, such as a tax rate or budgetary allocation, so choices are made as a matter of degree rather than by comparing distinct

---

[1] There are many excellent introductions to rational choice theory. The essays in Elster (1986) are particularly helpful.

alternatives. An individual can either prefer one alternative to another or be indifferent to a choice between them. We can represent preference in terms of *utility*, meaning happiness or satisfaction. More preferred alternatives give the individual greater utility than do their less preferred counterparts. Utility has been an important way of comparing incomparables – apples and oranges – in theory building since the nineteenth-century writings of Jules Dupuit (e.g., Dupuit, 1853). It underlies all the theory that we review in subsequent chapters.

The fundamental problem in rational choice theory is for an individual to apply his preferences when choosing among alternatives. In this paradigm, the individual retains exclusive judgment over her best interests. To make a rational choice, the individual chooses the best alternative she can given her preferences. Because preferences may differ among individuals, their choices may differ as well. When only some alternatives are available, as when you buy a different brand of toothpaste because your favorite is not on the shelf, preferences are not fully revealed. In this way, observed behavior may not tell us everything that there is to know about the preferences of an individual. Although there is much more to the rational choice paradigm than we can possibly discuss here, being able to define these basic concepts will assist the reader in understanding the material that follows and the broader literature beyond this book.

In this chapter, we articulate three general frameworks for analyzing governance problems. We begin with the most basic framework, the *principal–agent model*, and then discuss two important and related theoretical processes: *signaling* and *screening*. Their value is their ability to be applied to a host of governance situations, as illustrated through extended examples. Think of our present task as a briefing on internal combustion engines before undertaking an analysis of their carbon emissions.

2.1. THE PRINCIPAL–AGENT MODEL

Remind yourself of the last time you went to a physician's office. Unless you happen to be a physician yourself, it is probably safe to assume that your physician knew more about the workings of the human body than you did. By consenting to have your physician examine you, you allowed your physician to learn more about your own body than you, in fact, knew. Was your visit because of illness? If it was, your interest was in restoring your health. What was your doctor's interest? If it was not solely in restoring your health, you were presented with a principal–agent problem.

In jargon, you are the *principal*. A principal is someone (or some organization believed to have a unified preference structure) who wants something to be done but for one reason or another cannot do it himself. The reason for your visit to your physician was your physician's expertise; you did not have sufficient technical knowledge of the body to self-diagnose your illness. In other cases, the principal may lack some other resource capability such as time. Your doctor went to college and then medical school, spent time as a resident in a hospital, passed board examinations, and incurred a very large financial expense to develop relevant expertise. Your doctor is your *agent*, performing a service on your behalf. She offers diagnostic services to you in exchange for a fee. Because your physician sees a number of clients in addition to you, she is interested in exerting less, rather than more, effort in diagnosing your illness so that she may move on to other fee-paying patients.

Because in solving principal–agent problems, we are interested in mitigating opportunism, or "self-interest seeking with guile" (Williamson, 1985, 47), we shall make the ostensibly cynical assumption that your doctor is only interested in exerting the least possible effort in diagnosing your problem. You and your doctor have a *conflict of interest* in this transaction. You would like your doctor to be interested in restoring your health and not in those diagnostic choices that would minimize her effort. Note that your preferences are different from those of your doctor in the sense that different things make each of you happy (increase your utility) – your health versus your doctor's effort, induced by her desire to see more patients and increase her income. How do you bring your doctor's interests into alignment with your own? In the political economy literature, the answer is this: you must design a set of incentives that will compel your doctor to make diagnostic decisions as if your doctor's interest was solely in restoring your health. For the purpose of theory building, that incentive mechanism solves the principal–agent problem. Whether people respond to these incentives is ultimately an empirical question.

You are probably thinking that much of this incentive design has been done for you, and that is certainly true. Your doctor is bound to follow certain ethical guidelines. If you submit a claim to a health insurance provider, that company will ensure that the doctor's fees are not inappropriate to the effort she exerted in diagnosis.[2] Lawsuits targeting substandard medical practices that require low effort levels increase the

---

[2] Of course, the insurance company's interest in keeping its payments to doctors low creates incentives that may lead to a conflict of interest with your health restoration as well. We shall not discuss these problems, though the principal–agent model has been extremely influential in the analysis of insurance provision (e.g., Pauly, 1974).

costs to physicians of performing them. The list can get quite long. Nonetheless, we shall assume for the moment that you have to solve the problem for yourself, creating an incentive mechanism in the process.

There are really two companion problems that you must solve. Your concern that your doctor will make a diagnostic choice – which you do not have the technical expertise or even opportunity to observe – that runs counter to your interest in restoring your health is known as the moral hazard or *hidden action* problem. Hidden action refers to a situation in which an agent does something on behalf of the principal that the latter cannot observe. That your doctor has information you cannot easily learn can be used for her private benefit (minimizing the effort she exerts in your diagnosis). This is known as the problem of adverse selection or *hidden information*. This means that the principal cannot observe some trait that characterizes the agent, or, put differently, the agent's type. It may be that your doctor is not terribly adept at diagnosing lupus, and that may well be your problem given the symptoms you are experiencing. Creating incentives for doctors to reveal such deficiencies solves the hidden information problem. We turn first to hidden action, then to hidden information.

2.2. HIDDEN ACTION

Your interest (the principal's interest) is in your own health; the utility you derive – the happiness you get – from your health would be represented by the theorist as an increasing function of your actual health level. As your health improves, your utility function achieves higher values, implying simply that you like being healthier. Your doctor supplies her effort in restoring your health and is interested in exerting as little effort as possible on your case so that she can work on others and earn a better living. As effort increases, so does your health, but your doctor's happiness decreases. To make the problem simpler, let's assume that your doctor can exert one of two effort levels on your behalf: high and low. Having included both principal and agent preferences in our model, we may also specify the relationship between your doctor's effort and your health. This is done probabilistically; high effort is associated with a 90 percent chance of your recovery, whereas low effort correlates with only a 60 percent likelihood that you will recover. For the moment, assume that those probabilities and associations are known for certain, whatever their values.

You would like to offer your doctor a monetary incentive to induce her (or give her the incentive) to choose one level of effort rather than the other. This means that you wish to pay your doctor a higher wage for exerting more effort in your diagnosis than you would for a lesser effort level. How do you know that your higher payment will actually make her exert the higher level of effort in diagnosis? Remember that you know practically nothing about medicine and the human body. This means that there is a problem of information, as discussed in the preceding chapter. The higher effort level may involve a battery of tests of which you have never even heard. Recall, also, that we have assumed that your doctor will behave opportunistically. Suppose she just takes the higher fee, does not run the tests, and says that your case was just particularly difficult when the misdiagnosis becomes apparent? This result might well bring you into the world of litigation. You may hire a lawyer, who will argue to a court that the likelihood of correct diagnosis was 90 percent with the good treatment, for which you paid, and still you suffered harm that was only 10 percent likely. There is a real possibility that you won't win when all you have is such a claim. What nasty business! Might you have avoided it?

Solving the hidden action problem requires you to think about the potential for your doctor to behave opportunistically. You must tie your doctor's earnings to the likelihood that you will get well, that is, give her a performance bonus. If you pay your doctor some fixed fee plus a bonus if you get your health back, your doctor's incentives to behave opportunistically – or to shirk her duties, as the literature often describes it – change. Your doctor now sees the benefit of exerting the high level of effort as equal to the fixed fee plus the bonus, with the latter weighted by the probability that your health is restored, the condition for her getting the bonus, given high effort. Your doctor weighs this against the *opportunity cost*, the counterfactual in which she exerts low effort. This opportunity cost is the fixed fee, which your doctor earns regardless of effort level, plus the bonus weighted by the probability that you will recover given low effort. Even though you will still be misdiagnosed 10 percent of the time if she exerts high effort and 40 percent of the time if her effort is low, you have shifted the risk of misdiagnosis to her under this incentive scheme. This risk shifting has a very nice property, namely, that it is self-enforcing; that is, it does not require enforcement by an authority such as the police, the courts, or the Public Company Accounting Oversight Board. Simply by responding to the incentives in this scheme, your doctor would act in your best interest. No outside intervention, such as the aforementioned legal proceeding, would be necessary. Both you and your doctor would behave rationally, simultaneously maximizing your utility. Because each person's outcome depends on the actions, or strategy, of the other, this situation draws on a branch of mathematics known as *game theory*.

Your brilliant incentive scheme requires two things for your doctor to go for it. The first is known in the literature as an *incentive compatibility constraint*. To align your incentives, the bonus will have to be set such that your doctor's expected increase in fees will be at least enough to offset the opportunity cost of her increased effort. This offset lies at the heart of the solution to the hidden action problem: by compensating the agent (your doctor) for the higher effort, the conflict of interest dissolves. This dissolution requires one more thing, namely, you must make your doctor sufficiently intrigued by her potential earnings from your scheme that she does not throw you out of her office. A *participation constraint* is imposed by your doctor: her fee from your bonus scheme must yield at least as much as she requires to exert the higher effort level that, in turn, will make it more likely that you will return to good health.

You may be thinking, that is fine, but how much will I actually have to pay my doctor? Taken together, these constraints tell us that the fixed fee should be at most the wage you would pay for high effort less the bonus weighted by the probability of recovery associated with high effort. Because we have seen that offering a flat high-effort wage will not incentivize your doctor to do her best in your diagnosis, the bonus plays a role in that the wage can be reduced by the bonus payment your doctor expects to receive, namely, the bonus multiplied by the probability that she will get it. Let's assume that you want to pay your doctor the lowest total amount to induce her to take the higher effort – you wish to minimize costs. It is possible that the fixed fee you offer could be negative, meaning that your doctor would actually have to incur costs to have a chance at earning the bonus. The possibility of negative incentive payments can occur in the event that the high-effort wage is less than the probability weighted bonus. You might be skeptical about what a negative fixed fee implies. One interpretation is that it is the cost of the education, licensing, and other things that the doctor assumed to place her in a position to treat you and earn the potentially large bonus. This may be considered her human capital investment. Another view returns us to that unfortunate state of affairs in which you hired a lawyer after your doctor did not restore your health. The negative fee implies a penalty, exacted through your successful litigation, in the event of a misdiagnosis and your continued illness.

Our analysis suggests that your inability to understand what your doctor is doing in her diagnostic process is very costly. If you could perfectly observe her efforts, you could pay her a flat wage to induce the doctor to the higher effort level; rather, your inability to do this leads you to pay her a bonus that exceeds this flat wage. We shall call the difference between the wage you would have paid and what you actually pay under the bonus scheme an *agency cost*. In this case of hidden action, it is the cost that the principal (you) bears by hiring an agent (doctor) to perform a task in an area (medicine) in which the agent (doctor) has more expertise than the principal (you). Agency costs are essential to understanding the value of incentive mechanisms to those who are affected by them.

The principal–agent model gives us a map depicting how these facets of real-world problems work together to induce principals and agents to behave according to patterns that we observe. That is, of course, the goal of theoretical modeling. The incentive contract between you and your doctor is illustrative of the mechanisms behind a variety of theories that we discuss in subsequent chapters. To help us in applying these ideas and to suggest the relationship between hidden action and our next topic, hidden information problems, we next consider an example of incentive design in public policy decision making.[3]

2.2.1. Example: The Bridge to Canada

The Ambassador Bridge connects Detroit, Michigan, with Windsor, Ontario, Canada. This bridge over the Detroit River is the most traversed border crossing between the two nations[4] and has been privately owned since its opening in 1929. The Detroit International Bridge Company (DIBC) owns the bridge, and that company is in turn controlled by a single man, Manuel J. "Matty" Moroun, who made his fortune in trucking.

From the beginning, private ownership of the bridge was controversial. Having received a franchise to build the bridge from Congress at the end of the 1920s, New York financier and former Detroiter Joseph A. Bower fought bitterly with then Detroit mayor John W. Smith, who wanted the bridge to be built with public funds and jointly owned by the cities of Detroit and Windsor.[5] After voters approved a referendum endorsing private ownership, the bridge was built. The risk of hidden action on the part of the private owners underlies political arguments over the bridge to the present day.

---

[3] The example draws heavily from Zacharias (2007) and Davey (2007).

[4] More than 12 million vehicles crossed the bridge in 2000 (Davey, 2007).

[5] This joint arrangement turned out to be technically impossible under the municipal charters of Detroit and Windsor (Zacharias, 2007).

Writing just after the completion of the bridge, Parker (1931, 130) notes several ways in which the congressional franchising mechanism for toll bridges in place at the time protected the public interest. The first set of protections addressed the economic agency costs of centralized private ownership of toll bridges. In the language we have developed, Congress is the principal and extends a franchise (contract) to DIBC, the agent. Federal legislation had provided for tolls charged to be "just and reasonable" since 1906 (Parker, 1931, 132). As agents of the people, Congress as well as state and local governments face electoral incentives that provide them with incentives to respect the public interest in their actions. In the 1920s, when a private concern sought a franchise to construct such a span, "the subcommittee on Bridges of the House Interstate Commerce Committee demand[ed] that information be furnished concerning the likelihood [that] the state, county, or city" would construct the bridge on its own. Parker (1931, 130) notes that "no franchise is ever granted to private capital until the Committee is convinced that the bridge cannot or will not be erected and operated by a governmental authority."

The House subcommittee also promotes competition among private owners of crossings. Writes Parker (1931, 130), "even though a toll bridge already exists at a particular crossing, another franchise may be granted ... at approximately the same point of crossing if the density of traffic and other circumstances seem to warrant it." He continues, "Such a policy maintains the element of competition ... and hinders any bridge franchise from acquiring speculative value through the possession of monopoly characteristics."[6] Moreover, franchises are not perpetual, Parker (1931, 131) notes, but rather are limited by the state when conditions change. Though some spans, such as New York City's Williamsburg Bridge, made tremendous profits throughout the 1920s, "practically every toll bridge that has been authorized by Congress in the last few years can be condemned or recaptured" under governmental powers of eminent domain. In other words, a state or local government could buy a bridge that was being operated contrary to the public interest.[7]

---

[6] Indeed, Parker notes that the Ambassador Bridge was opened by DIBC, and less than one year later, the Detroit and Canada Tunnel Company opened a tunnel between Detroit and Windsor less than two miles away. Ferries on the river halved their rates, and DIBC floundered financially.

[7] This included profitable spans: "Generally, franchises for bridges are so drawn that in a condemnation proceeding ... nothing has to be paid for the earning power of the bridge nor for its value as a profitable going concern" (Parker, 1931, 131).

Regarding the safety and soundness of the building plans, Parker (1931, 132) would leave the check to the market for capital investment. He writes, "Before the toll bridge can be said to be soundly conceived, painstaking engineering and accounting investigations and reports" are necessary to encourage investors to devote their capital to the project. The market, then, provides a way of screening out bad bridges with insufficient engineering safeguards.

The events of September 11, 2001, and the collapse of the I-35W bridge in Minneapolis, Minnesota, in 2007 made the safety issue salient again. An October 2007 article in the *New York Times* observed that "with so much commerce depending on a single structure, people have begun to wonder what would happen if a terrorist were to attack it or if the Ambassador Bridge, approaching 80 years old, were to fail" (Davey, 2007). A battle ensued between the state of Michigan and Moroun over which party should build the bridge.

Michigan state senator Raymond E. Basham, a Democrat then representing a district south of the bridge's location, argued for public ownership, warning that "when it comes to dollars and cents, there is every incentive for [Moroun] not to tell us if something is wrong" (Davey, 2007). Moroun made a counterproposal to finance a six-lane structure and repair the Ambassador Bridge, which could be reopened in the event that the new span required repairs. Alan Cropsey, Republican Michigan Senate majority leader, saw merit in the private plan: "Why do they feel they need to put a bridge up and compete with the private sector? Why now?" (Davey, 2007). Why now, indeed. Michigan was in financial dire straits, as represented in a four-hour shutdown of its government in October 2007, when legislators could not agree on a budget bill.

Enhanced by the political realities, the characteristics of a principal–agent relationship seem evident in the controversy over who should control the bridge to Canada. Senator Basham is concerned with the potential for Moroun to behave opportunistically and, more specifically, with a hidden action problem that Parker (1931) had not considered in his focus on the economic consequences. DIBC can take advantage of the public through hidden action, but given the electoral connection, the problem is mitigated via a public bridge authority. Senator Cropsey appears interested in an incentive-based solution as well. Rather than building a publicly owned alternative, incentives might be offered to DIBC to provide information about the structural soundness of the span. Those incentives would have to satisfy participation and incentive compatibility constraints, and Basham may be concerned that such an agreement could not be written.

In the next section, we will provide explanations of Moroun's offer to build a new bridge and renovate the Ambassador, which we will call a (costly) signal to the governmental principal regarding the type of safety that he can provide. Moroun has hidden information about DIBC's ability to safely maintain the bridge. For Parker (1931), the incentives to reveal that information would come from the investment market. However, vibrant competition may be difficult to achieve in the market for bridges between Detroit and Windsor. It is to the revelation of hidden information in the absence of a competitive market that we now turn.

2.3. HIDDEN INFORMATION

The preceding section considered the problem in which an agent's action that could not be readily observed by the principal gave rise to the agency problem. However, yet as the case of the Ambassador Bridge suggests, the agent may possess some information that, if known, would affect the principal's decision making. In our example of the doctor visit, you might make your calculations differently if you know that your doctor is not terribly adept at medical diagnosis. Indeed, you might look around for other physicians who might be better suited to the task. You would like to screen physicians from a pool of candidates and select the best fit. These candidate physicians – a set that includes, say, all the physicians listed in the local telephone directory – are of different types. For simplicity, suppose that there are only two types: generalists and specialists.

How would you undertake this screening? You would need to design some incentive mechanism through which the potential physicians among whom you are trying to choose would reveal information about themselves. In that process, the physicians would provide signals as to their quality. They may, perhaps, provide a résumé that details the elements of their human capital investment. It should be apparent that the mechanism you design for screening physicians and the physicians' decisions regarding how to craft the signal (résumé) they send to you are two sides to the same problem. These problems are thorny. The primary difficulties are the information asymmetries that you and the physicians have. You don't know what type a given physician really is. Some generalists are exceptional at diagnosing illnesses but can't treat the most complex ones. If they could, your choice would be easy. Any given physician, for her part, doesn't know what type of physician you really need. You might be willing to pay less money for a generalist because you think that your illness is straightforward, or you may want a specialist because you believe your problem to be more localized, for example, your symptom is an earache. In any event, this mutual speculation leads to inefficient results and to the development of institutions that we see in the real world such as the myriad rules governing health plans. We eschew many of the complexities of signaling and screening problems and explain the logic of solving them in a simple way. To relieve you of thoughts of illnesses and bridge collapses, we turn our attention toward what Lipsky (1980) calls street-level bureaucracy.

Suppose that Audrey manages a group of line staff in the Department of Social Services (DSS). The governance task with which her group is charged is the placement of children into foster homes. In addition to her managerial responsibilities, Audrey is also in charge of hiring new and replacement staffers. In her long experience, Audrey finds that she receives applications from two types of graduate programs: master of social work (MSW) and master of public administration (MPA) programs. Audrey notes that the social workers she has hired over the years are deeply motivated to help children; they learn an exceptional amount about individual children and their family situations and understand their needs. Nonetheless, she finds that the social workers in her group are less interested in the bureaucratic organization and operations of the department. Time and time again, social workers will leave their front-line staff jobs for nonprofit organizations rather than accepting promotions to managerial levels at the DSS. Among public administrators, Audrey has observed a different pattern. These individuals reveal strong interest in bureaucratic organization and advancement in the DSS. Nonetheless, they tend not to stay in their front-line jobs in the foster care division when a higher-ranking position in another DSS division becomes vacant.

Audrey wants more stability in personnel in an organization that comprises both administrative and substantive skills; she wishes to have both types of individuals represented in the foster care group. She has a policy of keeping an equal balance of social workers and public administrators in her group at all times. When a position is vacated by a social worker, she hires another social worker, and vice versa. You might be thinking that Audrey's view is a bit skewed. Surely social work students take courses on organizations and public administration students study specific policy areas such as child welfare. Taking these sorts of classes – not to mention internships in these areas – certainly suggests that a student may have a commitment to both elements of the job. The mechanism she has designed does not screen candidates for the information Audrey really wants to know. That information is the candidate's likelihood of loyalty to the child welfare group in DSS. Audrey would like to screen out those individuals who wish to advance a career in either child welfare or public administration outside of the child welfare group. What type of hiring process – screening mechanism – should Audrey design to identify these applicant types?

One tactic is to focus on the implicit valuations of loyalty to the DSS and careerism implicit in the programs of study that the applicants undertake during their MPA or MSW studies. Suppose that there are two categories of courses, policy and administration, from which the applicants select and that both types are offered in MPA as well as MSW programs. Loyalists value a mix of courses in each category, whereas careerists prefer all classes in a single category. Theorists look for simple measures of behavior that evoke important elements of reality. These are the moving parts of formal theories. In this example, the ratio of the proportion of policy to administration courses taken tells us something about the degree of specialization that a student has acquired; we shall call it a student's specialization ratio. If the specialization ratio is equal to 1, the student is a pure generalist (having taken equal numbers of policy and administration classes). If it is greater than 1, the student is a policy specialist. If the ratio is less than 1, the candidate is an administrative specialist.

If students' underlying valuations of this specialization ratio are correlated, or associated, with their true types (loyalist or careerist), the value of the ratio is useful information to Audrey. Suppose that loyalist students assign the cost of pursuing a particular curriculum in the following way: as the specialization ratio deviates from 1 (a perfect balance of policy and administration courses), the subjective cost to a loyalist student of her academic program increases over and above the tuition that she pays. Careerists, by contrast, feel differently about their curricular choices. As the specialization ratio moves away from 1 in either direction, the careerists consider the subjective cost of their education to drop below the level of tuition they pay. The psychological basis for this determination may go something like this: taking specialized classes in either administration or policy makes careerist students feel as though they are already in their chosen career, and they trade off tuition dollars against that feeling of fulfillment.

These statements about the subjective costs of curricular choices reflect a difference in preferences between loyalist and careerist students. Costs reduce utility, permitting the use of cost functions to model the preferences of the students Audrey is considering for employment. Suppose that each student wishes to minimize the costs of his education. Loyalist students minimize their costs by choosing a perfect balance of courses in policy or administration, a situation that prevails when the specialization ratio is equal to 1. In contrast, that perfect balance of courses maximizes costs for careerist students. These individuals are better off as they take more policy or administration courses, indicated by a specialization ratio either greater than or less than 1, respectively.

Given knowledge of this kind of thinking on the part of graduating MPAs and MSWs, one possible screening mechanism that Audrey may use is to reward applicants who select a generalist curriculum with higher pay than the specialists. Audrey's intentions must be communicated to as many potential applicants as possible before they finish their course selection, that is, choose their final values of the specialization ratio. To do this, Audrey might place information on the DSS foster care Web site stating that successful applicants with a generalist degree will be paid starting salaries that are higher than those paid to holders of specialist degrees. Generalist degrees would be defined on the Web site as having a balance of policy and administration courses.

If Audrey succeeds, this result represents what is called a *separating equilibrium*. An equilibrium is a situation in which incentives are balanced in such a way that behavior will not change absent the introduction of some external force, for instance, a change in the partisan composition of the state legislature that foments opposition to DSS initiatives. A separating equilibrium is characterized by different types of individuals behaving differently such that each type is consistent with a specific behavior. By examining the number of specialist classes that an applicant lists on his application, Audrey can determine whether the applicant is a type likely to be a loyal DSS employee or a careerist. The types separate with respect to their specialization ratio, and separation requires Audrey's *credible commitment* to paying the different salaries for specialist and generalist curriculum choices that she announces on the Web site. Credible commitment simply implies picking a rule (institution) and sticking to it.[8] If Audrey could renege on those salaries, and the students knew this, they would not choose specialization ratios in ways that provide Audrey with the information she really needs.

---

[8] Nobel laureates Kydland and Prescott (1977) observed the importance of credible commitments in monetary policy. A clearly understandable rule regarding inflationary targets was better suited to its task than a specialized administrative agency entrusted with discretion.

Signaling by applicants also requires credibility. For a loyalist to let Audrey know that she is actually a loyalist, namely, the type of person Audrey wants to hire, the applicant must forgo the market opportunities afforded to individuals having specialist degrees and take fewer specialist courses. This is a costly action on the part of these individuals; though Audrey pays generalists more, there are likely to be lucrative opportunities for specialists that are now foreclosed. Such self-sacrifice makes the course selection signal credible.

The alternative to separation is *pooling*, in which both loyalists and specialists are paid the same amount. In a pooling equilibrium, all types of agents behave in the same manner, making it impossible for the principal to tell them apart. Suppose Audrey did not want to take a chance on offering a screening mechanism because fluctuations in the state budget and shifting political winds would likely make her salary commitments less than credible. Recent news accounts have also suggested that students are tending toward specialization in their educational programs. Given what she can glean from those accounts and from her own experiences, Audrey can place values on the probability that a generalist will graduate and the probability that a specialist will emerge. She uses these probabilities to calculate a pooled wage, the sum of the specialist and generalist wages we have discussed weighted by the probabilities that each type will graduate from MPA and MSW programs, and pays it to everyone. In this case, the pooled wage would not create an equilibrium because it depends on the graduation probabilities. If those values change, the pooled wage will not attract the right types of individuals to DSS. What is more, during an interview with Audrey, a student may reveal via an official transcript that she had taken five policy and six administrative courses – her specialization ratio is very close to 1 – and ask for a salary greater than the pooled wage. This should be a credible signal to Audrey of the loyalist type, leading her to make the hire with the larger salary. Of course, a student with a specialization ratio even closer to 1 could likewise ask Audrey for a higher salary, and so forth. The failure of the pooling wage to result in an equilibrium suggests the cost to Audrey of being unable to commit to the specialist salary that would induce separation in applicant types.[9] Without commitment, her mechanism fails to do what she wants it to do.

---

[9] In various applications, this cost can be extremely large, and uncovering an appropriate screening mechanism is of great value. The 2007 Nobel Memorial Prize in Economic Sciences recognized the value of solutions to this mechanism design problem. In

These hypothetical stories of the physician's visit and DSS recruitment illustrate the basic mechanisms that underlie the theories described in this book. We now consider another contemporary example of the role of hidden action and hidden information in the performance of a governance task to provide some additional context.

2.3.1. Example: Private Security Companies

Among the most controversial contracts in contemporary American governance are those going to private security companies (PSCs) (Singer, 2003). Consider the contract between Blackwater USA and the U.S. Department of State for protecting American diplomats in the Baghdad region during the Iraq War that began in 2003. The nature of Blackwater's contracts became the subject of public controversy in September 2007, when the Iraqi government attempted to expel the company after employees killed at least fourteen Iraqi civilians in a controversial and bloody confrontation (Ragavan et al., 2007). Subsequent congressional investigations heightened the debate by revealing that Blackwater employees underreported shooting incidents and Iraqi casualties, failed to stop and assess casualties after shooting incidents, and were subject to inadequate disciplinary measures. Moreover, Blackwater employees were found to have fired first in over 80 percent of shooting incidents, despite being barred from firing offensively (U.S. House of Representatives, 2007). The political controversy raised questions about the agency costs of contracts with PSCs.

Hidden action presents one problem. The U.S. Department of State (the principal) wants all diplomats protected from harm with no loss of civilian life. Blackwater USA (the agent) was contracted to protect certain individuals (diplomats) and was granted discretion to harm individuals, such as Iraqi insurgents, in the course of their protective duties. Although harm to noninsurgent Iraqis is clearly tragic and undesirable, it is not categorically avoidable under the intense conditions of war. As we have noted, incentive contracts must satisfy a participation constraint, and it would be difficult to convince Blackwater to undertake the task of protection in a war zone without the authority for its employees to protect

announcing the prize, the Royal Swedish Academy of Sciences noted in its press release that mechanism design theory "has helped economists identify efficient trading mechanisms, regulation schemes and voting procedures. Today, mechanism design theory plays a central role in many areas of economics and parts of political science."

themselves along with the diplomats they escort. It is in this sense that contracts distribute risk across parties.

Incentive compatibility is the source of the controversy. In its contracts, which, between 2004 and 2006, exceeded $832 million, Blackwater USA was authorized to use force only in defense against "imminent and grave danger" (U.S. House of Representatives, 2007). Owing to the difficulty of discerning insurgents from noninsurgents before an attack occurred, Blackwater employees had incentive under the contract terms to err opportunistically on the side of assuming more rather than less imminent danger from unknown individuals to adequately protect diplomats. Passionate arguments have been made that given existing contractual provisions, harm to diplomats is far more likely to incur penalties than harm to insurgents, rightly or wrongly identified. As a result, Blackwater could reasonably assume that the consequences of its involvement in Iraqi civilian casualties would be mitigated as long as diplomats remained safe. Blackwater employees thus had the incentive to maximize protective measures for diplomats at the expense of carefully distinguishing insurgents from civilians. This hidden action problem materialized in the form of multiple civilian deaths because incentive compatibility was not achieved.

The contract must formally tie compensation, continuation of the contract, or other incentives to Iraqi civilian deaths to give the PSC tangible motivation to accurately distinguish insurgents. Although a variety of mechanisms could potentially be used in a contract, political feasibility is an important element to consider. For example, setting a quota on the number of civilian deaths in which Blackwater can be involved might well have been too politically difficult for the State Department to consider. Alternatively, imposing stiff penalties for civilian deaths that could have been avoided through reasonable caution as identified in the contract and enforced in court might have induced Blackwater to exercise greater effort in identifying insurgents.

As Blackwater USA is not the only PSC with which the State Department might contract, the question arises as to whether the department might screen for PSCs that are less likely to use excessive force. Significant discrepancies existed in the rates at which different PSCs in Iraq fired first during shooting incidents (Ragavan et al., 2007). These discrepancies suggest that some PSCs may have encouraged higher levels of effort among employees in distinguishing insurgents, making employees less likely to use excessive force. The level of effort that a given PSC is capable of exercising constitutes hidden information.

One possible mechanism may seek information from PSCs regarding their suitability solely to the specific task of protecting diplomats versus their ability to contribute to the broader U.S. mission in Iraq. Blackwater has been accused of impeding progress in the mission overall by focusing exclusively on its protective duties (Singer, 2007). If a PSC's primary ability is as a protection service, its concern for the effect of Iraqi deaths on the overall Iraq mission might be lower than the government requires, and efforts to limit collateral casualties may likewise be lower. The U.S. military, by contrast, is capable of a much broader involvement in the war. An agent that can contribute to various aspects of achieving a stable government and facilitating peace in Iraq will in all likelihood take into account the negative impact of civilian deaths on the mission and will work diligently to avoid such casualties. Consequently, screening PSCs is another theoretically sound possibility for inducing incentive compatibility.

2.4. CONCLUSION

This chapter introduced the reader to rational choice theory, focusing attention on individuals with preferences over alternatives. We began with the key approach to theorizing in the chapters that follow: the principal–agent model. We discussed how screening and signaling are two sides of the same problem of choosing the right agent for a principal's purposes. The key difference between these approaches was that screening required credible commitment to an incentive mechanism, whereas signaling did not. Commitment will play an important role in subsequent chapters.

We shall next extend its reach to include delegations of governance tasks to administrative agencies. When the U.S. Congress (principal) delegates policy-making authority to an administrative agency (agent) that can learn more about that policy area than Congress knows, it faces a hidden action problem. Within agencies, when a politically appointed supervisor must rely on expert career bureaucrats to implement policy, he, too, faces a principal–agent problem. As we increase the reach of these theoretical issues, and with it, our understanding of contemporary governance, we must frequently return to the foundational ideas that we have developed here.

PART I

THEORY

This part begins by introducing the basic tools used in building the theories at the heart of this book. Our attention is drawn toward two areas in which the political economy approach has provided considerable explanation of governance. Chapter 3 considers the allocation of resources for performing governance tasks. Chapter 4 synthesizes theories of the delegation of authority over those tasks to be legitimately performed. The literature in this area was developed primarily in the context of American political institutions. As a result, our context in this part will be federal policy making in the United States. Although the implications of this literature have a much broader geographic reach, we focus on the United States while briefly discussing comparative implications.

3

The Power of the Purse

> The people take part in the making of the laws by choosing the lawgivers, and they share in their application by electing the agents of the executive power; one might say that they govern themselves, so feeble and restricted is the part left to the administration, so vividly is that administration aware of its popular origin, and so obedient is it to the font of power. The people reign over the American political world as God rules over the Universe. It is the cause and end of all things; everything rises out of it and is absorbed back into it.
>
> – Alexis de Tocqueville ([1835] 2000, 60)

In Tocqueville's view of the antebellum United States, the connection between the sovereign authority of the people and the administration of the laws that shape their behavior was a defining feature of its democracy. As we consider the political economy of public sector governance, the connection between the people and public managers will always be at the center of our story. In the narrative of American public management that developed with its practice beginning in the nineteenth century, the need for administrators to exercise rational, balanced judgment that is accountable to the public through its elected representatives was seen as a requirement for the people to govern themselves (Bertelli and Lynn, 2006). Thus the lessons of the analytical models that we review in this and subsequent chapters will reveal themselves as corresponding to the broadest and most trenchant themes of public management: what it is, what its practitioners do, what they should do, and what a democratic public expects of them when they do it.

Pursuant to the U.S. Constitution, "bills for raising Revenue shall originate in the House of Representatives" (Art. 1, Sec. VII). James Madison

39

wrote in *The Federalist*, no. 58, that this language implies that "the house of representatives can not only refuse, but they alone can propose the supplies requisite for the support of government. They in a word hold the purse," which "may be in fact regarded as the most compleat and effectual weapon with which any constitution can arm the immediate representatives of the people, for obtaining a redress of any grievance, and for carrying into effect every just and salutary measure" (Hamilton et al., 1982 [1788], 296–297). Moreover, Congress has the sole authority to legislate (Art. I, Sec. I) and the authority to "lay and collect Taxes, Duties, Imposts and Excises, to pay the Debts and provide for the common Defence and general Welfare of the United States" (Art. I, Sec. VIII). A strong collective reading of these provisions implies that if Congress does not finance a policy initiative, it cannot be undertaken by the government. Because no administrative task is costless, public management can happen only when Congress appropriates budgetary authority to it. A substantial amount of administrative deviation from the policy interests of Congress (hidden action) may seem to be correctable by funding constraints, and such constraints respect the formal authority given to Congress by the Constitution.

It is with this "power of the purse" (Hamilton et al., 1982 [1788], 297) that we begin our exploration of what has come to be known as the political control of bureaucracy, or the ability of the political branches – Congress and the president, which face direct election – to constrain the policy choices of administration. As the American administrative state grew in the early twentieth century, a tension between the strength of the power of the purse held by Congress (as principal) and the ability of expert administrative agents to produce good public policies became significant. This tension became more acute throughout the beginning of the twentieth century and ultimately engaged the legislative, executive, and judicial branches in a "constitutional moment" that redefined the relationship between the theory and practice of the constitution (Ackerman, 1998).

To motivate the political control problem, we first consider how the power to determine policy comes to be concentrated in the agency, rather than in its constitutional superiors, through uncertainty and expertise. This takes us into a discussion of the nature of bureaucracy as policy implementer. We tie the question of bureaucratic control to the elevated constitutional position of Congress, as lawmaker, over agencies. Throughout the early intellectual history of public management, this de jure constitutional superiority was placed in tension with the agency's de facto power over what policy is chosen. In Chapter 6, we see that the tension between expertise and democracy is yet unresolved. It centers on the professional obligations of administrators who affect our daily lives and how their action can be checked in the absence of an electoral connection. Embedded within the traditional literature of public administration as well as the contemporary political–economic models we survey is a profound respect for the democratic pedigree of Congress. An example of scholarly opinion within the public administration community illustrates the problem in our present budgetary context.

3.1. THE BUDGET AS POLITICAL CONSTRAINT

William F. Willoughby was a Princeton University professor, experienced manager, and first director of what would become the Brookings Institution. In an essay presented at the annual meeting of the American Political Science Association in 1912, he took a particularly strong view of the power of the purse:

Congress seeks by law to give precise and detailed instructions to the executive as to exactly how the money appropriated shall be spent, just what stations, agencies, and offices shall be maintained, how much money shall be spent for the remuneration of personnel, the number of persons that shall be employed, the compensation that shall be paid to each, the character of the work that shall be undertaken, and the expenditure that shall be made for each item, the amount of money that shall be spent for this or that. (Willoughby, 1913, 78)

Willoughby (1913, 78) argued against so broad a construction and, in doing so, elaborated the conditions for the hidden information problem that motivates the analytical models reviewed in this chapter. "This method ignores," Willoughby wrote, "as far as it can, the fact that the efficient conduct of affairs necessarily involves the exercise of discretion from day to day by those actually in charge of the work to be performed" (78). He argues that the public's money is used inefficiently if Congress does not allow the administration to develop expertise in administrative matters and to use that expertise in determining the precise funding levels required to implement the policies legislated by Congress.[1] The

---

[1] This problem is broadly applicable to organizations that centrally prepare the budgets of their subunits. "Efficiency dictates that an organization's resources be channeled to the most productive subunits. Yet productivity is notoriously difficult to measure, especially within the public and private sectors. . . . Central planners must often estimate output and cost figures. These estimates are often derived from information provided by the subunits themselves, which have obvious incentives to depart from candor" (643) (Pollack and Zeckhauser, 1996).

reader should recall here that the ability of the administrative agent to gain and use expert information presents a principal–agent problem to Congress. Willoughby was more specific, positing a budgetary version of the *incomplete contracting problem*: "it is impossible to estimate in detail the precise sum [of money] that will be required for each subdivision of a work" and "that contingencies impossible to forsee will constantly arise" (Willoughby, 1913, 78). The contract is incomplete because it leaves some possible outcomes unspecified. As with your doctor in the last chapter, you cannot forsee every contingency that might occur during your treatment. If something unforseen does arise, you may need to rely on the courts to provide remedial action or compensation. The courts in that situation function like the monitors in the models described in this chapter. These gaps, he maintained, must be filled by administrative discretion expertly employed.

Willoughby (1913, 80) did not believe that Congress meant to "usurp the functions of the administrator and to deprive the latter of all initiative and discretion" but rather that it had not been able to discover a better way of "supervising and controlling" administration of the laws. Solving the principal–agent problem was for him a problem of policy design. Willoughby (1913, 81) recommended that Congress "formulate a general plan of work, place at the disposal of managers funds sufficient to permit of the carrying out of such program, and then exercise supervision over the manner in which this trust is discharged." Willoughby was grappling with a central theme in democratic public administration that would, in a broader form, become enshrined in the Friedrich–Finer debate that we engage in Chapter 6. That issue is the extent to which public administration should be responsible to the public through elected officials. While maintaining some flexibility, Willoughby's respect for the positive authority of Congress is readily apparent.

To gain traction on this problem, we consider a variety of models that depict a relationship between two unitary actors; a politician and a bureaucrat. The politician could be characterized as a pivotal actor in the legislature, the median member of an oversight committee, or even the electorate itself.[2] The bureaucrat is a unitary actor characterizing an administrative agency, as we later detail. We shall see that the incentives uncovered by the models we review not only reflect Willoughby's concerns but suggest a more specific version of his recommendation as the

---

[2] In the study of legislatures, the median member is important as pressures to moderate policy choices under majority rule institutions are predicted in many cases (Black, 1958; Hotelling, 1929).

solution to the problem of how Congress might effectively use the power of the purse. The incentives uncovered are manifest in the structure and behavior of contemporary monitoring institutions in American politics. We describe these in a fuller example. Before turning to this question of political control, we must develop a foundation for understanding the character of bureaucratic authority as controlled by Congress. As we shall see later in this and in the following chapter, the degree to which Congress shares effective power with administration is a result of the incompleteness of delegations to those authorities. The first aspect of bureaucratic discretion we examine is what Madison considered the threshold power to expend resources to perform governance tasks.

3.2. THE CHARACTERISTIC BUREAUCRAT

Perhaps no theory that we shall discuss draws more ire or is the subject of more confusion in some academic public administration communities than the line of inquiry that began William Niskanen's (1971) *Bureaucracy and Representative Government*. Its role in the modern political economy of public sector governance is not central; indeed, the literature discussed later in this chapter evolves from a critique of it. Yet we spend time with it here to help understand the parsimonious approach to theorizing about complex realities that is employed in this book. To develop a theory of bureaucratic behavior, Niskanen (1971, 22) centers on a characteristic bureaucrat, "the senior official of any agency with a separate identifiable budget." For example, one might think of the Administrator of the Environmental Protection Agency (EPA) or the Secretary of Education as the bureaucrats characterizing their respective departments. This is the first of many models we review in which a complex organization is represented by a *unitary actor*, essentially a single individual having preferences over alternative policies. Because this reductionism is both important to this book's theoretical project and potentially disquieting to readers, we explore the structure of bureaucratic organizations in the next few pages as a means toward assessing the reasonableness of such an assumption. After doing so, we discuss the bureaucrat's preferences and the core claims of the theory.

3.2.1. Legitimate Authority in Organizations

In their classic textbook, Simon et al. (1950, 85) define a formal organization as "the pattern of behaviors and relationships that is deliberately and legitimately planned for the members of an organization." The complex patterns we see in government – both within a large bureaucratic organization like the Department of Defense and throughout a network of collaborating agencies – have formal, planned components that gain legitimacy by virtue of the position of the planner. An organization holds legitimate authority when it receives general approval from those subject to its actions and decisions.[3] The positive authority of the creator of an organization is a source of legitimacy; Congress has the democratic pedigree to legitimately create administrative agencies.

Of formal authority, Simon et al. (1950, 85) observe that in government agencies,

Legitimacy flows ultimately from the action of the legislature in creating the organization (or the larger structure of which it is part) by statute, and providing a procedure by which an executive or board is appointed to direct it. The legally constituted executive, in turn authorizes more detailed plans for the structure of his organization, and appoints principal subordinates to positions of formal authority within it. This process may be several times repeated down through the structure of the organization.

For example, the EPA administrator holds legitimate authority dating to President Nixon's Reorganization Plan No. 3 of 1970, which called for the grouping of congressional delegations relating to environmental protection scattered throughout various agencies into a single, independent agency. EPA Order 1110.2 created the Office of the Administrator, stating that "responsibilities of the Agency are carried out under the supervision and direction of the Administrator." Given this broad grant of legitimate authority, the administrator is appropriately the characteristic bureaucrat for the EPA. Nonetheless, the EPA presently employs about seventeen thousand people in offices across the United States, and readers may need more encouragement to accept that a single office might capture the incentives facing the EPA for analytic purposes.

Through formal organization, legitimacy is preserved. The canonical conception of a legitimacy-preserving, formal organization is the Weberian bureaucracy. Wrote Weber (1964, 333) of his ideal-type, "only the supreme chief of the organization occupies his position of authority by virtue of appropriation, of election, or of having been designated for the

---

[3] Weber (1964) considered three types of legitimate authority, but modern democratic systems of government focus primarily on one: legality. Writes Dahl (1964, 28), "legitimacy rests on a belief that power is wielded in a way that is legal; the constitutional rules, the laws and powers of officials are accepted as binding because they are legal; what is done legally is regarded as legitimate."

succession." Thus the secretary of labor heads the Department of Labor by designation of the democratically elected president of the United States. The secretary of state of North Carolina heads her department by direct popular election. Nonetheless, Weber (1964, 333) continues, even the authority of the head of the bureaucratic organization "consists in a sphere of legal 'competence.'"

The expertise of an agency is vested in a cadre of administrators. The canonical Weberian bureaucracy places them within a system that employs their expertise while ensuring that the legitimate authority of the "supreme chief" – a good candidate for the position of characteristic bureaucrat – is maintained. Weber's ideal type of bureaucracy imposes a strict hierarchy of power and responsibility on the organization, with accountability to the top. Administrators in a Weberian bureaucracy have the following characteristics:

1. They are... subject to authority only with respect to their impersonal official obligations.
2. They are organized in a clearly defined hierarchy of offices.
3. Each office has a clearly defined sphere of competence...
4. The office is filled by a free contractual relationship...
5. Candidates are selected on the basis of technical qualifications [and] are appointed, not elected.
6. They are remunerated by fixed salaries in money... the official is always free to resign... [and t]he salary scale is primarily graded according to rank in the hierarchy...
7. The office is... at least the primary [ ] occupation of the incumbent.
8. ... There is a system of "promotion" according to seniority or to achievement, or both. Promotion is dependent on the judgment of superiors.
9. The official works [are] entirely separated from ownership of the means of administration...
10. [The official] is subject to strict and systematic discipline and control in the conduct of the office. (Weber, 1964, 333–334)

These formal institutions coexist to preserve the legitimate authority of the "supreme chief." On the basis of this type of formal structure, a unitary actor at the top of an administrative hierarchy can also be seen as a reasonable choice of characteristic actor.[4] But the reality of agencies

---

[4] Niskanen (1971, 21–22) is nonetheless critical of the Weberian conception of a bureaucratic organization.

is somewhat messier than this ideal type. Indeed, the formal organization can achieve neither legitimacy nor the organization's goals without, wrote telecommunications executive and management theorist Chester Barnard (1938, 139), "the willingness of persons to contribute their individual efforts to the coöperative system." The way in which this is achieved, he continued, is through the very mechanisms we explored in Chapter 2. Cooperation among members of an organization is achieved through well-designed incentives. For Barnard, complex organizations are glued together by solving incentive design problems:

The contributions of personal efforts which constitute the energies of the organizations are yielded by individuals because of incentives. The egotistical motives of self-preservation and of self-satisfaction are dominating forces; on the whole, organizations can exist only when consistent with the satisfaction of these motives, unless, alternatively, they can change these motives. The individual is always the basic strategic factor in organization. Regardless of his history or his obligations he must be induced to coöperate, or there can be no coöperation. (Barnard, 1938, 139)

Barnard warns that the organization may not be what its formal structure suggests. Incentives shape behavior in ways that may be inconsistent with formal rules. Although we shall see in Chapter 4 that delegating tasks to a public manager is central to solving the collective action problems of governance, the inducements of which Barnard writes imply that the manager's leadership can only influence those who are open to influence. This should remind you of the incentive compatibility and participation constraints in principal–agent problems that is discussed in Chapter 2. Incentives are generated by formal institutions, but the effectiveness of these incentives is tied up with informal institutions prevailing in specific groups of people. Management books-of-the-moment postulate strategies for effectiveness, but their success in practice is tied up with the correspondence between informal institutions in specific workplaces and those recognized by the authors.[5] We need to make such distinctions because different governance tasks involve different actors and norms.

---

[5] Take, for example, a maxim from the internationally best-selling *The Rules of Management*: "And that is basically the secret of good management. Give 'em a job to do and let them get on with it. Check once or twice to make sure they've done it the way you want it done and next time just let them get on with it.... Sometimes this will backfire...and hey, that'll be entirely your fault because you're the manager and it's your team.... Read on and we'll find ways to make sure it doesn't happen – well not often anyway" (Templar, 2005, 24). This simply references the principal–agent problem of the last section. Templar's example is a gardener, and the norms of gardeners who work on-site without supervision as a rule may be different than those of a reader's firm.

To capture this deviation between formal and informal influences, Simon et al. (1950, 87) define an informal organization as "the whole pattern of actual behaviors – the way members of the organization really do behave – insofar as these actual behaviors do not coincide with the formal plan." Deviation from the formal plan for organizational behavior can occur for two reasons. The first arises when "the formal plan [is] incomplete – it may not include the whole pattern of behavior as it actually develops" (Simon et al., 1950, 87). Incompleteness of the plan is a fundamental problem of the delegation of governance tasks by politicians to public managers, the subject of Chapter 4. When, as Willoughby suggested at the outset of this chapter, the politician inevitably cannot anticipate every contingency involved in policy implementation, he embeds incentives in statutory language to manage discretion ex ante. In this way, incentives can help to bring the informal organization into line with the formal plan and reduce the need for monitoring of agency behavior ex post that may or may not detect hidden action.

When such incentive mechanisms fail, a second source of deviation occurs, namely, "some portions of the actual pattern of behavior may be in contradiction to the plan" (Simon et al., 1950, 87). For Leibenstein (1966, 413), this implied simply that "for a variety of reasons people and organizations normally work neither as hard nor as effectively as they could." Because competitive market discipline – the forces of supply and demand that determine the success or failure of business organizations – does not adhere to administrative agencies as it does to private firms in neoclassical economic theory, the potential exists for disharmony between the informal and formal organizations:

> Where competitive pressure is light, many people will trade the disutility of greater effort, of search, and the control of other peoples' activities for the utility of feeling less pressure and of better interpersonal relations. But in situations where competitive pressures are high, and hence the costs of such trades are also high, they will exchange less of the disutility of effort for the utility of freedom from pressure, etc. (Leibenstein, 1987, 3)[6]

The (Barnardian) role of incentives in nonmarket situations is to increase the costs of these "trades" as they represent a key reason why incentives work differently in the public and private sectors.

---

[6] In transactions cost economics, markets and firms are both means of organizing transactions. The price mechanism coordinates production without the existence of a firm, yet the firm is built to supercede the price mechanism to reduce transactions costs (Coase, 1937).

Employing a characteristic bureaucrat to represent an administrative agency in a theoretical model requires the formal and informal organizations to orient toward the agency's goals as interpreted by the head of the agency. To the extent that the formal and informal organizations provide divergent goals and incentives, the characteristic bureaucrat is less attractive as a unitary representation of bureaucratic preferences. Two points are worth making crystal clear. First, incentives both inside and outside organizations are studied similarly. Second, the assumption of a characteristic bureaucrat is at times good enough to explain behavior, while at other times, it is not. This is an empirical question. The importance of this abstraction of the agency to the tractability of our examination of its position within an institutional environment, such as the U.S. separation of powers, will become apparent.

3.2.2. Budget-Maximizing Bureaucrats

Niskanen takes a *public choice* approach to developing a theory of administrative agencies rooted in the power of the purse. In the public management literature, the idea behind public choice theories is often misunderstood, particularly in normative terms. In neoclassical economics, the price and quantity of goods supplied are a product of the incentives and constraints facing consumers and firms. Likewise, public choice accounts have as their "central insight... that the provision of government services is an incidental effect of the incentives and constraints of voters, politicians, and bureaucrats" (Niskanen, 1991, 14).[7] In this setup, agencies represented by the characteristic bureaucrat provide policy outputs to a single "buyer," the legislature that passed the laws that enable it. In effect, then, the "demand for the output of an agency is that of this political sponsor [the legislature], rather than that of the ultimate consumers of the service" (Niskanen, 1991, 16). Institutions specified in the Constitution establish a representative democracy, and this renders Congress, not the people, the principal for our analytical purposes.

Niskanen (1971, 24) assumes that an agency is the sole supplier of a particular governance task; that is, only the Department of Defense produces a particular national security output. The relationship between agency and legislature is that of a bilateral monopoly rather than a

---

[7] Mueller (2003, 362) notes that while Downs (1967) and Tullock (1965) employ economic analysis to study bureaucratic organizations, Niskanen (1971) provides "the first systematic effort to study bureaucracies within a public choice framework."

competitive market: "The primary difference between the exchange relation of a bureau and that of a market organization is that a bureau offers total output in exchange for a budget, whereas a market organization offers units of output at a price" (Niskanen, 1971, 25). This also implies that tasks are pooled. This arrangement, Niskanen (1971, 24–25) notes, is "characterized by both threats and deterrence, by both gaming and appeals to a common objective... [,] hardly more unlike the rational-legal, impersonal relations which Weber finds characteristic of a bureaucracy." Ironically, as we have seen, Weberian bureaucratic rationality supports Niskanen's claim that the agency can be reasonably characterized by a unitary actor at the top of the organizational hierarchy. Goal conflict between the characteristic bureaucrat and the politician represents the means of understanding budgetary politics in Niskanen's model.

This bilateral monopoly has attributes with which we became familiar in the last chapter. Writes Niskanen (1991, 16–17), "the sponsor's primary advantages in this bargaining are its authority to replace the bureau's management team, to monitor the bureau, and to approve the bureau's budget. The bureau's primary advantage is that it has much better information about the costs of supplying the service than does the sponsor." If we consider the sponsor as principal and the administrative agency as agent, then we can draw on the lessons of the preceding chapter to understand the impact of the information asymmetry on the performance of governance tasks.[8] Recall that the solution to the incompatibility of incentives owing to your doctor's informational advantage was solved by offering her an incentive contract. Hiring, firing, and monitoring agents are the features of the institutional environment of the signaling and screening approaches we review in the following sections.

Recall that the solution to the hidden action problem involved paying your doctor a linear reward scheme, namely, a flat fee with a bonus that increases with the effort she puts into diagnosing your medical condition. Another common example of such a scheme arises when the chief executive officer (CEO) of a publicly traded corporation receives a bonus that depends on his performance. This is easily accomplished by a private firm because the CEO can be given stock options having value that is contingent on the quality of the management choices she makes on the job. Yet incentives for administrative agencies are different.

---

[8] Careful readers will note that we are not treating this as a bargaining problem analytically, though Niskanen called it one.

Government agencies have various important differences from private firms; the inability to distribute residual claims to the firm, such as stock options, is one key distinction.[9] This is of central importance to Niskanen's claim about the power of agencies vis-à-vis their sponsors in Congress:

Even in large corporations, a substantial portion of the income of senior managers is in the form of stock options. In such organizations a manager can maintain or sell his property rights in the firm, independent of the decision to maintain or change his managerial position. Consequently, these managers are significantly motivated by the expected future profits of the firm... A bureaucrat's "property rights," however, are specific to his managerial position, and any value of these rights can be appropriated by the bureaucrat only during the tenure in the position.... The coterminous relation of a bureaucrat's rewards and his position implies that a bureaucrat will maximize the total budget of his bureau during his tenure as head of the bureau. (Niskanen, 1971, 113–114)

In his original model, Niskanen (1971, 38) motivated bureaucratic behavior by assuming that the characteristic bureaucrat seeks to maximize the total budgetary allocation because "salary, perquisites of the office, public reputation, power, patronage, [and] output of the bureau" all increase with total budgetary allocations.[10] The sponsor politician is concerned with the output of the agency. Because the public is concerned with air and water quality, not any particular regulatory activity performed by the EPA, the politician who wishes to be reelected is likewise interested in these environmental outcomes. Nonetheless, the budget includes funds for any regulatory activities that the EPA undertakes. The bureaucrat knows the means by which budget is translated into the outcomes the politician desires, but the politician does not. Because of the bilateral monopoly, the bureaucrat's objective is to maximize his budget subject only to the constraint that the budget received must at least

[9] A substantial literature exists that characterizes the differences between public and private organizations as essential to understanding the public sector (e.g., Bozeman, 1987; Dahl and Lindblom, 1953). Organizational scholars have claimed alternatively that these differences are not important to understanding organizations generally (e.g., Pugh et al., 1969).

[10] Responding to criticism regarding the budget maximization assumption for theoretical purposes, Niskanen (1975, 619) constructs the microfoundations of the bureaucrat's preferences: "The bureaucrat is not, in this formulation, assumed to have any direct preferences for the budget, output, or efficiency of the bureau." He continues, "The relations between the conditions valued by the bureaucrat and the performance of the agency are determined by the reward structure of the institution, as established by the government review group." His core claim of oversupply likewise follows from the revised model.

cover the cost of generating the policy outcome that the politician seeks. Without this constraint, the agency would be doomed by an "unfunded mandate."[11]

Most memorable in Niskanen's theory was the claim that bureaucratic organizations separating from the political branches leads to an over-supply of the governance tasks they perform. For example, if an agency's task was to inspect businesses for ergonomic workplaces, it would always perform more than the efficient number of inspections needed to make workplaces ergonomically sound. Moreover, if the market for a public service is assumed to be competitive, the monopolistic agency is antici-pated to oversupply it in relation to the level of private provision. This type of claim connected Niskanen's theory of bureaucratic behavior to arguments favoring the privatization of government services (e.g., Miller and Simmons, 1998).

Governance covers a wide range of subjects from health care to envi-ronmental protection to civil defense. Niskanen claims that if the demand for the agency's output in one area becomes satiated, the characteris-tic bureaucrat may encroach into other policy areas by proposing addi-tional tasks (outputs) to be performed by the agency.[12] Writes Mueller (2003, 365), such encroachment "could take the form of radical inno-vations, or more plausibly, infringements of one bureau onto another bureau's domain, or onto the domain of the private market." In essence, Whitford (2003, 164) writes, competition among agencies "reveals information by allowing comparisons" that can help agencies avoid failure, that is, termination, bad publicity, and so forth. Moreover, entrepreneurial agencies can develop autonomy from their political prin-cipals through (1) divergent policy preferences from their political spon-sor; (2) organizational capacity "to create new programs, to solve prob-lems, to plan, to administer programs with efficiency, and to ward off corruption"; and (3) legitimacy in the sense that political authorities believe that the agency can provide "benefits, plans, and solutions to national problems found nowhere else in the regime" (Carpenter, 2001, 14). Because Congress must delegate powers to the agency, and because the president and courts play several roles in policy implementation, a broader politics is involved that we shall gradually unmask as this book progresses.

---

[11] While outside our present scope, an interesting body of theory on unfunded mandates has developed in the literature on federalism (e.g., Volden, 2005; Cremer and Palfrey, 2000).

[12] In Chapter 5, we discuss the related concept of strategic capacity building.

3.3. THE POLITICAL ECONOMY OF BUDGETING

Various challenges to Niskanen's model followed, with much constructive reexamination in the 1980s and 1990s yielding a new theory of the congressional power of the purse. The strongest challenges to the Niskanen model have been to its premises: first, that the characteristic bureaucrat maximizes its budget, and second, that a bilateral monopoly in which the agency can make take-it-or-leave-it offers to its sponsor is an appropriate model of budgetary politics (Conybeare, 1984, 483). Migué and Bélanger (1974), for example, argue that bureaucratic structure compels the bureaucrat to focus on the discretionary budget – the difference between the total budget maximized by the agency in Niskanen (1971) and the total cost of implementing the governance task.[13] Regarding process, Breton and Wintrobe (1975) focused attention on a legislative oversight function that is designed to reduce the sponsor's uncertainty about the agency's cost of production and weaken the agency's bargaining position. It is this oversight function that plays a central role in the theories to which we now turn.

3.3.1. Screening Approaches

By focusing on the superior authority of Congress in making appropriations to agencies – the power of the purse – political economists have developed an important picture of the incentives for Congress to control the bureaucracy via budgetary incentives. This more appropriate theory emerged in response to the Niskanen (1971) approach, and we begin to examine it in this section. We review efforts to understand the budgetary control of bureaucracy by viewing the power of the purse as providing Congress with the ability to credibly commit to budgetary increases or cuts designed to reward efficiency.

With Niskanen, Bendor et al. (1985) begin by observing that agencies have informational advantages over Congress that flow from two sources. First, bureaucratic performance of governance tasks can be difficult for Congress to observe, making the monitoring that Willoughby proposed quite difficult. When an agent of the U.S. Federal Bureau of Investigation is following a suspect, it is important that the steps he takes in pursuit be clandestine (from the suspect at a minimum). The need for unobservable process creates a hidden action problem. Second, bureaucrats develop

---

[13] Niskanen (1975, 619) incorporated the discretionary budget into its decision making.

expertise in "the relation between programs and consequences" or how successful or unsuccessful particular implementation practices are likely to be for particular governance tasks (Bendor et al., 1985, 1041). These problems create two policy design dilemmas for Congress. Niskanen addresses the first: Congress must know precisely how much output is produced, and the agency must produce exactly the amount it promises to Congress. Recall that Willoughby (1913) considered this a very difficult informational burden for Congress, suggesting that the agency's administrative expertise must be consulted.

But agency expertise yields a second problem. In an important paper, Miller and Moe (1983) note that "the most instructive and far-reaching criticism of Niskanen's work" centers on the fact that "budgets and service levels, after all, are not really bureaucratic decisions – they are joint decisional outcomes that arise from bureau-legislative interaction, and should be modeled as such." They focus on the role of oversight committees, recognizing that it is difficult for Congress to know how much effort the agency must exert to generate the promised output. Committees, they claim, develop rules of thumb or conjectures regarding the cost of bureaucratically produced outcomes, forcing a bureaucrat to "package his supply information within a framework imposed by the committee, and... this requirement will tend to block him from achieving budgets and outputs as large as he would like" (Miller and Moe, 1983, 319). This means that the principal–agent problem between Congress and the agency is solved in such a way that agencies cannot maximize their budgets. This is a very important critique indeed, but is it correct? Can Congress develop an incentive mechanism to learn whether its agent will efficiently implement the policies with which it is charged?[14]

One possible solution is to study the problem as one of hidden information. Suppose that two processes exist to perform a particular governance task: one that is highly efficient, and one that is inefficient. Bendor et al. (1985, 1043) postulate that Congress uses its constitutional power of the purse to create a screening mechanism under which the agency will have the incentive to act in a way that reveals its true marginal cost for

---

[14] An important response to this question from the certain strands of the policy implementation literature has been negative. Lindblom (1968, 26) notes that "what is feasible politically is policy only incrementally... different from existing policies." Because the legislature cannot choose an optimal revelation mechanism due to cognitive and organizational constraints, i.e., because they are boundedly rational, policy generally changes only incrementally. Various accounts of budgetary politics take this view (cf. Jones and Baumgartner, 2005, chapter 3; Wildavsky, 1984).

performing the governance task – the efficient or inefficient process – and be unable to use its expertise and private information.[15]

Like Audrey in Chapter 2, Congress achieves this by designing incentives for the agency. The screening mechanism central to the Bendor et al. (1985) argument is the budgetary appropriations process, a procedure that Congress has the authority to create in the way it chooses (by making a law).[16]

The budgetary process Bendor et al. (1985) model has five sequential steps:

1. The agency provides information of the possible ways in which it can use any budget resources to perform a governance task, that is, its production costs.
2. Congress unilaterally approves or disapproves an allocation of budgetary authority.[17]
3. The agency performs the task.
4. The agency's performance is monitored by an agent (the monitor) that Congress creates.
5. Congress imposes a penalty in proportion to the agency's "bias."

Agency bias is defined as the difference between the possible resource allocations promised in step 1 and the monitor's information about the true allocative possibilities in step 4. It is an example of an agency cost. It is driven by misinformation about the performance of a governance task and is the reason why monitoring is warranted. Because monitoring is costly, Congress does not use it on every occasion nor always in the same amount. It is also possible that monitoring will fail to uncover the cost of undertaking a governance task.[18] In an example of monitoring the production technology, albeit on behalf of the president, the Office of Management and Budget (OMB) has used the Program Assessment

---

[15] The marginal cost is that needed to produce an additional unit of output. Because this incorporates information about any inputs to production, e.g., equipment, additional staff, it is a critical concept for determining the agency's response to legislative demand for its output. Efficiency demands that marginal revenue, in this case, the marginal increase in appropriations due to congressional policy demand, equal marginal cost.

[16] Note that this model does not consider the presidential veto.

[17] This abstracts from the budgetary decision-making process established by statute in 1974, where overall spending levels are set by Congress and committees are kept within those bounds (Ferejohn and Krehbiel, 1987).

[18] To capture this, Bendor et al. (1985) make the logically equivalent claim that the monitor always discovers the agency's bias but audits the agency's activities with some nonzero probability. Monitoring every action the agency takes increases the probability of detecting the true bias – it eliminates the information asymmetry – but is costly.

Rating Tool (PART) as a mechanism for evaluating the management of agencies, including the efficiency in budgetary resource allocation that Bendor et al. (1985, 1044) describe. According to OMB, the PART's "overall purpose is to lay the groundwork for evidence-based funding decisions aimed at achieving positive results" (as quoted in Gilmour and Lewis, 2006b, 744). Higher scores are meant to be associated with larger budget increases, whereas lower scores are not meant to justify cuts but rather smaller incremental increases.[19] We discuss the PART initiative in more detail in Chapter 6.

If bias is detected, the penalty in step 5 is not exacted through budgetary reductions. The nonbudgetary penalty that results from the monitor's activity compels the agency to "trade expected budget against expected penalty," while a punitive reduction in resources may, in fact, "hurt Congress by reducing output" (Bendor et al., 1985, 1044). Budgetary authority makes it possible for an agency to undertake governance tasks that have constituency benefits that legislators need to be reelected. As Ting (2001, 264) puts it, "the tension behind the power of the purse is made clear: punishing an agency by cutting budgets may also hinder [a politician's] ability to realize her own policy goals." This is an important reminder that politicians value governance tasks for the policies they create, something made explicit in the spatial conceptions of policy conflict on which we focus in the next chapter.

Bendor et al. (1985) show that agencies' deceptive practices depend on the price elasticity of demand for their output.[20] If a change in demand due to a change in price is disproportionally greater than the change in price, the output is said to be elastic. Only agencies with inelastic outputs, such as the Department of Defense, overestimate their costs. We more carefully examine two sets of results from the Bendor et al. (1985) model. The first set depicts what might be called a politics of mutual deception between Congress and agency. By exploiting their asymmetric information, the actors are able to affect budgetary outcomes. Congress may well know more about demand for a governance task than the agency; after all, it has an electoral connection that creates incentives for its membership to

---

[19] A cautionary note about the objectivity of monitors is sounded by Gilmour and Lewis (2006b, 750), who find that PART scores affected budgeting but only in Democratic programs during fiscal year 2004 under Republican president Bush: "Advocates of Democratic Party budgetary goals can take some solace in these findings. They should expect that a Republican administration will reduce funding for programs that Democrats care about." This will be considered further in Chapter 6.

[20] The price elasticity of demand is defined as the percentage change in demand divided by percentage change in price.

understand the policy wants and needs of voters. It also has the ability to define penalties for bias detected by its monitors. If the agency faces uncertainty about congressional demand for the governance task as well as the penalty Congress might exact for bias – for example, because of ambiguous representations by Congress in statute – Bendor et al. (1985) claim that two effects are possible. These and other interesting results from the models we review in chapters 3 and 4 will be presented as propositions.[21] These propositions are also collected and reproduced in Appendix A.

Proposition 3.1. *Increases in demand uncertainty yield decreases in agency bias.*

Proposition 3.2. *Increases in penalty uncertainty yield decreases in agency bias.*

Because the agency has superior information about its cost efficiency in performing governance tasks, it, too, can behave strategically in creating uncertainty. These results depend on the degree of risk aversion characterizing the agency. In this case, *risk aversion* implies that the agency's marginal utility rises as the budget decreases: the first \$1 million in budget cuts matters more than the second, and so forth.[22] More generally, risk aversion implies that an actor has preferences not only over governance tasks but also over the likelihood that they will affect policy. Risk-averse actors may prefer a more certain policy impact with a lower payoff than a riskier outcome with a higher payoff.

Proposition 3.3. *In risk-averse agencies, increases in supply uncertainty yield increases in agency bias.*

Proposition 3.4. *In risk-seeking agencies, increases in penalty uncertainty yield decreases in agency bias.*

---

[21] Readers who are familiar with literature in formal theory will quickly notice that the form of these propositions is designed to incorporate the intuition behind the results rather than the results on their own. This is done to maintain the nontechnical style of this book, while highlighting the importance of specific predictions.

[22] While claims of the bureaucrat as deeply interested in preserving his organization and status exist throughout the literature, Krause (2003) constructs a statistical test of the risk propensities of the Securities and Exchange Commission (SEC). He finds that the SEC displays risk aversion with respect to its congressional appropriations but risk neutrality with regard to its own outputs. Essentially, the SEC displays a greater risk tolerance with respect to the resource under its control.

In sum, these propositions predict an interesting set of behaviors. If an agency is not sure about the value Congress places on a governance task it performs, it has the incentive to perform that task precisely as Congress expects. When Congress is unclear about the penalty that it will impose on an agency for nonperformance, the agency also has the incentive to do what Congress wants it to do without injecting any bias. Yet when an agency is risk averse, volatile production of its governance task keeps Congress fearful that it may not be performed. This allows the agency to bias outcomes in its favor.

3.3.2. Monitoring Institutions

Because an agency's superior information can permit bias, Congress has the incentive to create monitoring institutions that can collect information on its behalf. What is the effect of these institutions on the manner in which agencies use their budget? In the preceding chapter, we noted that an important characteristic of principal–agent relationships is that monitoring is not required when incentives are properly designed before a governance task begins. Specifically, we noted that Audrey could design a mechanism to determine whether applicants to the Department of Social Services have loyalist or careerist tendencies. Monitoring – even when credibly threatened but not carried out – can be part of such a mechanism. We begin with an abstract discussion of these mechanisms in both the screening and signaling contexts. Then we move to a discussion of federal monitoring institutions and their behavior to contextualize this discussion.

A preliminary step toward understanding the incentives inherent in monitoring regimes was taken by Bendor et al. (1985, 1053). They began with a very simple characterization of the ways in which administrative agencies use their budget. Their characterization assumes that it can be used in three ways:

1. Performing governance tasks, thereby creating "more of just what Congress wants."
2. Enabling constituency service, or "embodying resources in an inefficient production process to please a powerful constituency."[23]
3. Creating perks for bureaucrats, a scenario they labeled "plush-carpet syndrome."

---

[23] In the congressional politics literature, constituency service is an important way for individual legislators to curry favor, develop an incumbency advantage, and have more leeway to do what they would like to do in policy terms (Fenno, 1978; Cain et al., 1987).

Given these budgetary usage categories, the conflict of interest between politicians and bureaucrats is easily seen. The more the agency deviates from the way Congress intended the money to be used, the more important monitoring becomes, and the more willing Congress is to invest in it. The preferences of Congress over the bureaucratic disposition of budgetary resources can be captured in an ordering of these three possible uses. Bendor et al. (1985, 1054) characterize congressional preferences by ranking the loss Congress suffers when agencies use resources in each of these ways. As such, perquisites are assumed to produce the greatest loss – effectively squandering resources that could have been used to perform governance tasks. Task production presents the least loss to Congress because overproduction provides the only possible contradiction with congressional preferences. Constituency service falls somewhere in the middle. The agency's core constituencies may not be the same as those of Congress. For example, a Democratic Congress may be at odds with constituencies represented in legislation and executive action from a prior Republican Congress and administration.[24] Bendor et al. (1985, 1054) analyze a scenario in which Congress knows the type of use preferred by the agency and designs budgetary allocations and monitoring to get the best outcome it can given the loss it will suffer from that use.[25]

Bendor et al. (1985, 1054) show that the amount of monitoring that Congress undertakes depends on the particular governance task being performed by the agency. Below some maximum value, the relationship between monitoring and type can be summarized in the following way.[26]

Proposition 3.5 (Task-Type Monitoring Principle). *Congress monitors administrative agencies with a penchant for perquisites more than*

[24] We shall describe such influence in more detail in the next section as it is an insight derived from the signaling approach to budgetary politics. Moreover, evidence suggests that bureaucratic influence over the allocation of funding from federal programs is not merely policy analytic, partisan, or dictated by legislation. Bertelli and Grose (2009) find large impacts on resource allocation due to the ideological leanings of heads of departments (the characteristic bureaucrats we have discussed) when compared with members of Congress.

[25] In a recent paper, Grossman and Helpman (2008, 423) develop a model that permits Congress to design "the budget bill, which can include a cap on spending and earmarked allocations to designated projects." In this way, the bureaucratic preference ordering described here is superceded by congressional action, and budgetary politics becomes a version of the politics of delegation of powers and bureaucratic discretion.

[26] Congressional monitoring investments for each bureaucratic type – task production, constituency service, and perquisites – converge toward a maximum value, meaning that there is some maximal monitoring investment that Congress considers worth making.

constituency service agencies; the least monitored agencies are those that expend additional resources performing more of the governance tasks they were created to perform.

The task-type monitoring principle tells us something interesting about monitoring, namely, that among the types of agency loss that accrue when granting discretionary budget authority to administrative agencies, Congress favors overproduction, as Niskanen predicted, over constituency service and perquisite seeking. Congress can claim credit for punishing pork barrel spending that benefits individual members to the exclusion of larger constituencies and can certainly do so when attacking administrative featherbedding.

While this claim has some intuitive appeal, it is easily seen to be the product of the assumed ordering of congressional preferences described earlier; this is a very strong assumption. To improve the generalizability of their theory, Bendor et al. (1987) subsequently examine a more general version of the model. This analysis also examines a more nuanced budgetary procedure having the following stages:

1. The agency requests a budget for performing some governance task, and Congress cuts it by some amount.
2. A monitor gives Congress a signal about agency bias.
3. Congress uses the information in this signal (1) to penalize the agency for bias in its reported cost of production and (2) to update the budget it would like to allocate to the agency.
4. Congress changes the budgetary allocation subject to a "degree of irreversibility" arising from statutory restrictions or political realities (Bendor et al., 1987, 802–803).

Note here that the bureaucrat is uncertain about the cut, signal, and irreversibility. In this more general setting, Bendor et al. (1987, 803) find something different.

Proposition 3.6 (Monitoring Accuracy Principle I). *When monitoring provides accurate information for Congress, the agency provides accurate information about its cost of performing a governance task. However, if monitoring provides inaccurate information, the agency provides a cost estimate consistent with budget maximization.*

The importance of high quality monitoring is clear. When the agency is uncertain about what Congress will do to its budget, it will truthfully reveal its cost structure as long as monitoring is accurate. This is an example of the screening result we discussed in the case of Audrey and her Department of Social Services hiring practices in the last chapter. Creating an accurate monitoring scheme does not mean that it has to be used. It creates sufficient ex ante incentives for the agency to provide the information Congress needs to avoid overbudgeting the governance tasks assigned to it. Because the agency's characteristic bureaucrat knows that if Congress chooses to monitor, it will learn the true costs of undertaking a governance task, the agency runs the risk of a possible permanent budgetary penalty for misrepresenting its costs in that circumstance. Gambetta (1994) provides an excellent example of this idea through the case of the Sicilian Mafia. The Mafia ensures transactions on the part of buyers and sellers. It demands payment for this protection and uses a threat of force – an incentive mechanism – to ensure it. It does not need to break many kneecaps; it merely has to break enough to maintain the credibility that it will do so in the future. The ability of Congress to credibly commit to penalizing an agency that misrepresents its costs is the primary criticism of this approach. We take up this critique in the next section.

Some results differ under the latter approach of Bendor et al. (1987, 804). Among these are the predictions for the agency's misrepresentation given different agency tolerances toward risk.

Proposition 3.7. *When the agency is risk neutral, its bias in reporting costs decreases regardless of the penalty that Congress will impose. When the agency is risk averse, its bias increases.*

This finding is counterintuitive because the more risk-averse agency engages in the risky behavior of lying to Congress about the costs of policy production. The reason lies in the penalty that Congress imposes for detecting agency bias. Changes in the budget cuts anticipated by the agency have no impact at all on the penalty that Congress enacts on the agency, but they do affect the thinking of the characteristic bureaucrat. If she is risk neutral, she expects that stringent review will be followed by stringent process. Once Congress seeks to understand costs, deception matters less, and her expectation is that the agency will lose money. A risk averse bureaucrat perceives the situation differently. In the face of larger expected budgetary reductions, she is "willing to sustain a larger expected penalty in exchange for protecting part of its revenues from harsher cuts" (Bendor et al., 1987, 805). Risk propensities affect the agency's tolerance for budget cuts; risk neutral agencies can accept them, while their risk-averse counterparts circle the wagons and protect what they have.[27]

Since the outset of this book, we have been concerned about the governance tasks that agencies perform. Bendor et al. (1987) provide a set of predictions that allow us to gain traction on task distinctions across agencies.[28] *Project agencies* produce policies that are not separable into clear tasks. Their outputs are complex bundles of factors. It is difficult for school administrators to catalog every classroom activity in which their teachers engage. Similarly, diplomats in the State Department engage in a variety of activities, some clandestine. It is also the case that the administrative process, teaching or diplomatic negotiation, might not map conveniently onto student learning and goodwill toward the U.S. government abroad. In such areas, the costs of monitoring will be quite substantial. By contrast, *task agencies* perform governance tasks that, while complex,

---

[27] What happens if the agency is more uncertain about congressional action? Before, the model predicted a reduction in bias when uncertainty increased, but here, certain types of agencies respond to demand uncertainty by increasing their bias. More risk-averse agencies increase their distortions, and only the moderate levels behave as expected and decrease bias. Again, the agency is trapped and cannot reduce uncertainty.

[28] Readers may be familiar with a famous typology of organizations given by Wilson (1989, 158–171). He argues that the substantive ambit of the agency may make it extremely difficult to learn how the administrative process is undertaken, as in the case of craft and coping organizations. Wilson (1989, 165) defines a craft organization as one in which the activities of bureaucrats "are hard to observe but whose outcomes are relatively easy to evaluate." The antitrust division of the U.S. Department of Justice gives its attorneys substantial discretion in developing cases. Cabining that discretion might be unwise, as creativity in the case development process is important to enforcing antitrust laws. Yet supervisors can make the final decision on whether to take cases to trial, monitoring each case for overzealousness and outcome appropriateness (Wilson, 1989, 166). Coping organizations, such as public schools and the U.S. Department of State's diplomatic corps, present a situation in which outcomes are likewise difficult to monitor (Wilson, 1989, 168). Monitoring costs are lessened somewhat in the case of procedural organizations in which "managers can observe what their subordinates are doing but not the outcome (if any) that results from those efforts" (Wilson, 1989, 163). In the U.S. Armed Forces, peacetime operations are characterized by detailed inspection of every conceivable weapon-related procedure by a hierarchy of superiors. Yet Wilson (1989, 163) notes that "none of this tells us in fact what we really need to know: Do these weapons deter enemy aggression and, if fired, will they explode as planned on enemy targets?" Thus monitoring can be performed, but it may not lead to better outcomes. In production organizations, the costs of monitoring are lowest because "managers have an opportunity to design (within the limits established by external constraints) a compliance system to produce an efficient outcome" (Wilson, 1989, 160–161). There is some correspondence between this typology and that employed by Bendor et al. (1987). Craft and coping agencies correspond to the project category described later, while task and procedural agencies are similar to those in the task category.

can be subdivided. U.S. Postal Service supervisors, for example, can monitor the actions of sorters and carriers to calculate the extent to which they are meeting a target of so much mail delivered so quickly. Bendor et al. (1987, 810–811) produce the following prediction for these two types of agencies.

Proposition 3.8. *When they become more uncertain about the budgetary penalty that Congress will impose, project agencies increase their bias, while task agencies reduce it.*

The logic behind this claim is as follows. Because project agencies use a mix of factors to complete the governance tasks with which they are charged, it is more difficult for them to scale down production in response to congressional changes in the demand for those tasks. Moreover, highly technocratic agencies have a harder time retaining specialists in uncertain budgetary times; their skilled staff may find enticing career opportunities in the private sector, for instance. Like risk-averse agencies, project agencies protect their budgets when they become uncertain. Interestingly, then, increased monitoring by Congress only has its desired effect – reducing bias – when that monitoring has already been careful, penalties have been harsh, and agencies have been risk neutral. The same pattern induces very risk-averse agencies to increase bias. When monitoring and penalties have been weak, the perverse result that increased monitoring induces more bias follows: "If political realities are such that Congress cannot or will not impose proportional increases in sanctions for proportional increases in deception, then it would be wasting its time revamping its monitoring technology" (Bendor et al., 1987, 811).

Finally, Bendor et al. (1987, 813) examine optimal legislative strategies in choosing budget cuts and monitoring strategies. They distinguish two types of scenarios: reward budgets, where the agency truthfully reveals its cost information, and that is what Congress learns, and penalty budgets, where the agency misrepresents its cost structure and Congress uncovers the deception. When Congress can commit to such reward and punishment, the screening result is striking (Bendor et al., 1987, 818).

Proposition 3.9 (Strategic Budget Uncertainty Principle). *If Congress can increase uncertainty over reward or penalty budgets only when agencies request large (not small) budgets, then the agency always reduces its bias. When Congress does impose budget cuts, both project and task agencies are always less likely to bias their cost information.*

Commitment to reward and punishment strategy strikingly reverses the bilateral monopoly view of Niskanen (1971). The Strategic Budget Uncertainty Principle states that Congress controls the agency if it can control the latter's uncertainty over its resources and, as the next proposition suggests, its monitoring strategies.

Proposition 3.10 (**Monitoring Accuracy Principle II**). *Improvements in monitoring technologies always lower the value of deception for the agency, producing truthful cost information.*

Improved oversight gives agencies with efficient technologies no incentive to exaggerate their resource requirements for performing governance tasks. Because it improves the likelihood of detection, the penalty budget can be increased by Congress. If the cost structure of an agency is truly high, the agency is of the inefficient type, and better monitoring reveals to Congress that the agency is not engaging in deception. This ability to remove such congressional doubts reduces the incentive of these truly high cost agencies to bias their reports. As a result, Congress only monitors when the agency announces that it is the high-cost type (Bendor et al., 1987, 818).[29] In sum, the benefits of credible commitment for Congress are substantial, namely, it gets accurate information about the costs of performing governance tasks. It can then allocate budgets according to the true needs of agencies. Citizens get the governance tasks that their elected representatives decide on their behalf to provide and their tax dollars are allocated efficiently.

3.4. SIGNALING APPROACHES

Can Congress really make a commitment to reward and penalty budgets? Important realities of American politics suggest that it might not be able to do so. Congress is an elected body, and as such, the electoral connection provides information about the public's interests in governance. What may seem like a program worthy of budget reductions at one time may be politically infeasible at another. In such a sequence of events, Congress could commit to something that does not serve its members' interests in reelection. Elections themselves provide another commitment problem. Suppose an election precipitates a change in the partisan control

---

[29] Monitoring in this model is not costly, but if it were, this decision would remain unchanged as Congress would have a stronger incentive to avoid monitoring and its associated costs.

of Congress. In causing that shift, voters show that they want changes to governance. Credible commitments would require stable resource choices across elections. Although the benefits of commitment for Congress are substantial, they may not outweigh its costs. The culprit in this problem is the electoral connection as defined in the Constitution.

3.4.1. The Benefits of Monitoring

In an important response to the screening approach developed earlier, Banks (1989) moves away from commitment and toward a signaling approach. This corresponds to Audrey's inability to commit to hiring based on the ratio of generalist to specialist courses. Congress can once again monitor the agency in this approach, but only at a cost. This means that Congress may decide not to audit the agency if monitoring costs outweigh the informational benefits to be gained (Banks, 1989, 693).

Banks (1989) examines two types of budgetary procedure. Under the closed procedure, an administrative agency knows its true cost structure and requests a budget from Congress. Being presented with an agency budget request, Congress may take one of three possible actions: (1) allocate the requested amount; (2) reject the request and supply a status quo budget, for example, last year's appropriation; or (3) monitor the agency at a cost in attempt to learn its true cost type. Readers should recognize this as the process embodied in the screening models discussed in the last section. By contrast, the open procedure allows Congress a fourth alternative, namely, to make a counterproposal – a budget cut, for instance – that the agency may accept or reject. If the agency rejects the budget cut, the governance task is not completed, and the agency receives no budget from Congress. The governance task is not undertaken if that occurs.

Recall that a key feature of signaling results is the separation of types. A signaling mechanism would be successful for Congress if high- and low-cost agencies were to behave differently when making their budgetary requests. Like Audrey, Congress is looking for signals that are correlated with the true type of an agency. Banks (1989) finds the following.

Proposition 3.11. *Under a closed rule and as long as monitoring costs are not excessively high, the agency signals its true cost type in making its budgetary request. The agency types separate through the budgets each type request.*

Monitoring creates a set of incentives that keep the agency from fully using its informational advantage, namely, its knowledge of the true costs of performing the governance tasks with which it is charged. In other words, monitoring is effective in achieving congressional interests even without commitment under the same process that yielded Propositions 3.6–3.10. The results under an open budgetary procedure with costly monitoring are strikingly different.

Proposition 3.12. *When Congress is permitted to make a counterproposal under an open rule and monitoring costs are not excessively high, the agency's budget request reveals no information about its true cost type in this scenario.*

Without the possibility of commitment to reward and penalty budgets, Congress should not make a counterproposal to the agency. Doing so generates a pooling result and no distinction between agency cost types, efficient or inefficient. As a consequence, Congress finds itself with the incentive to impose a procedural solution. As long as monitoring costs are moderate or low, Congress can get more information from the agency by creating a monitor and eliminating its own option to make a counterproposal. Essentially, Congress replaces one form of commitment with another. By eliminating the counterproposal, Congress regains its advantage over the agency despite not being able to commit to reward and penalty budgets. Though beneficial, auditing does place substantial financial demands on the public fisc. We should emphasize that Propositions 3.11 and 3.12 require that the costs of monitoring be moderate. If Congress must pay more to set up accurate monitoring than the agency's cost information is worth, it will choose not to do so. The aforementioned monitoring accuracy principles describe incentives that cannot be accessed by Congress for free.

Because monitoring does have the strong informational benefits we have described, it would be beneficial for Congress to create institutions that engage in it. This is an important lesson from both the signaling and screening approaches. We now turn to a brief description of three institutions that are involved in budgetary monitoring in the U.S. government. These provide important examples of the complexity of monitoring mechanisms we have been describing in practice at the federal level.

3.4.2. Three Federal Monitors

The Budget and Accounting Act of 1921 required the president to submit to Congress a proposed budget for the federal government each year. It created two organizations to aid in the process: the Bureau of the Budget, the president's monitor, and the General Accounting Office, the congressional monitor (Saturno, 2000). Prior to the act, Congress exerted primary influence over budgetary outcomes through the Legislative Appropriations Committee (Committee on the Budget, U.S. Senate, 1998). Yet the Constitution does not establish any specific process for the consideration of budget-related legislation. In 1939, the Bureau of the Budget expanded its mandate from preparation to execution of budgets, clearing executive orders, and circulating codes of management (circulars) to agencies. A 1970 reorganization plan and enlarged mandate was accompanied by a name change to the current Office of Management and Budget (OMB) (Shuman, 1992). OMB's current mission is to "assist the President in the development and execution of his policies and programs" through the "development and resolution of all budget, policy, legislative, regulatory, procurement, [electronic government], and management issues."[30]

3.4.2.1. Office of Management and Budget. Monitoring costs are considerable. OMB receives the largest appropriation and has the largest staff of any unit within the Executive Office of the President. The office is organized into four central Resource Management Offices, each headed by a politically appointed associate director, as well as the Office of Federal Financial Management, which develops and directs the implementation of financial management policies and systems (Tomkin, 1998). Program divisions of OMB review agency proposals, while the Budget Review Division (BRD) coordinates the budget process for the executive branch and assembles the budget proposals that the president submits to Congress (Tomkin, 1998). Unlike the Resource Management Offices, BRD is headed by a career official. The Budget Analysis branch of the BRD, composed of financial, fiscal, and policy analysts, works to produce deficit, economic, and budgetary forecasts used in the budget formation process. OMB's Budget Review branch coordinates the final form of the president's budget before its submission to Congress and tracks the changes made during the congressional appropriations process (Tomkin, 1998). The budget concepts and systems branches prepare process guidelines and instructions that agencies must use when submitting budget requests to OMB, respectively, and track agency budget formulation processes and budgetary activity in Congress (Tomkin, 1998).

OMB gives estimates and projections used to analyze agency budget requests each year. During initial budget formulation, agencies receive

[30] See http://www.whitehouse.gov/omb/organization/index.html.

estimates from OMB, the Treasury Department, and the Council of Economic Advisors, which they use to formulate their formal requests. From April through June, OMB, along with the Treasury Department and the Council of Economic Advisors, reviews major governance tasks, updates long-term forecasts of revenues and expenditures, and presents the president with a projection of economic conditions (Maltese, 2000). During July and August, OMB uses the directives of the president's decisions to create ceilings to aid agencies in forming their requests for presentation to OMB during September and October. OMB then reviews the requests and prepares issue papers and recommendations for the OMB director's review. Decisions are then given to the agencies, which can either accept or appeal. If OMB and the agency cannot reach a decision, the matter is resolved by the president. When OMB informs agencies of their final decisions, agencies revise their budgets to include the decisions in the president's formal request to Congress by the first Monday in February (Maltese, 2000).

3.4.2.2. *Congressional Budget Office.* The Revenue Act of 1941 was an early congressional attempt to centralize its budgetary oversight capabilities. It created the Joint Committee on the Reduction of Federal Expenditures, which was composed of the members of the House and Senate appropriations committees. The staff of the joint committee tracked congressional action against the president's budget request (Committee on the Budget, U.S. Senate, 1998). The Congressional Budget and Impoundment Control Act of 1974 established a congressional budget procedure, instituted annual adoption of a concurrent resolution on the budget, and created the House and Senate Budget Committees and the Congressional Budget Office (CBO) to provide Congress with budgetary information independent of OMB (Saturno, 2000).

In the 1970s and 1980s, the workload assigned to OMB by the administration compelled a dramatic politicization of the organization. Rather than providing neutral information to aid the administration's decision making, OMB became an advocate for favored policies (Tomkin, 1998). Shuman (1992, 21) calls the act that created CBO "the creature of crisis." He continued,

The crisis had two components. One was the struggle for power between the Congress and President Nixon, the only major transfer of power – this time from the president to the Congress – was occasioned by an attempt to abuse power. The other component was the Congress's guilt over its inability to discipline itself and to bring the budget under control.

A report by the Senate Budget Committee (1998) notes that Congress began to realize that it had no institutional framework with which to address budgetary approval. A monitoring problem existed. The president and Congress both had interests (as political principals) in controlling the actions of administrative agencies. The president was gaining the upper hand with the changes in OMB behavior and was using that advantage against Congress in separation-of-powers politics. Rather than establishing its own spending priorities, Congress could only react piecemeal to presidential budget requests. A dispute between President Nixon and Congress developed in 1971 amid severe inflation in the national economy. Then OMB deputy director Caspar Weinberger told a Senate subcommittee that the president had authority to impound, or refuse to appropriate, funds to administer programs enshrined in congressionally enacted statutes "derived basically from the constitutional provisions which vest executive power in the President" (Stone, 1991, 388). On this view, President Nixon sought to impound up to $15 billion of previously approved agency appropriations (Committee on the Budget, U.S. Senate, 1998). Through the Congressional Budget and Impoundment Control Act and its subsequent revisions,[31] "Congress required itself to pass a budget resolution that set targets for both revenues and expenditures for the coming year (making a statement about the level of deficit that it is willing to accept)" (Gosling, 2006, 39–40). This requires the CBO. If the OMB finds that a particular legislation will fail to meet the deficit target or discretionary spending limits, the president must issue a sequestration order, reducing or cancelling budgetary authority (Maltese, 2000).

The CBO is divided into seven branches – Management, Business, and Information Services; Macroeconomic Analysis; Tax Analysis; Budget Analysis; Microeconomic Studies; Health and Human Resources; and National Security – and its staff comprises primarily economists and public policy analysts. The Macroeconomic Analysis Division creates economic projections using the estimates and budget projections prepared in-house by the Budget Analysis Division and the Tax Analysis Division and policy and program analyses prepared by the program divisions – Health and Human Resources, Microeconomic Studies, and National Security. Despite its history, the CBO describes its role as analytic, not to make policy recommendations.[32] It submits an annual report on fiscal policy to

---

[31] These were incorporated in the Balanced Budget and Emergency Deficit Control Act of 1985 and 1987 and the Budget Enforcement Act of 1990.

[32] http://www.cbo.gov/aboutcbo.

the budget committees of the House and Senate that estimates the budgetary impact of alternative revenue and spending patterns, including the status quo (Maltese, 2000).

The story behind the creation of these agencies presumes a conflict of interest between the executive and legislative branches of the U.S. federal government. They are *multiple principals* of administrative agencies. As principals, the president and Congress each seek to incentivize administrative agencies to produce policies they desire. When partisanship and ideology differ between those actors, their preferences about the execution of governance tasks can likewise diverge. Readers can gain traction by thinking about these interests separately, though models that completely integrate them can be difficult to construct with generality.[33] As we will see in the next chapter, the constitutional role of each of these principals gives rise to a strategy for modeling their influence over the performance of governance tasks. Does the conflict of interest manifest itself in the reports of OMB and CBO? Figure 3.1 shows differences between budget deficit projections of OMB and CBO as well as their reporting bias, measured as the difference between the projection each monitor provides and the actual deficit (Krause and Douglas, 2005). If monitoring were impartial, we would not expect to see differences between these deficit projections. Nonetheless, the solid black line denoting OMB and CBO differences is not flat at zero. During periods of divided party government – when the president and at least one chamber of Congress do not share affiliation with a political party – the difference in OMB and CBO projections is larger.[34] Consistent with the story behind the creation of OMB and CBO as separate monitors, these data suggest that conflicts of interest in the separation of powers between the executive and Congress are present.

The figure also suggests that electoral incentives have an impact on information quality. Differentials between OMB and CBO are largest near presidential elections. In particular, note the spike in the solid black line near the 1984 election that pitted President Reagan against Democrat Walter Mondale. OMB projected larger deficits as Republicans sought

---

[33] One way of thinking about the difference between principals is in terms of their influence technologies, or capabilities to offer incentives to the agency that actually shape behavior. This idea has its roots in common agency approaches such as that of Grossman and Helpman (2000). Bertelli and Lynn (2004) provide an example of interest groups being considered as multiple principles to a human services agency.

[34] This claim is based on a simple difference of means test ($t = 2.38$). I thank George Krause for generously providing the data for Figure 3.1.

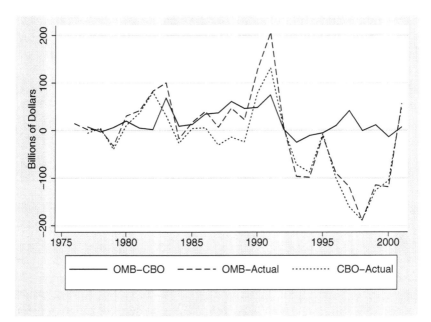

FIGURE 3.1. Differences in deficit projections between monitoring agencies, 1976–2001.

to rein in spending by a Democratic Congress until the end of President George H. W. Bush's administration. CBO projected greater deficits when the Republicans took control of the House of Representatives in 1994, with the opposite projections noted during the campaign between President Clinton and Republican senator Robert Dole. Represented by the dotted lines, bias peaked near the end of presidential administrations. Dramatic overestimates by both monitors near the end of the Bush administration gave way to even greater underestimates during the Clinton administration. CBO bias was also noticeably lower during President Reagan's second term and during the term of his successor, with both bias and differentials being very high in the George H. W. Bush years. These patterns suggest that OMB and CBO understand that they are agents of different principals but must also maintain credibility in their forecasting.

3.4.2.3. Government Accountability Office. The Government Accountability Office (GAO) began as the General Accounting Office in 1921. The Legislative Reorganization Act of 1946 required that GAO send reports to the House and Senate Committees on Government Operations, rendering GAO a congressional agent. World War II and then the Cold War further expanded its role. In 1950, Congress passed the Budget and Accounting Procedures Act, which called for GAO to engage in large-scale audits of government efficiency. GAO changed the composition of its workforce to reflect the new mandate, hiring more professional auditors and accountants (Brown, 1970). In the 1960s, GAO renewed its focus on financial management and program evaluation (Mosher, 1984).

GAO emerged as a response to the budgetary chaos following World War I; wartime spending had increased the size of the national debt, and Congress realized that it needed more information and control over government expenditures.[35] GAO was created to be independent of the executive branch and to investigate how federal money was spent on congressional request (Brown, 1970). Though GAO depends on Congress for its powers, resources, and general oversight, it also has a number of delegated governance tasks that it can undertake independently (Mosher, 1984).

GAO is distinct from OMB and CBO in that its evaluations are not part of the budget formation process. Instead, it performs work in ex post expenditure monitoring, that is, receipts were properly recorded and controlled, financial records and statements are complete and reliable, and so forth (Mikesell, 2007). GAO investigates whether agency practice adheres to current laws, regulations, and the auditing standards it establishes (U.S. General Accounting Office, 2007).

3.4.3. Mitigating Monitoring Costs

Given the Gordian structure of the federal monitors just discussed, the cost of monitoring cannot reasonably be seen as low or nonexistent. How does Congress control monitoring costs? To address this question, Banks and Weingast (1992) build on the claim in Proposition 3.11 regarding the closed procedure by incorporating a role for interest groups in supplementing information that a congressionally created monitor might provide. Organized interest groups such as the AARP or the National Resources Defense Council spend a great deal of time and resources monitoring the policy-making activity of administrative agencies. If Congress could create incentives to align those efforts with its own monitoring needs, then the resource savings could be substantial.

---

[35] http://www.gao.gov/about/index.html.

Proposition 3.13 (Monitoring Cost Principle). *As monitoring costs become larger, Congress uncovers less information about an administrative agency's cost of performing a governance task.*

Consequently, an incentive exists for Congress to supplement monitoring with other sources of information. In Chapter 4, we describe some conditions under which Congress passes vague laws but requires agencies to make complex administrative procedures. Moreover, the Administrative Procedure Act of 1946 provides courts with substantial authority to review agency rulemaking when affected parties seek to challenge it. The self-interest of the aggrieved parties making these challenges generates information about the activities of administrative agencies that Congress can take into account (McCubbins et al., 1989). In other words, the watchful eyes of groups and individuals can reduce monitoring costs.

To understand the congressional response to this incentive more fully, Banks and Weingast (1992) provide a far more sophisticated picture of politicians than does Niskanen (1971, 1975). Assuming that politicians are interested in being reelected, and that the electoral gains they can achieve are influenced by the governance tasks assigned to administrative agencies, they characterize an agency in terms of monitoring difficulty and interest group cohesion in the domain of the governance task (Banks and Weingast, 1992, 519).[36]

Interest group cohesion is a simple idea. Each governance task attracts attention from a different constellation of interest groups. In other words, groups monitoring different agency policy choices are themselves different. For example, a Department of Labor mandate to regulate the ergonomics of the workplace may attract the attention of the National Federation of Independent Businesses (NFIB), who want to ensure that any rule that the department adopts does not place an undue financial burden on small business, and labor unions wishing to ensure safe working conditions for their members. Other groups may be allied with small business and worker interests, respectively, but those sides of the issue stand in opposition to one another. If many more groups ally with the unions and worker interests than with the NFIB and small business, workplace ergonomics is an area of high-interest group cohesion. Alternatively, if the groups involved in the policy area are relatively balanced

---

[36] Banks and Weingast (1992) provide additional predictions regarding agency provision of constituency benefits as well as electoral gains to politicians and the degree of interest group cohesion.

on both sides, the governance task is undertaken in an environment of low cohesion.

Congress, in the Banks and Weingast (1992) model, seeks to incentivize these groups to provide monitoring on their behalf. Democrats may share the interests of the unions on this issue, while Republicans share the interests of small business. In any monitoring scheme, a majority coalition in Congress would likely want to concentrate incentives on the groups that best represent its policy position. Banks and Weingast (1992) provide the following prediction.

Proposition 3.14 (Group Cohesion Principle). *Given the difficulty of monitoring the actions of an administrative agency, greater interest group cohesion in the governance task environment decreases the costs of monitoring.*

Proposition 3.14 suggests a mechanism through which interest groups help Congress police the performance of governance tasks. The general idea is this: more cohesive groups interested in a particular governance task, either pro or con, will generate better information. Because of their keen interest in the substance of the governance task and the policy it is capable of producing, Congress can rely on them to do this. If the groups find the agency doing something that goes against their interests, Congress can, through hearings and statutory provisions that elicit their input, give groups the opportunity to inform their members about what the groups have observed. While the groups have an interest in biasing their findings in favor of their policy positions, Congress is aware of the bias and can provide the opportunity for the groups supporting its position to "sound fire alarms" when the agency violates their positions. Should Congress want less bias, it can intentionally incentivize such information from groups on both sides of an issue, that is, the labor unions and NFIB in our example. This *fire alarm oversight* is of great value to Congress; the interest groups perform and incur much of the cost of monitoring bureaucratic policy making (McCubbins and Schwartz, 1984).

Figure 3.2 provides a look at an important implication of the Group Cohesion Principle that reaches beyond budgetary politics. Depicted there is attention by the GAO to the policy-making activities of two agencies operating in different environments of interest group cohesion.[37] The

---

[37] Attention to policy-making actions is measured as $\ln(1 + k)$, where k is the count of GAO reports issued in each year in reference to each agency's activities. These data are used in Warren (2010), and I thank Patrick Warren for his generosity in sharing them.

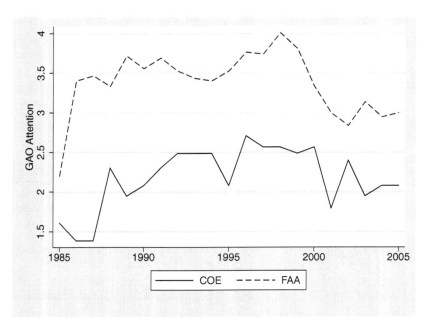

FIGURE 3.2. GAO attention to the Corps of Engineers and Federal Aviation Administration, 1985–2005.

U.S. Army Corps of Engineers (COE) plans, engineers, and maintains a variety of public works, including dams and canals throughout the United States. Their work is highly technocratic, as are the groups and professional associations interested in the governance tasks it performs. By contrast, the Federal Aviation Administration regulates civil aviation. While also highly technocratic, its regulations, for example, place for-profit carriers into conflict with safety advocates. With more cohesion, the Group Cohesion Principle anticipates that less attention would be paid to the COE by the GAO as such attention represents costly monitoring expenditures. For COE tasks, Congress can rely on fire alarms, such as those sounded in regard to flood control in New Orleans in the wake of Hurricane Katrina in 2005. By contrast, the FAA, with less cohesion, is a more problematic candidate for fire alarm oversight. After the costly and bitter strike in 1981 that ultimately led to the decertification of the Professional Air Traffic Controllers Association as the union – organized interest – representing air traffic controllers in U.S. airports, cohesion in this area decreased. It is striking to note the increase in GAO attention as a new union, the National Air Traffic Controllers Association, was formed in 1987 (Beik, 2005).

Since more cohesion implies more effective oversight, Banks and Weingast (1992, 521) note that "there exists a strong selection effect at work in the process of agency creation: while bureaucratic discretion [to shape policy] is a big problem for some potential agencies, politicians are far less likely to create such agencies." Because fire alarm oversight is more effective when agencies are delegated governance tasks in areas of strong interest group cohesion, Congress can place those tasks in the hands of agencies and use interest groups as an important part of the incentive mechanism. When groups are less cohesive, monitoring is more difficult and costly. Even in the case when interest groups are not cohesive, Congress may create an agency. As an illustration, Banks and Weingast (1992, 520) provide the example of the Consumer Product Safety Commission (CPSC). The safety of products is of interest to a very diffuse constituency, namely, consumers. Yet that constituency is of essential interest to politicians. If a monitoring technology, for example, the ability of citizens to sue the CPSC for failure to adequately address safety concerns, is designed such that even a diffuse constellation of interests can decrease monitoring costs, the agency will still be created because some monitoring can provide information to keep the agency's budgetary authority at more efficient levels. The problem is one of incentive design, and agency creation – the congressional delegation of powers – is the core subject of the next chapter.

3.5. CONCLUSION

We began this chapter with a constitutional provision, namely, that which locates the power of the purse in Congress. At its end, we saw how the performance of governance tasks by administrative agencies rather than by Congress itself makes it difficult for Congress to gain a clear picture of the resources required. This is an essential lesson in American government: the separation of powers creates interbranch conflict that renders the power vested in one branch contingent on the actions and authority of another. It is precisely what James Madison meant when he wrote in *The Federalist*, no. 51, that "ambition must be made to counteract ambition." Barnard (1938) envisioned such incentive-based checks as central to an organization, and we know from Chapter 1 that the federal government can be seen as an organization for theoretical purposes. The collective action problems inherent in our government are addressed by creating institutions that place incentives on politicians and public managers. We discussed the analytic traction we can gain on the separation of powers by considering an organization as acting with unitary interest, assuming that these collective action problems are solved.

This chapter brought our first look at the importance of credible commitments in American government. If Congress could commit to pecuniary punishments of administrative agencies, those agencies would reveal accurate information about the cost of performing governance tasks so that policy goals might be achieved without wasting tax dollars. Commitment, in this milieu, forms the basis of the enforcement required in effective incentive design. While this claim establishes an important benchmark for further analysis, the nature of the congressional electoral connection makes such commitment impossible. Various current members may lose the next election, and a newly constituted Congress may well make entirely different choices. One crucial institution in the budgetary process is the ability or inability of Congress to make a counterproposal to an agency once the agency has stated the costs it anticipates for producing the policies Congress wants. A counterproposal stage in the process induces the agency to reveal no information about the true costs it faces when producing policy. Removing that stage creates a form of commitment by Congress, and the agency provides good information about true cost of governance. This has an important effect on the quality of information revealed by the agency.

A critical feature in our discussion was the role of monitoring institutions in providing incentives for agencies to provide accurate information about the resources needed for governance. The CBO and GAO were created to perform such monitoring roles for Congress. Interbranch conflict with the president's OMB suggests that the separation of powers figures centrally in the design of monitoring agencies. We saw that the nature of the interest group environment can assist Congress in performing its monitoring tasks thanks to the well-defined policy preferences of groups and their cohesion on a policy issue. When groups are cohesive, monitoring becomes easier for Congress. Knowing the ideological direction of groups' biases and permitting them opportunities to alert Congress of agency activity that troubles them generates a low-cost monitoring scheme. Where there is disagreement among groups in less cohesive environments, Congress has to invest in a monitoring technology of its own to better understand governance and its costs.

The distribution of interest groups around a policy implemented by an administrative agency can be intuitively understood by reference to a continuum of policies, arrayed from liberal to conservative, with groups most preferring a particular policy being placed along that continuum.

Such is the nature of the spatial model that forms the basis for the theories discussed in the next chapter. With it, we will explore the incentives involved when Congress decides to create the administrative agencies that gave it such difficulty in this chapter. We will also explore the design of those agencies and the important, but heretofore implicit, role of the president in American separation-of-powers governance.

4

Delegation and Discretion

Detailed legislation and judicial control over its execution are not sufficient to produce harmony between the governmental body which expresses the will of the state, and the governmental authority which executes that will.... The executive officers may or may not enforce the law as it was intended by the legislature. Judicial officers, in exercising control over such executive officers, may or may not take the same view of the law as did the legislature. No provision is thus made in the governmental organization for securing harmony between the expression and the execution of the will of the state.

– Frank Goodnow (1900, 97–98)

We now consider the central institutional design problem for democratically sound public management, the delegation of legitimate policy-making authority to responsible officials. At its essence, this is an agency problem: Congress passes a law that is signed by the president. The coalition of actors supporting the law, or the enacting coalition, now wishes it to be implemented by an administrative agency, in keeping with the policy intent of the actors in that coalition. As in the agency problem arising between you and your doctor in Chapter 2, the problem may be one of effort, or it may be that the agent has different policy preferences from the enacting coalition. This particular conflict of interest lies at the core of this chapter.

The epigraph suggests that this conflict of interest is not resolved simply by specifying the actions that an administrative agency should take in the text of statutes. In Chapter 3, this incomplete contracting problem created incentives for Congress to expend resources on monitoring agency compliance to preserve its interests and to ensure that the budgetary resources an agency received were being used in a way that Congress intended. When read together, the Monitoring Cost and Group Influence principles state that an administrative agency receives greater discretion to complete a governance task as the legislature's opportunity for and cost of monitoring and sanctioning the agency increase. In this chapter, our understanding of the congressional–bureaucratic relationship broadens substantially from this starting point.

To begin our exploration of delegation, we briefly describe a view of politics that has much in common – indeed, is rooted in – our approach to governance from Chapter 1. Political institutions can impose costs on key actors in the policy process or the manner in which changes to the status quo occur. Those actors also receive benefits from the incentives the institutions create. As institution building, delegation has its benefits and costs, which are more fully considered in the following section. After considering these benefits and costs, you may wonder why, if indeed a conflict of interest is the problem, the congressional enacting coalition does not seek to solve it in the same way that Audrey sought to hire the right type of Department of Social Services (DSS) employee in Chapter 2. We discuss why the incentives facing the enacting coalition are such that screening does not make sense even in the presence of substantial conflicts of interest. This will have normative implications, to which we shall return in Chapter 6.

To analyze delegation problems, scholars have made use of what are known as spatial models. The canonical model we discuss later has a broad substantive reach. This is because it considers the implementation of delegated governance tasks as inducing policy preferences. If the National Park Service makes a rule (a governance task) that permits snowmobiles in Yellowstone National Park, its decision is favorable to some liberal as well as some conservative members of Congress. The policy it induces is likewise processed by interest groups and citizens across an ideological spectrum. Libertarian conservatives may welcome it, whereas environmental liberals may challenge it vociferously. The notion that a policy can take a position along an ideological continuum, or policy space, allows the models in this section, spatial models, to make predictions about a tremendous range of governance tasks. Because the spatial model is such an important facet of the approach, we develop its intuition carefully before turning to the canonical delegation model.

The canonical delegation model in the political science literature is exemplified by the Epstein and O'Halloran (1999) theory of congressional policy making. We review key features of their influential model in detail. The core problem we study in this chapter occurs when a legislature delegates policy-making authority to an administrative agency in a separation-of-powers system. As a general approach, the canonical model lends itself to various extensions with important substantive implications for understanding contemporary governance. We concentrate our efforts on a careful characterization of the process by which policy is implemented as this is precisely the job of public managers. These extensions to the canonical model have implications for the ideological affinity between political principals and key public managers, the incentives for administrators to acquire expertise that makes them specialists in specific governance tasks, and the ability of administrative agencies to gain policy-making autonomy from their political principals.

Though this chapter offers a large number of arguments and predictions that help us analyze public management problems, it presents only a small selection of the work that has been done. The concluding section offers a brief list of extensions. Additional contributions are also discussed in Appendix B.

4.1. AGENCY PROBLEMS IN U.S. GOVERNMENT

A variety of actors and relationships are important in understanding modern governance in the United States, and relationships between them give rise to a host of agency problems studied in the political economy literature. A map of these problems is depicted in Figure 4.1. Key actors in the political process are represented as boxes, and the connected boxes represent agency relationships that have been studied in the literature. Though we will not examine all these problems in this book, it is important to recognize the breadth of the literature. One way to think about these relationships – sometimes called *transaction cost politics* – is that each box in Figure 4.1 represents an actor that has the ability to impose transactions costs on the other actors to which it is connected. In solving these agency problems, institutions are designed to mitigate these transaction costs (Dixit, 1996). Such costs are not a bad thing. For instance, we want voters to have the ability to create friction in governance as it is necessary for popular accountability.

The theories that we discuss in this chapter focus primarily on one linkage: the relationship between Congress and agencies, though the president also emerges as an active player. Important characteristics of this relationship generate an incomplete contracting problem when Congress considers delegating a governance task to an agency. As Goodnow's

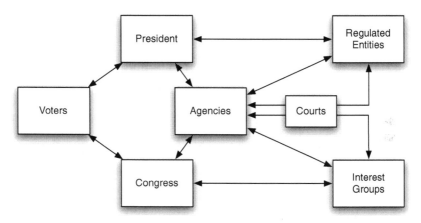

FIGURE 4.1. Key relationships examined in delegation models.

epigraph makes plain, it is impossible for a piece of legislation, no matter how detailed it may be written, to specify every contingency that may confront an administrative agency as it implements the statute. Yet an incentive based solution is workable. The methodology developed in Chapter 2 allows us to see a statute in the same way that we see the contract between you and your doctor, and Goodnow is telling us that any delegation contract will be incomplete.

Congress is considered the principal and an administrative agency the agent in the relationship formed by the statute that represents the delegation contract. The solution to this incomplete contracting problem is a statute that includes a set of *ex ante controls* – so named because they are put in place before the administrative agency begins a governance task – that create incentives for the administrative agency to act in the interests of Congress. This is, of course, something you know well after reading the previous two chapters, and it remains important to our present story.

Because the Constitution requires the president to sign proposed legislation before it becomes law, theories that seek to understand this relationship also incorporate the role of the president and his veto. In many cases, the president has the power to appoint top agency officials and members of independent commissions. This is an important presidential power over administrative agencies and is considered carefully when studying this relationship. Of course, the Senate has the constitutional authority to "advise and consent" to these administrative appointees, and this confirmation process is incorporated into models of congressional delegation. Two important types of administrative agencies are defined in terms of the ability of the president to remove top managers in them at will. In executive agencies, namely, the fifteen cabinet-level departments such as the Department of Defense or the Department of the Interior, the president also has the authority to remove top managers at his pleasure. In contrast, the president does not enjoy discretionary removal power in the case of independent agencies such as the Federal Trade Commission or Federal Reserve Board.[1] As we discussed in the previous chapter, Congress can provide for *ex post controls* over administrative agencies through monitoring and oversight provisions. Such provisions are described in this way because performing governance tasks can trigger review and, possibly, punishment. All these elements of congressional delegation have been incorporated into political–economic theories of administrative delegations.

We saw the influence of interest groups and regulated entities in the delegation of powers through our discussions of fire alarm oversight in the preceding chapter. These incentives relate to the Monitoring Cost and Group Influence principles. We thus considered the portion of Figure 4.1 that forms a triangle of Congress, agencies, and interest groups at the end of Section 3.4. Interest groups were involved in the ex post monitoring of governance through what we called fire alarm oversight. As groups are influential in the formation of statutes, they can be relied on for their continued interest in the subject and can provide valuable information to Congress regarding the performance of governance tasks. Scholars have studied the role of groups in a variety of ways. We give some attention to the implications of interest group activity in specific policy areas to appointment and confirmation incentives for administrative officials in Section 4.4. However, much more work has been done to provide a framework for understanding the role of interest groups in governance.

One influential approach treats interest groups as multiple principals that aim to influence an agency as it undertakes governance tasks. In this framework, various interest groups have a common agency relationship with the administrative agency, and each attempts to offer the agency a menu of incentives from which the agency chooses.[2] You should recognize this as the screening problem facing Audrey in recruiting for the DSS. By providing different compensation to specialist and generalist graduates, Audrey was able to learn something about the type of employee she

---

[1] This was the source of controversy about the delegation to the Public Company Accounting Oversight Board noted in Chapter 1.

[2] The most complete statement of this theoretical approach is Grossman and Helpman (2000).

was getting in her applicant pool. In common agency models of interest group influence over administrative agencies, bureaucrats aggregate support from various groups when performing governance tasks. This creates both incentives for groups to align with each other to concentrate their influence and free-riding incentives for groups to expend no influence effort while those with similar resources exert influence on their behalf.

Some political–economic models explicitly incorporate the voter into the governance landscape. Approaches in which a voter is considered a principal and an elected official her agent are known as *political agency theories*. They examine incentives related to the electoral connection between citizens and their elected representatives. These theories are used to understand relationships on the left side of Figure 4.1. As with the bureaucracy in Chapter 3 and Congress in some subsequent instances, the government as a whole is considered a unitary actor agent to make these models tractable. After all, an enacting coalition must form for legislation to occur, and such models can be interpreted as seeing these coalitions as themselves agents of the people rather than principals with policy interests all their own. In political agency models, the government maximizes social welfare, acting as a benevolent caretaker for the general interest.[3] Laffont and Tirole (1993) have used such models in influential studies of the incentives involved in business regulation. To develop their arguments, theories in this camp make assumptions about the way that governments aggregate citizen preferences beyond the ballot box and majoritarian institutions like legislative voting.

Congress can nonetheless make policies that reduce social welfare even to the point where its benefits fall below its costs. It does this by responding to interests that are not consistent with some broader public interest. A very famous result known as the Arrow (1963) impossibility theorem shows that it is impossible to reveal society's preferences through a mechanism that, at once, (1) avoids dictatorship, (2) allows citizens to state their beliefs freely, (3) achieves unanimity, (4) remains robust to the consideration of irrelevant alternatives, and (5) produces the same result whenever applied. It is institutions, then, that solve these shortcomings. This creates a divide between the public economics literature in which they are situated and that of *positive political theory*, which is a term often used to describe the mode of theorizing we use in this book. Public

---

[3] Readers with some background in political philosophy will recognize that the government is seeking the greatest good for the greatest number of individuals, which Jeremy Bentham believed was the appropriate moral action. Thus my statement about the general interest is true in a utilitarian sense.

economics and positive political theory share much common ground in the questions they seek to address, but positive political theory has developed richer depictions of political institutions and the policy process, whereas public economics has concentrated on the distributional consequences institutions impose on markets and economic life.

This section has presented a high-altitude overview of the basic agency problems present in contemporary American governance and the scholarly literatures that consider them, highlighting the central place of administrative delegation in that picture. The relationship between political principal and administrative agent is the central problem in democratic public management. We now turn to an important threshold question for understanding this important relationship: what are the costs and benefits of delegation to Congress? Indeed, we should anticipate that if delegation is more costly than it is beneficial, Congress would have no incentive to do it. From the outset, it must be understood that delegating powers is a decision, not a requirement for Congress. As it does in many policy areas, Congress may retain policy-making authority as provided to it by Article I of the Constitution. Delegating power to administrative agencies in a policy area presents associated costs and benefits that are important to consider.

4.1.1. The Benefits and Costs of Delegating Powers

Congress can benefit from delegating governance tasks to administrative agencies in several ways. Two of these benefits are principally technocratic. First, delegation saves time and reduces workload for members of Congress and their staff, leading to *effort reduction*. Second, delegating allows Congress to take advantage of knowledge and skilled practice that the agency develops in connection with implementing a governance task, helping to make sound public policies. This expertise rationale motivated you to consult a doctor in Chapter 2. Alexander Hamilton relied on it in *The Federalist*, No. 23, when arguing for the delegation in the area of national defense: "It is impossible to forsee or to define the extent and variety of national exigencies, and the correspondent extent and variety of the means which may be necessary to satisfy them." Note the manner in which Hamilton echoes Goodnow's sentiment from the epigraph, reminding us that statutory delegation is an incomplete contracting problem.

Another benefit of delegation accrues only if Congress has a certain type of preference toward policy. In Chapter 3, we defined a risk-averse actor as one who prefers a more certain outcome with a lower payoff to a riskier outcome having a higher payoff. If Congress is risk averse with regard to outcomes from an agency's implementation of a specific governance task, then the *reduction of uncertainty* is an advantage that flows from delegation to experts in that area of substantive policy. As we shall see later in this chapter, the propositions following from the canonical model of delegation do not depend on a requirement that Congress be risk averse, but it is not unreasonable to think that it is in relation to some governance tasks. Suppose that Congress is interested in curtailing highly skilled immigration into the United States as a means of encouraging business firms to give highly paid jobs to American citizens during an economic downturn. In addition to its intended effect, that policy may lead businesses to move their capital elsewhere to take advantage of lower-cost labor markets. If Congress delegates responsibility for implementing these immigration restrictions to Immigration and Customs Enforcement within the Department of Homeland Security, that agency may well implement the policy in a way that keeps jobs and capital in the country. Yet it is also possible that the implementation of such a rule will be very difficult and could lead to bad outcomes that have a low payoff for Congress. In this case, it may be reasonable to assume that Congress is risk averse and would benefit directly if the agency were to acquire substantial expertise to minimize the risk that this policy will drive out good jobs or business capital. Such interpretations are important for you to consider as you apply the ideas in this chapter, and in this book, to the problems you study and confront.

Two additional benefits of delegation are political in nature. Delegating policy-making authority permits the *protection of special interests* because they can be incorporated into statutes and even the structure of bureaucratic organizations. We have discussed the impact of interest groups on oversight, of course; incorporating them into the structure and process of administrative agencies may provide opportunities for fire alarm oversight. It is important to recognize the source of administrative agencies, namely, the statutes in which Congress delegates authority. Moe (1995, 143) describes the creation of administrative agencies as being the outcome of what he calls *structural politics*, whereby agencies emerge from the legislative process "as a jerry-built fusion of congressional and presidential forms, their relative roles and particular features determined by the powers, priorities and strategies of the various designers. The result is that each agency cannot help but begin life as a unique structural reflection of its own politics." The agency's life, Moe observes, continues this politics, and interest groups play a primary role. Groups who oppose the agency's actions look for ways to keep it from performing the governance task it was delegated (or changing the way it is executed), while "the winning group must constantly be ready to defend its agency from attack – but it may also have to launch attacks of its own" (Moe, 1995, 146).

When Congress writes a statute that delegates, it can incorporate administrative procedures – ex ante controls – that incentivize or even compel public managers to perform governance tasks in ways that favor the winning group. This rule-bound, institutional advantage has been termed *deck stacking* (McCubbins et al., 1989). In environmental regulation, the choice between command and control regulation that places specific requirements on polluters and cap-and-trade schemes that produce markets has this effect. Specific requirements invite organized interests as they intensely affect some polluters and not others. The same effect occurs in social policy when Congress authorizes in-kind transfers, such as child care, rather than cash equivalents, such as food stamps, or when it provides subsidies to providers of services rather than vouchers to consumers.

A final benefit of delegation is not related to the completion of governance tasks per se but to the interest of Congress to preserve favor with the electorate by *shifting blame* to administrative agencies for doing tasks that yield unpopular policies. This is a not problem relegated to the delegation of powers by a political actor but, as Hamman et al. (2010, 1847) claim, is present in many agency problems and works to the advantage of both principal and agent:

A principal may hire an agent to take self-interested . . . actions that the principal would be reluctant to take more directly. The principal may feel more detached, and hence less responsible, for such an action if it is delegated, while the agent may feel that he or she was "just carrying out orders" or merely fulfilling the requirement of an employment contract. Through the use of agents, therefore, accountability . . . can become vertically diffused with no individual taking responsibility.

The important part of this behavioral concept of blame shifting is that it suggests how delegation may redirect responsibility from both Congress and the administrative agency with which it has charged a governance task. While the electoral connection gives members of Congress the incentive to avoid responsibility for governance tasks yielding bad policy, an administrative agency can rely on a restrictive delegation to locate blame.

Delegation does not come without its costs, of course, and we have already discussed the first among these. In the preceding chapter, agency costs accrued to Congress in financial terms, just as they did in health and financial terms in the contract you made with your doctor in Chapter 2. In what follows, we generalize the notion of agency costs in the delegation costs to incorporate *policy conflict*. Such conflict means that Congress and the administrative agency have different views of what policy the delegated governance task should generate. As policy conflict increases, then, Congress becomes worse off. In the next section, we will show that this can be intuitively represented as ideological disagreement between Congress and the agency through a spatial model.

A primary reason behind the delegation of authority is the acquisition of expertise by the agent. However, as we saw in Chapter 2, the expertise that an administrative agency develops can also contribute to agency loss because it creates *information asymmetries* between the expert agency and nonexpert Congress. Because the agency knows more about the environment surrounding and technology for implementing a governance task, Congress is at a disadvantage. In Section 4.4, we address this problem in some depth by considering models that shed light on the question of when administrative agencies have the incentive to acquire the expertise that creates this informational agency cost. Even when the administrative agency acquires expertise, another cost is generated because the agency can, quite simply, make mistakes. These mistakes are not a political problem – Congress can and does blame agencies for them – rather, they are a technological problem for the agency. In other words, the transformation between the effort an agency devotes to a governance task and any particular policy is not perfect. This refers to the *capacity*, or technical capability, of the agent to execute the task. Increases in agency capacity reduce the uncertainty surrounding the completion of a governance task, but low capacity agencies present Congress with considerable uncertainty about the policy that will ultimately result from the delegation.

The final cost is also one that we have discussed in the preceding chapters. *Monitoring* is an ex post review of agency actions that requires resources. The Congressional Budget Office and Government Accountability Office require large operating budgets to effectively perform the monitoring functions with which they are charged. An important lesson of your encounter with your doctor in Chapter 2 is that if ex ante incentives are appropriately designed, the cost of this monitoring can be reduced. Our discussion of the role of interest groups in oversight suggests another way to mitigate these costs. Reducing ex post oversight costs by improving incentive design is a central theme of this chapter. In the models that follow, Congress weighs the costs and benefits of delegation in the case of each governance task and makes the choice to grant administrative discretion when the benefits dominate.

4.1.2. Policy Windows

Think back to Audrey's predicament in hiring the right type of DSS employee. Recall that the solutions to screening problems involve the provision of a menu of incentives – or to develop rules or institutions that generate such incentives – for the agent to reveal its true type or to dispatch tasks in a way suitable to Congress. Gailmard (2009) compares the delegation problem with the screening approach in terms of the ability of two types of statutes to provide good outcomes for Congress. In so doing, he provides an important result that gives insight into why Congress has the incentive to delegate rather than to create a screening mechanism to find the optimal agent.

The first type of statute is known as a *menu law*. Like Audrey's pay scale, a menu law associates observations that an agency might make with a set of actions that the legislature requires the agency to take. Throughout this chapter, we shall refer to conditions that the administrative agency observes as *states of the world*. Thus a menu law requires the following policy process: (1) the agency observes the state of the world and chooses a policy by performing a governance task and then (2) the legislature observes the policy and transfers some benefit – such as budgetary resources, as discussed in the preceding chapter – to the agency according to the menu (Gailmard, 2009, 28). For instance, a trigger pricing mechanism established in a 1978 statute was meant to speed up action by the Department of Commerce and the U.S. Customs Service when they were investigating an influx of cheap steel produced internationally on the domestic market. These agencies had been collecting an index of foreign steel prices, and the new legislation simply required that if that index produced a price that was below a certain level, investigations should be conducted in an expedited manner (Gailmard, 2009, 26). Note that this menu law requires a commitment by the legislature to the index value in the same way that Audrey had to commit to a wage level in Chapter 2 and Congress to the penalty or reward budgets in Chapter 3.

The second type of statute creates a *policy window* for agency action. After observing the state of the world and applying its expertise to the governance task, the agency may create any policy within some restrictions. The policy window, then, is simply a set of outcomes that an administrative agency can implement that will not be overturned by Congress.

Enforcement occurs only outside the policy window and is done through corrective congressional legislation. The discretion that the agency has in performing its governance task is represented by the size and location of the policy window. As long as its discretionary action does not produce a policy that is too far from what Congress would like, that policy will remain in place.[4] Under the Toxic Substances Control Act, for instance, the Environmental Protection Agency (EPA) is required to issue a rule when it observes a certain state of the world, defined by Congress as a "significant new use" for a toxic substance where exposures could raise public policy concerns. Within a reasonable interpretation of "significant new use," the EPA can make any rule.[5] It may, for example, require fully fluorinated alkyl sulfonate-containing compounds that have no less than four and no more than ten carbons to be regulated. Making this rule – a regulatory governance task – is fine if it produces a policy within the window. Although it is legal, it is important to note that this agency-created requirement provides an entry barrier for new suppliers but would be supported by incumbent producers. The burden of proof is on the new use supplier, but for current suppliers, the burden of proof rests with the EPA. Policy window restrictions are far more common in practice. They are the mechanism studied in the canonical model of delegation in Section 4.3.

The key shortcoming of a menu law is that it requires Congress to commit to the incentives that the statute lays out. This was noted as a problem with penalty budgets for agency noncompliance in Section 3.4. As you will recall, one of the benefits of delegation is blame shifting. By delegating policy-making authority, Congress is able to avoid taking responsibility for governance tasks producing policies that prove unpopular with the electorate. Commitment to a punishment scheme may place Congress in a precarious position if it means that an administrative agency doing something popular must be punished. Members of Congress may complain that the rules are unwise and things should be changed, and given its constitutional power to enact corrective legislation, an enacting coalition may form to change the statute. If that happens, the agency

---

[4] Gailmard (2009, 33, 35–38) shows that the policy window does not have any gaps. Though a gap could provide useful information to the legislature when agencies pool their policy choices near the edges of the gap, the legislature must commit to allowing the agent to use its information in what Gailmard calls an "unattractive" way.

[5] The interpretation of reasonableness is an important question of administrative law that political economists have not ignored. It is, however, outside the scope of our present discussion.

cannot appeal to a more sovereign authority to restore the terms of the original statute, as you could do in court if the contract with your doctor were abrogated. The credibility of the policy commitment is tarnished.

Because of this problem, the choice of statute that Congress makes when delegating a governance task to an administrative agency is between a no-commitment menu law and a policy window. This difference becomes particularly relevant when it is considered as a function of the policy conflict between Congress and the administrative agency, and Gailmard (2009, 40) shows an important reason why the policy window approach is employed in the canonical model we discuss in Section 4.3. Congress is always better off when it uses a policy window to delegate a governance task to an agency than when it attempts a menu law to which it cannot commit for the reasons just described.

Proposition 4.1. *Congressional utility is greater when it uses a policy window delegation than under a menu law regardless of the degree of policy conflict with the agency performing the governance task.*

Because the policy window allows the agency to use its expertise about the state of the world in ways that it finds appealing, albeit within bounds, it gives the agency the incentive to truthfully reveal its own policy values. This is critically important: an agency in these theories is not a neutrally competent technocrat but a policy-motivated strategic actor (Hammond and Thomas, 1989). For instance, if a preponderance of officials in the EPA believe that emissions-reducing rules are required to mitigate global warming, the agency will let Congress know those views. Implicit within the policy window statute, then, is a different kind of commitment; Congress cannot veto the agency's policy choice if it falls within the window.[6] However, this commitment is not always effective (Gailmard, 2009, 41). Back in the DSS, Audrey may not be able to reject an application from a friend of the governor regardless of her commitment to incentivizing potential loyalists and improving the stability of her organization. This kind of patronage scheme will not be kept secret over time as applicants will learn that Audrey does not always reward the behavior she claims to reward. The incentives flowing from her salary commitments to candidates through advertising will be lost. In congressional delegations, the administrative agency may perform governance tasks so

---

[6] Legislative vetoes are unconstitutional; *INS v. Chadha*, 462 U.S. 919 (1983). Though the Supreme Court's opinion in that case was quite formalist – in the sense of legal reasoning being separate from policy implications – its rule did preserve an aspect of commitment that assists Congress in making more effective delegations of governance tasks to administrative agencies.

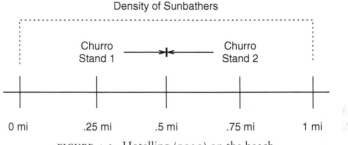

FIGURE 4.2. Hotelling (1929) on the beach.

as to produce policy outcomes that make Congress quite unhappy because neither ex ante controls (fire alarms) nor ex post oversight (police patrols) provides it with sufficient information about what the agency is doing. As a consequence, agency loss will remain an important consideration in the canonical model.

Before presenting a version of the canonical model in some detail, we must represent the policy window in a way that is both intuitive and mathematically tractable. The solution that the literature has developed employs a clever analogy to geographic distance. To see this, we take a trip to the beach on a sunny day.

4.2. THE SPATIAL MODEL

The spatial model of policy disagreement taken in this chapter is due to Hotelling (1929), who developed a model of firm competition on the basis of geographical, or spatial, positioning. Hotelling examined the question of why retailers locate near each other rather than in locations where they face no visible competition. Customers, who live all around town, would be advantaged if retailers were more scattered because they would not have to travel as far to buy their goods. Quite apart from this question, the importance of Hotelling's contribution is a simple mathematical representation of geography.

While there are more inviting pictures of a sunny, Southern California beach on a summer day, Figure 4.2 will have to do for now. People get to the beach by car, and the parking lot they use is located at the left edge of the space; the beach continues along for one mile. Sunbathers are symmetrically distributed around the half-mile mark such that they are scattered rather evenly across the beach. The distribution used in Figure 4.2 is the uniform distribution; regardless of where an observer looks along the beach, she sees the same number of sunbathers. With all those leisure-seeking sunbathers around, market opportunities are certainly present.

Two churro vendors have arrived to sell their equally delicious snacks to the sunbathers from carts that can be moved freely along the beach. Where should they locate?

We begin the analysis with two important assumptions about the preferences of the sunbathers. First, they choose the churro stand they wish to visit on the sole basis of its geographic proximity to where they are situated on the beach. This may be because they dislike walking, because they do not wish to disturb their sunbathing more than is necessary, or for a variety of other reasons. When choosing a vendor, our sunbathers seek to minimize the spatial distance between their own position and the churro stand. Ideally, then, the vendor would come to them, but since that doesn't happen, they simply walk the shortest distance to buy a churro. Second, in health-conscious California, our sunbathers only want one churro, regardless of how far they walk to get it. In economics, their demand for the churro is called *inelastic*: as the cost of buying a churro (price plus effort walking to the stand) increases, demand stays the same. We will return to these assumptions in a moment as they are useful in understanding the political behavior that interests us in this chapter.

Suppose that the two vendors initially locate at the 0.25 and 0.75 mile markers along the beach. This would allow the vendors to command half the market share. Yet this is not a stable equilibrium. If stand owner 2 moves his stand 0.10 miles toward the center of the beach, he would gain 10 percent of stand owner 1's market share. Owner 1 would (literally) not stand for this and would rationally move toward the center to recapture the customers she lost to owner 2's encroachment. This would continue until equilibrium is reached, with the stands located side by side at the 0.5 mile marker. In equilibrium, the stands retain their 50 percent market share, but the sunbathers are not benefited by the competition. Rather than having to walk, on average, 0.125 miles from the original stand positions, they must now walk 0.25 miles.

Sensing importance far beyond churro sales, Hotelling (1929, 54–55) suggests the importance of spatial analysis for understanding political behavior with an example of candidate competition:

Each [political] party strives to make its platform as much like the other's as possible. Any radical departure would lose many votes, even though it might lead to stronger commendation of the party by some who would vote for it anyhow. Each candidate "pussyfoots," replies ambiguously to questions, refuses to take a definite stand in any controversy for fear of losing votes. Real differences, if they ever exist, fade gradually with time though the issues may be as important as ever.

Downs (1957) built on these ideas to produce a theory of candidate behavior in electoral competition that remains important in contemporary electoral studies. This version of the spatial model gives us the tool we need to make the policy window analytically tractable. Rather than physical distance between churro vendors on a beach, the Downsian spatial model uses the horizontal line in Figure 4.2 to represent a continuum of policies from liberal to conservative. Voters are distributed symmetrically as before, but this time, their distribution is the recognizable normal bell curve.[7] Most voters have *ideal points*, or most-preferred policies, that are moderate, though extremists certainly exist.[8] Like the sunbather who has unrolled his beach towel in some spot along the beach and craves a churro, it would be fantastic in the eyes of a voter if a candidate would locate in the same place ideologically that she finds herself. As the policy represented in that candidate's campaign diverges from the voter's ideal point, she gets less value from voting for that candidate. The voter chooses the candidate that is closest to her ideal point for the same reason that the sunbather becomes a patron of the nearest churro stand. Voters and sunbathers have *Euclidean preferences*, so named because the value the voter gets diminishes as the (Euclidean) distance from her most-preferred policy outcome increases. Like our sunbather who only wants one churro, political institutions require that in U.S. congressional districts, voters are represented by only one House member and can only vote for one candidate for the House of Representatives. Thus voters' Euclidean preferences remain inelastic. This is a simple way – the remainder of the chapter deals with much more complex instances – in which institutions shape behavior.

Figure 4.3 depicts the Downs (1957) spatial model of candidate competition. Suppose one Democrat (candidate 1) and one Republican (candidate 2) enter the race with distinctly Left- and Right-leaning campaign policies, respectively. Because party and ideology are correlated in American politics, we can use a spatial model to investigate partisan

---

[7] Careful readers will quickly see that a normal distribution is not required for the result, but it is shown here for simplicity in exposition.

[8] An important means for testing these models was developed by Poole and Rosenthal (1997) that is similar to the revealed preference idea from demand theory in economics. When political actors engage in certain actions – for instance, when members of Congress cast roll-call votes – they reveal some information about their preferences in the same way that you do when you buy an iPod Touch, but only when its price drops from $299 to $229. The iPod makes you better off at the lower price than the status quo of $229 in your pocket and a train commute without music. An example later in this chapter will make use of estimates that are based on this measurement of revealed ideology.

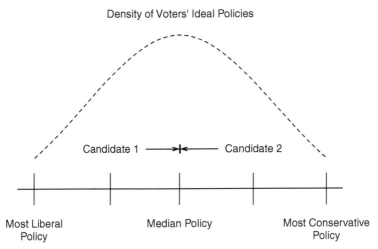

FIGURE 4.3. Downs (1957) and the median voter.

conflicts as well (Poole and Rosenthal, 2007). Like our churro vendors, a moderate move by the Republican candidate can win some of the Democratic votes, creating an incentive for the Democrat to respond by moving to the center to recapture those voters. It is easily seen that this equilibrating process will end at the center of the policy space, the location preferred by the *median voter*, who splits the distribution of voters in half. In equilibrium, both candidates offer similar, moderate policies to voters. Indeed, the median voter's position is extremely powerful in this model. Given a choice between the median voter's ideal point and some policy to the left, for instance, candidate 1's position in Figure 4.3, the median will be preferred by the median voter, of course, but also by all voters more conservative than the median. Likewise, a more conservative position such as that of candidate 2 will be preferred by the median and all voters who prefer more liberal policies. Though the literature on campaigns and elections has progressed considerably since this model, it is useful in explaining the way in which spatial models operate.

While not by any means an accurate portrait of the contemporary scholarly literature on party positioning, the spatial representations at the heart of the simple median voter model allow us to understand policy conflict as ideological disagreement, which will be valuable as we interpret the predictions that constitute a political–economic theory of delegating governance tasks. More good news is that we now have all the basic building blocks necessary to understand the canonical model of delegation, to which we now direct our attention.

4.3. THE DECISION TO DELEGATE

We have now arrived at the heart of this rather complex chapter. Epstein and O'Halloran (1999) develop an influential model of congressional delegation, and we explore that model in some detail to understand the basics of a canonical approach to theorizing about delegation. To understand the question answered by the model, it is important to note an institutional fact about Congress. Although most readers will know something about congressional committees, their importance in the theory of delegation comes in the expertise of highly specialized subcommittees, which provide an alternative to administrative agencies in the delegation of governance tasks.[9] The House Subcommittee on General Farm Commodities and Risk Management states on its Web page[10] that it is responsible for "program and markets related to cotton, cottonseed, wheat, feed grains, soybeans, oilseeds, rice, dry beans, peas, lentils," among other things. Should Congress wish to delegate a governance task related to, say, lentil markets, it has a choice. It might delegate the task to an administrative agency such as the Department of Agriculture, or alternatively, it may choose to keep the task in congressional hands and have the subcommittee handle implementation of specific lentil market regulations. This choice is important in understanding the characteristics of delegations.

Costs and benefits to the handling of governance tasks within congressional committees must be weighed. Some benefits from delegation described earlier likewise accrue because the task is essentially being performed by a subset of legislators who can reduce efforts for Congress as a whole, develop substantive expertise, be incentivized to consider special interests, and take blame for unpopular decisions. The costs of delegation are similar to the administrative agency scenario, but one important additional agency cost arises. Committee or subcommittee members, after all, have geographically circumscribed constituencies – congressional districts – and may seek benefits for those voters to the exclusion of all others.[11] This may involve targeted (or pork barrel) spending, which may be generally unpopular or nonsalient but extremely popular among a

---

[9] The committee system plays an important role in the development of coalitions in Congress (Weingast and Marshall, 1988) and has been heavily studied by political scientists.

[10] The page can be found at http://agriculture.house.gov/singlepages.aspx?NewsID=30&LSBID=44.

[11] This is an important reason why political scientists are less enthusiastic than economists about government aggregation of individual preferences through the social welfare functions we described in connection with public economics.

particular committee member's constituents. Should Congress delegate lentil regulation to a subcommittee or to the Department of Agriculture?

Epstein and O'Halloran (1999) model delegation by taking the statute as the unit of analysis. This means that the relevant decision for Congress is not the creation of a multipurpose administrative agency like the Department of Labor but rather a choice of whether to delegate a specific governance task or related cluster of tasks to an administrative agency – existing or created anew – or to keep the task in Congress by assigning it to a committee or subcommittee. For the completion of each governance task, Congress faces what industrial organization economists call a *make-or-buy decision* (Williamson, 1996, 41). It could give responsibility to a committee and make (insource) policy within Congress, or it could delegate the task to an administrative agency and buy (outsource) it by incurring the political and pecuniary (i.e., budgetary) transaction costs. Congress chooses the option that provides a benefit that outweighs its cost.

One caveat is required before proceeding: our original story in Chapter 2 of your doctor visit included only a single principal (you) in the problem. The separation of powers in the U.S. Constitution implies that an administrative agency has more than one principal, as we discussed briefly in Chapter 3. Epstein and O'Halloran (1999) incorporate presidential influence but do not distinguish between the preferences of the Senate and the House of Representatives. Other authors make this distinction. For instance, Huber and Shipan (2002, 256) offer a bicameral model and reveal conditions under which the chamber with preferences closer to those of the president can extract benefits in the performance of governance tasks. Important extensions of this approach are possible, and several exist in the literature. A sampling are discussed in Appendix B.

4.3.1. The Canonical Model

The Epstein and O'Halloran (1999) model involves four strategic actors: the congressional floor median, a congressional committee, the president, and an administrative agency. We assume that each has induced preferences over public policy outcomes. Though we assume that members of Congress prefer being reelected to losing their seats, the interest of the voters in particular outcomes compels, or induces, their own interest in such policies. Each policy outcome can be arrayed along a unidimensional policy space just like the candidates' campaign positions in Figure 4.3. Each actor has an ideal point in this space. The median member of the

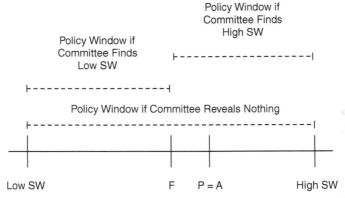

FIGURE 4.4. Understanding the Epstein and O'Halloran (1999) model.

legislature is important for the reasons we discussed in the preceding section; this makes her a reasonable characteristic member to represent Congress in the model (Epstein and O'Halloran, 1999, 54).[12]

Policy outcomes depend on the policy passed by Congress and the impact of the state of the world on the enacted policy. This very abstractly describes the *policy implementation process* by which statutory enactments are implemented to yield outcomes that voters value. To represent this in a way that makes our policy space most useful, we simply consider policy outcomes as equal to the enacted policy plus the impact of the state of the world. When performing a governance task, an agency produces policy in this way, which is similar to the use of inputs to produce outputs through a production function or technology in microeconomics. Looking at Figure 4.4, suppose that the value of the enacted policy is F. If the impact of conditions in the world is positive, the policy outcome drifts rightward from the enacted value, whereas if it is negative, it drifts leftward from F. The highest and lowest values to which policy can be pushed by the impact of the state of the world are denoted along the line as "High SW" and "Low SW," respectively.

The legislative process at work in the Epstein and O'Halloran (1999, 55) model begins with the action of the congressional committee; it learns some information about the governance task being delegated, including the state of the world, and prepares a bill to be considered on the floor of the legislature. In this stage, the committee interviews witnesses,

---

[12] Actors other than the median can be pivotal, depending on congressional rules such as the Senate filibuster rule and the presidential veto override provision in the Constitution (Krehbiel, 1998).

commissions and collects reports, and engages in other information-collecting and -processing activity. Such action places the committee in a relatively expert position when compared to the floor median's knowledge of the details and implementation possibilities of the governance task at issue. You should recognize this as what we have called an information asymmetry.

When deciding whether to endorse the bill, the floor median has a choice over two things. First, it must decide the position of the enacted policy in the policy space over which we have said the actors have induced preferences. This is a key characteristic of spatial models. Second, the floor median must choose the amount of discretion the agency has in performing the delegated governance task. Taken together, these actions define a policy window that constrains subsequent implementation decisions that will be taken by an administrative agency. Recall, however, that Congress faces a make-or-buy decision. Epstein and O'Halloran (1999) treat the situation in which the administrative agency is given zero discretion as a failure to delegate any authority to an agency – a nondelegation. In that case, the floor median sets policy, and it is implemented by an agency performing a governance task, producing a policy according to the implementation process we have specified earlier; the sum of the enacted policy and the state of the world. For Epstein and O'Halloran (1999, 58), this is equivalent to a situation in which an agency must still perform the governance task, but it is sufficiently constrained in its discretion that it cannot effectively change public policy. Providing some income tax relief for individual taxpayers who purchase new hybrid cars is an example. While the Internal Revenue Service (IRS) must decide whether a vehicle purchase qualifies as a hybrid car, that information is rather easily discoverable – Congress could even supply a list of models – and it would be difficult for IRS auditors to move policy perceptibly away from the congressional enactment.

If the administrative agency does receive discretion, a delegation occurs. The president can then use his appointment power to choose an administrator or agency head, who serves as the characteristic bureaucrat for the agency.[13] In the preceding example, the president may choose a new chief IRS administrator or even a new secretary of the treasury. The ideal point of that appointee will determine the most preferred policy, or

---

[13] Presidential appointments can occur in the nondelegation case, but the policy window so constrains the agency's action that the president cannot use appointments to gain a policy better than the congressional ideal point.

ideal point of the agency in the policy domain, relevant to the governance task at hand. In the case where the statute creates a new agency to handle the governance task, the president is granted the authority to choose a head administrator. If the delegation is given to an extant agency, the president may choose to change the agency head in light of the new governance task that has been charged to it.[14] In either the new or extant agency case, the president is not able to commit to a policy outcome in advance because he has the incentive to wait and see where the policy window lies and how large it is before choosing an administrator. His appointment powers allow him this luxury of time, and Congress, as a result, will most likely not consider his commitment to appoint a particular person to head the relevant agency beforehand. Since the characteristic bureaucrat for the agency is assumed to have Euclidean policy preferences, she will also want to move policy as close to her ideal point as possible. As a result, a delegated governance task will produce an outcome that is the sum of the enacted policy, the state of the world, and the ideal point of the agency. The choice of actor to implement the governance task is central to understanding the policy outcome.

Beyond the role of the agency's ideal point in determining the policy outcome, there is an important difference between congressional and agency policy making in the ability to acquire information about the state of the world. Information that the committee can learn about the state of the world is much coarser than that which can be acquired by the agency. In 2008, the EPA employed eighteen thousand bureaucrats.[15] Though this number is small by federal agency standards, the EPA's informational infrastructure is much larger and more sophisticated than even the most heavily staffed congressional committee. Individual members of the House of Representatives are limited to eighteen full-time and four part-time staff members.[16] Because of such considerations, the model assumes that the committee can only learn whether the state of the world is positive or negative given the policy space in Figure 4.4. The agency, conversely, can learn its precise value. Another reason for the agency advantage in

---

[14] The role of a loyal administrator may be to change revealed beliefs when the president informs him that the agency is going to take a new direction. One way to think of the ally principal that we describe later in this section is that the agent simply follows the president's orders, implementing the governance task such that policy moves to the point in the policy space where the president's induced preferences lie, namely, the president's ideal point.

[15] Figures for all federal executive and independent agencies for 2008 can be found at http://www.bls.gov/oco/cg/cgs041.htm.

[16] See http://www.rules.house.gov/archives/jcoc2s.htm.

gaining information is that "some time will elapse between the passing of the law and making regulations, giving the agency access to new information revealed in that period" (Epstein and O'Halloran, 1999, 55–56). Whatever the reason, Congress faces a trade-off with which we are now familiar. It may delegate and take advantage of the superior expertise that can be acquired by the administrative agency but must balance such gains from expertise against the possible policy drift that is introduced because the agency wants to pull policy toward its ideal point when performing its part in governance.

The key elements to be determined in this model are the following:

1. The congressional policy enactment written into the statute
2. The policy window, or the bounds of the agency's discretion
3. The agency's ideal point that results from the president's appointment of an agency head, the characteristic bureaucrat

Figure 4.4 illustrates these important aspects of the equilibrium. To understand the substantive implications of that picture, we begin by considering the agency's problem of choosing policy. We start at the end not because of our public management interests but because the actors making decisions at earlier stages in the policy process, namely, Congress and the president, anticipate the behavior of those at later stages.[17] The administrative agency would, of course, most prefer policy to be located at its ideal point, but it must work within the policy window that is embodied in the statute delegating the particular governance task that we are considering. Thus the agency will rationally use the full width of the policy window to implement a policy as close to its ideal point as possible. For instance, for a policy window corresponding to "Low SW," the agency in Figure 4.4 will choose a policy at the rightmost edge of the policy window. Put differently, the agency fully uses its discretion to get the best outcome it can for itself.

Given this anticipated agency behavior, the president will appoint an agency head that will perform the governance task in a way most faithful to his own policy interests. Recall the agency's expertise advantage; it will learn the true state of the world and will know, as a consequence of the simple, additive policy process we have specified, the precise location of the implemented outcome along the policy space. The president, like Congress, does not have this information and cannot learn it with the

---

[17] Those with some understanding of game theory will recognize this as backward induction to find a subgame perfect equilibrium.

same precision as the agency. Knowing this, and wanting an outcome as close to his ideal point as possible, the president will choose an agency head who will use her discretion to perform the governance task in a way that produces outcomes consistent with what the president himself would produce if he had the capacity to implement policy himself. The best choice of agency head is thus a person whose ideal point is identical to that of the president. This result is shown as $P = A$ in Figure 4.4 and is the first manifestation of what we refer to as the Ally Principle.

Proposition 4.2 (Ally Principle I). *The president will choose an agent who precisely shares his ideology to implement a delegated governance task.*

Do presidents really appoint agency heads that share precisely their ideological leanings? Bertelli and Grose (2011) develop measures of the ideal points of the president, cabinet secretaries who head the fifteen executive agencies under the closest presidential control, and members of Congress that allow us to examine this manifestation of the Ally Principle for a series of recent Congresses.[18] For the period between the 102nd (1991–1992) and 108th (2002–2004) Congresses, Figure 4.5 shows the average absolute difference – meaning a difference in either a positive (conservative) or negative (liberal) direction – between ideal point estimates for cabinet secretaries (A) and presidents (P). This is a measure of the policy conflict that Ally Principle I predicts will be zero and is represented by a solid dot. This executive branch policy conflict can be compared with the absolute difference between an average cabinet secretary (once again, A) and the median member of the House of Representatives (HM), the median member of the Senate (SM), or the senator whose vote is needed for cloture on a filibustered bill (the so-called filibuster pivot, or SFP).[19] Moving from left to right in each row of the figure, the first three panels represent these average differences within the presidential administration labeled, while the bottom right panel shows the measures for the entire 1991–2004 period.

---

[18] The method that Bertelli and Grose (2011) use to estimate ideal points uses positions that cabinet secretaries take on bills before Congress that receive a roll-call, or recorded, vote in either chamber during the year of the testimony. The positions facilitate a relative comparison of yea and nay votes on the congressional roll call with the positions taken by cabinet officials just mentioned. McCarty and Poole (1995) provide similar presidential "votes" from public positions (see also http://voteview.com). The statistical method follows Clinton et al. (2004).

[19] Krehbiel (1998) defines the pivotal congressional actors.

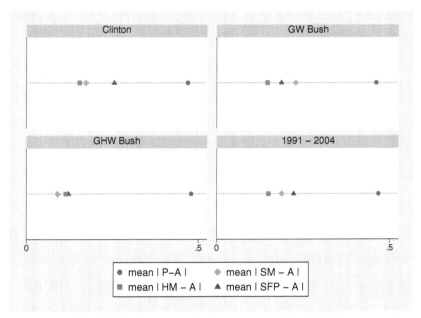

FIGURE 4.5. Cabinet secretary appointments, 102nd–108th Congresses.

It is straightforward to see that Ally Principle I is not supported by the figure. All these solid dots are associated with positive values, indicating divergence in the ideal points of the president and his appointees. In fact, the average cabinet secretary differs from the president in either a liberal or conservative direction ($|P - A|$) considerably more than she differs from any key congressional actor. This can be seen because the solid dots lie to the right of the triangles, diamonds, and squares that represent the congressional divergence. What is more, this version of the Ally Principle fails even in the case of executive agencies, which are headed by cabinet secretaries who can be fired at will because they serve at the pleasure of the president.[20] We should not hastily dismiss the usefulness of the entire model because the presidential version of the Ally Principle does not appear to explain the relevant behavior. While Bertelli and Grose (2011) provide statistical tests that support the graphical evidence here, there may be, for instance, something peculiar about the period captured by the data presented in Figure 4.5. Nonetheless, there is a clear pattern of divergence,

---

[20] Extending the canonical model to incorporate a fuller appointment procedure, Volden (2002) shows that divergence might be possible in the case of independent agencies. However, his model agrees with Ally Principle I in the case of executive agencies, where the Bertelli and Grose (2011) evidence exists.

or diversity, in the ideological portfolio of the executive branch. Selected extensions shedding light on this violation of Ally Principle I are discussed in the following section.

Returning to the Epstein and O'Halloran (1999) model, our next step is to consider the floor median's decisions that determine the size and location of the policy window. Regardless of the ideal point of the president and, consequently, the appointment decision that we have just described, the floor median writes a statute that includes a policy enactment and grant of agency discretion to produce a policy outcome at its ideal point. However, recall that she makes this choice on the basis of information that is provided by the committee. While we shall turn to the committee's recommendation momentarily, recall that the committee can learn less precise information about the state of the world than the agency. Because of this limited information, the floor median can only define the policy window on the basis of what it expects will be the outcome of the policy process. This is an important disadvantage of the coarse information that can be provided to the floor by a committee.

To ensure that the administrative agency has the discretion to achieve an outcome the floor median desires, it enacts policy at its most preferred point.

Proposition 4.3. *The floor median sets its ideal point as the enacted policy when delegating a governance task.*

The reason for this has to do with the committee's recommendation and its capacity to learn about the implementation environment of the governance task. Suppose the committee fails to provide reliable information about the state of the world. This may happen either because the committee reports nothing at all or because it provides information that the floor median simply does not believe. If the committee's report is unreliable, the floor median can only rely on its prior information about the state of the world. In Figure 4.4, this means that the realized state of the world can drive policy in the liberal direction to the point labeled "Low SW," in the conservative direction to "High SW," and anywhere between. In other words, the floor median has a considerable amount of *outcome uncertainty*. Though this range includes some policies that are quite distant from its ideal point, the floor does not want to ignore the expertise gained by the agency, which, as we know, can observe the state of the world perfectly. Consider the position of the agency in Figure 4.4. If the agency learns that the state of the world lies just to the right of the lower bound, the floor median would not want to restrict the agency's discretion too much. This is straightforward to see because the floor median's ideal point adjusted by the state of the world is actually quite good from the floor median's perspective. That policy outcome also improves the agency's welfare. We now know why an agency should receive more discretion when outcome uncertainty is high.

Proposition 4.4 (Uncertainty Principle). *As outcome uncertainty increases, the amount of discretion an agency is granted by Congress to perform a governance task likewise increases.*

This uncertainty principle makes intuitive sense when looking at Figure 4.4. Ally Principle I means that the president and the administrative agency are ideologically simpatico ($P = A$). As depicted, their ideal points are not far away from the floor median. The informational advantage gained by allowing the agency the discretion to learn the true value of the state of the world and to use that information freely when implementing policy makes outcomes better for the floor median. Agency expertise reduces outcome uncertainty and prevents outcomes more distant on either side of the agency's ideal point. Although this is the situation that occurs because of the configuration represented in Figure 4.4, it does not always represent the environment surrounding the delegation of a particular governance task. You might imagine that in situations of divided party government – where Congress is controlled by the political party opposite the president – the floor median and the president would have ideal points that are much farther apart. The situation represented in Figure 4.4 is consistent with unified government, which prevails when the president's party controls Congress.

A more general statement of effect of the location of congressional and executive ideal points on the size of the policy window is thus in order.

Proposition 4.5 (Ally Principle II). *As the preferred policies of the legislature and administrative agency diverge, statutory discretion for performing a governance task is more restricted.*

Ally Principle I captured the incentives for presidential appointments of agency heads. This second manifestation represents an important concern for Congress regarding ideological allegiance. Recall that discretion is zero when the policy window tightly restricts agency discretion to a single point. In other words, Ally Principle II suggests that if the ideological distance between the floor median and the administrative agency is sufficiently large, Congress will choose to make rather than buy the governance task.

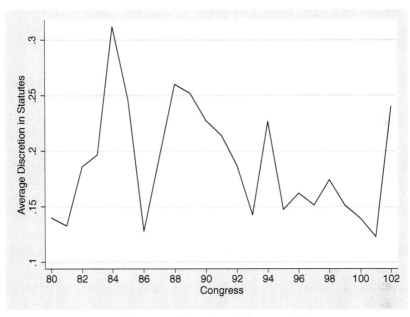

FIGURE 4.6. Statutory discretion, 80th–102nd Congresses.

You may well be asking whether this proposition explains patterns of discretion among administrative agencies in periods of unified versus divided government. Does Congress choose to make rather than buy governance tasks during periods of divided government? Epstein and O'Halloran (1999, 107–112) developed a measure of the discretion granted to administrative agencies to perform specific governance tasks in 257 statutes passed between 1947 and 1990.[21] Figure 4.6 plots an annual average value of their discretion measure between the 80th Congress (1947–48) and the 102nd Congress (1991–1992). During this period, divided government prevailed in the 80th, 84th–86th, 91st–94th, and 97th–102nd Congresses. Figure 4.6 shows low discretion in the divided 80th Congress, followed by a subsequent rise. After divided government returned in the 84th Congress, discretion dropped dramatically until the 86th Congress, when it rose steeply again. While discretion dropped

---

[21] The Epstein and O'Halloran (1999) discretion measure comprises two parts. For each bill, they construct a measure of delegation, a ratio of provisions in the bill with executive delegation to total provisions (93), and one of constraints, the ratio of the number of administrative constraints in a bill to the total number of possible constraints (103). A measure of relative constraints is the product of these two ratios (104). Discretion is measured by the difference between the delegation and relative constraint measures (111). I thank Stephane Lavertu for generously providing the data.

steadily as Republican president Nixon faced a Democratic Congress, it sharply rose after his resignation due to the Watergate scandal and remained volatile and somewhat lower during unified government under Democratic president Carter. Discretion declined to quite low levels under Republican president Reagan and the Democratic Congress but increased sharply on the election of President George H. W. Bush, who, while also Republican, was widely perceived to be more moderate than his predecessor. Figure 4.6 is overall quite consistent with the prediction of Ally Principle II, which appears to be helpful in understanding delegation patterns in postwar federal policy making. While not a statistical test, the graph is consistent with the congressional version of the Ally Principle. It suggests a discretion profile that could occur if that principle were correct.

The equilibrium of the Epstein and O'Halloran (1999) model has not yet been fully described. To complete our discussion, we must return to the beginning and the bill sent to the floor by the congressional committee. As we have noted, committees are created by the floor to collect information that can be advantageous, but they have their own constituency interests and may not reliably report on the state of the world (Krehbiel, 1991). Just as policy conflict can exist between the floor median and the administrative agency, it can also arise between the floor and a committee. Epstein and O'Halloran (1999, 64) illustrate this conflict of interest between committee and floor with an agriculture committee weighing evidence of upcoming weather forecasts and anticipated crop yields: "If members of the committee want greater subsidies for their constituents, then they are liable to report that bad weather is ahead, no matter what the actual forecast conditions. The committee, then, will resemble a broken record, always reporting the same thing, and is therefore useless to the floor as a reliable source of information."

This type of policy conflict diminishes the usefulness of a committee report. In equilibrium, the committee only reports the truth about the state of the world to the floor, or it remains silent. Beyond this, the committee only reports the truth if that report would help the floor reduce agency discretion in a way that would improve the committee's welfare. If the committee anticipates that a narrower policy window will bring the outcome of agency implementation closer to its ideal point, it will send a truthful report to the floor; otherwise, the committee says nothing, and the floor median chooses its ideal point as the policy enactment. Thus the final component of Figure 4.4 is revealed. When the committee credibly reports that the state of the world is lower or higher than the floor median's ideal point, the statute restricts the policy window to the appropriate side of the policy space. Put more generally, the model expects that when internal committee reports about the state of the world are credible, agency discretion for performing a governance task is reduced. Credibility, however, depends on committee policy preferences.

Before we turn to extensions that more realistically depict the policy implementation process, a few words about robustness, or maintenance of the predictions when certain assumptions are violated, are warranted. The model that we have just described makes important assumptions about the nature of legislators' preferences and the policy-making process. Bendor and Mierowitz (2004) provide important caveats and extensions to this story by generalizing the canonical model. Though their treatment is thorough, we only concern ourselves with two very general results.

The first of these relates to the nature of congressional policy preferences. Bendor and Mierowitz (2004) show that assuming that Congress is risk averse, namely, that it dislikes uncertainty in policy making regardless of what outcome is produced, is not necessary to produce the results we have discussed. In other words, Propositions 4.2, 4.3, and 4.5 are robust even when Congress is not risk averse with regard to a governance task. The uncertainty principle described in Proposition 4.4 is not entirely irrelevant given this finding, but it has an alternate explanation. In the delegation model, "more risk means that outcomes are farther from the ideal point, hence less desirable" (Bendor and Mierowitz, 2004, 297). It may well be that Congress displays risk aversion in a particular policy you are trying to understand, and in that case, Proposition 4.4 will serve you well. However, if that assumption is too strong, another logic preserves the prediction. This logic is as follows: because the agency will learn about the true state of the world if given discretion, the floor median trades off outcome uncertainty about the location of an outcome against the bias due to bureaucratic drift. In task areas having greater outcome uncertainty, the *distributional benefit* to the agency that comes when reduced agency discretion allows the floor median to get a better outcome in the policy space is outweighed by the *informational benefit* it gets when the agency's expertise can help it to produce policies it prefers. A distributional benefit accrues to the congressional principal when governance tasks are dispatched to produce policies closer to its ideal point. The principal receives an informational benefit when agent expertise in performing the governance task improves the welfare of the principal. Separately, Ally Principle I maintains that the president will choose an ideologically allied agency head to minimize the distributional benefit to the agency.

A second important result regards the form of the policy implementation process, which, in the canonical model, provides that a policy outcome equal to the enacted policy plus some random shock from the state of the world can be made more general. Bendor and Mierowitz (2004, 298) "require only that together the policy and shock create some uncertainty in outcomes." This means that more than one outcome can arise from a single policy choice, and that outcome can be better or worse than Congress thinks. This, it turns out, holds the key to understanding delegation in the canonical approach. Delegation occurs because Congress is ignorant of the state of the world and its ability to produce a better or worse outcome than Congress expects. Because the agent can condition its policy choice on the state of the world it observes, the agency is able to pull outcomes toward its ideal point. Once again, Ally Principle I allows the president to mitigate policy drift through appointments, though presidents do not seem to be responding strictly to this incentive (Bertelli and Grose, 2011).

The nature of the policy implementation process is central to the study of public management; indeed, in a delegation model, it *is* public management. Several extensions of the canonical model have been made that provide insight for public managers. These also provide some rationale for why Ally Principle I appears not to hold. We now begin a discussion of these extensions.

4.4. MODELING POLICY IMPLEMENTATION

Approaches outside the political–economic literature that we have been considering recognize that the policy process is made up of a complicated web of actors that interact over quite long periods of time (Sabatier, 2007, 3). In those literatures, the policy process begins when policy ideas are formed and includes an entire trajectory through the legislative process, implementation, and even feedback to politicians and administrators afterward. Our scope has been narrower.

The canonical model says little about issue formation or the process by which an issue emerges from the public to the government's policy agenda. This may be seen by some as a serious limitation, but it does give delegation theories the important advantage of broad applicability. The canonical model begins its work when an issue has reached Congress; that body must consider how to implement a governance task that it believes government must perform. In individual policy areas, the manner in which legislators become convinced that a specific governance task is an appropriate function of government is important to understand. The profound usefulness of accounts of the formation of particular issues and their path to the congressional policy agenda cannot be overlooked. With respect to the canonical delegation model, these things are exogenous, occurring outside – in this case, before – the modeled events. Such information allows us to understand, for example, the configuration of ideal points along the policy space in Figure 4.4. As we have noted, that configuration may work well to explain one policy area but not another. It is essential for public management scholars and practitioners to understand such exogenous concerns before applying the logic of the model. Once they are understood, the model and its extensions can tell us quite a lot.

Our focus in this chapter is not on issue formation but rather on the other end of the process. It is this postdelegation, implementation process that lies at the heart of public management research and practice. Scholars of the policy implementation process, or the implementation of governance tasks, would be far from pleased with the way in which the canonical model has captured it. The notion that an administrative agency learns the state of the world perfectly and applies that knowledge to a clear policy enactment to produce an outcome is quite inadequate. In that process, the agency interacts with no one as it performs the governance task after Congress imposes its ex ante controls. We should ask whether and how interest groups influence the performance of governance tasks because we know that they do. It also seems unrealistic to expect that an agency will always have sufficient expertise even to roughly support the assumption that the agency learns the state of the world precisely. Indeed, expertise is developed over time, as agencies hire more and better staff, refine their organizational procedures and structures, and otherwise evolve. It is thus important to ask whether the agency always acquires substantial expertise and what incentives exist for it to do so. Though a large number of studies extend the canonical approach, the sampling we engage in this section provides important insights that we apply in subsequent chapters. It also gives us some understanding of why the presidential version of the Ally Principle as stated in Proposition 4.2 does not seem to explain presidential appointments. Our focus first turns to the role of interest groups and then to the acquisition of expertise.

4.4.1. Implementation Bargaining

Public managers and students of the policy process know very well that the role of organized interests does not stop when a bill is signed into law by the president. Recall that one form of ex ante control known as deck stacking explicitly creates roles for group involvement in the execution of governance tasks. Such roles can be quite direct. Consider the negotiation of guidelines for mitigating risks from specific products that the Consumer Product Safety Commission (CPSC) negotiates with manufacturers. Monitoring by consumer and other groups as well as agency monitoring alerts the CPSC to violations of standards or regulations. A bargaining process between the agency and a manufacturer over compliance measures then ensues, with the CPSC able to threaten cease and desist orders, civil suits, or civil fines in the event that negotiations do not bear fruit. When manufacturers violate standards, the CPSC frequently negotiates consent decrees, which, like contracts, are negotiated agreements enforceable by courts. Judicial enforcement permits the CPSC and the manufacturer to credibly commit to the agreement reached in this example of implementation bargaining.

Another example of implementation bargaining can be found in the EPA's Office of Enforcement and Compliance Assurance (OECA). Under most federal environmental statutes, a polluter is first ordered to cease and desist by the EPA. If violations persist, the OECA begins negotiations with the polluter, but the EPA can sue the polluter in civil court if negotiations produce an impasse. A federal district court has interpreted one such statute as requiring an agency like the OECA to consider any reasonable offer from the polluter, though that offer does not have to be accepted.[22] Deck stacking and interest group involvement more generally give shape to the policy implementation process and imply that it differs considerably from that represented in the canonical model.

To capture institutional features such as those described in the forgoing examples, Bertelli and Feldmann (2007) incorporate implementation bargaining into a simple delegation model. They find that Ally Principle I does not hold in its presence, and the president makes strategic appointments away from his ideal point to counteract the influence of interest groups while the agency performs a specific governance task. The logic of strategic appointments is simple to understand by considering a single dimension of policy like the policy space in Figure 4.4. Congress has delegated a governance task that, when completed, produces an outcome on the policy space. The president desires an implemented policy outcome as close to his ideal point as possible. If the administrative agency were permitted to choose policy without any influence from groups, the

---

[22] *Pinkus v. Reilly*, 178 F. Supp. 399 (D.C.N.J. 1959).

president would be made best off by appointing an agency head having the same ideal policy preferences. In other words, Ally Principle I should hold. Suppose, rather, that the agency produces a policy outcome after negotiation with an interest group. That group may be more liberal or more conservative, but what is important is that its ideal policy is located somewhere else in the policy space. The bargaining solution that Bertelli and Feldmann (2007) employ requires that the negotiated policy outcome wind up somewhere between the group and agency ideal points, depending on the strength of the interest group in influencing the agency. Most important is that the policy outcome that emerges from implementation be a weighted average of the group and agency preferences, where the weight is the magnitude of the group's influences.

The essential reason for the impact of implementation bargaining on the president's choice of agency head is simple. Let's do this as a pencil exercise using the most basic spatial model.[23] On a sheet of paper, draw a horizontal line segment to represent the policy space for a particular governance task. Draw a point near the middle of the policy space, and label it "P" to represent the president's ideal point. Suppose that the policy space represents environmental protection, with liberal, conservation-oriented policies on the left and conservative, market-oriented policies on the right. The president is, thus, moderate in our example. Suppose that the main organized interest in the implementation stage is the conservation-oriented Natural Resources Defense Council (NRDC). Draw a point somewhere on the left side of the line segment and to the left of the president, and label it "G" to denote the group. Suppose that the president chooses an ideological ally to head the agency under Ally Principle I, and note on your graph that $P = A$. Bertelli and Feldmann (2007) show that the policy outcome will be a weighted average between the president's and the group's ideal points. Suppose that the group's influence is strong enough to move policy to a perfect compromise in bargaining. In that case, the outcome is simply the midpoint between $P = A$ and G, which lies, as you can see, to the left of the president's most preferred policy. Ally Principle I fails to deliver the president's ideal policy.

---

[23] Pencil exercises such as this one are a very simple yet powerful way to think about, for instance, the effect of different configurations of ideal points on outcomes in a spatial model. After finishing this exercise, you might consider returning to Figure 4.4 and the surrounding text, changing the location of the key actors based on your knowledge of an interesting governance task, and seeing the impact on outcomes of this change.

Can the president improve his distributional benefit by appointing a different agency head? Yes, he can. By appointing an administrator whose preferences oppose, or offset, those of the group, the president can produce an outcome at his ideal point. To see this, draw a point on the policy space the same distance to the left of P as G lies to its right and label it "A_2." The midpoint between A_2 and G represents the negotiated outcome, and that now lies exactly at P. If the agency's ideal point is chosen to exactly offset the group's influence, the president's ideal point becomes the implemented outcome. In our example, this means that the moderate president had to appoint a rather conservative agency head to negotiate effectively with the NRDC. Notice, also, that regardless of the group's bargaining strength, the president's optimal choice of agency head lies on the opposite side of his ideal point than the group. If a stronger group than the NRDC emerges on the left, the logic we have seen suggests that the president's best choice of agency head will be even more conservative, falling to the right of A_2. The president cannot obtain his best outcome by following Ally Principle I unless agency policy choices are entirely independent of interest group influence.

Bertelli and Feldmann (2007) incorporate several institutional features of American politics into their delegation model, but the most important is the Senate's constitutional power to "advise and consent" to presidential nominations. Though the president may wish to appoint a very extreme agency head so that the governance task will be performed so as to yield his ideal policy outcome, Congress may block such an appointment. Look again at your diagram. Suppose that the Senate median is located to the left of G; indicate this by drawing a point and labeling it "SM." At this location, the Senate median prefers the NRDC's ideal policy to that of the much more conservative president. Presidential appointees who are very conservative and market oriented in our environmental case are unlikely to be confirmed because the Senate would most prefer an appointee even closer to G than P and so considerably more liberal. Now return to Figure 4.5 and note that the absolute distances between the Senate median and the average cabinet secretary are always less than the presidential differences. Senate influence in the confirmation process is an important institutional consideration in refining the presidential version of the Ally Principle.

The bargaining process in Bertelli and Feldmann (2007) does not incorporate any specific institutional features of implementation bargaining such as the sanctions and court review in the CPSC and OECA examples with which we began this section. As a result, the model is sufficiently general to apply to a variety of forms of interest group influence in the policy implementation process. Because interest group influence in implementation leads to policy outcomes that, in one way or another, resemble negotiated agreements between administrative agencies and key groups, a simplified version of the logic in Bertelli and Feldmann (2007) suggests reasons why Ally Principle I seems not to explain the data. These can be summarized in the following proposition.

Proposition 4.6 (Group Influence Principle). *The president appoints agency heads strategically and, to the extent permitted by the confirmation process, chooses them to offset the influence of interest groups in the implementation of governance.*

You might have noticed that there was no outcome uncertainty in the Bertelli and Feldmann (2007) model. The outcome was simply generated by the weighted average, which leaves out the impact of the state of the world in the policy implementation process. Consequently, this section has only considered the distributional benefit of delegation. In the next section, we return to the informational benefit and review two approaches that take more care in understanding how agency expertise affects that aspect of delegation.

4.4.2. Administrative Capacity and Policy Expertise

An essential element of the policy process has to do with the internal operations of an administrative agency as it acquires the capacity for making expert decisions. Federal agencies differ in their capacity for performing governance tasks, differences across U.S. state agencies are even more striking, and international differences are yet more substantial. Cross-national, comparative interest in bureaucratic capacity generated an important study by Huber and McCarty (2004). Does bureaucratic capacity affect the likelihood of delegation and the discretion that agencies receive? An important result in their model is that agencies with greater capacity are more likely to be delegated governance tasks even though their policy preferences are farther from Congress than those of lower capacity agencies.

It is straightforward to understand this by returning to your pad of paper and thinking once again about appointments. As before, draw a horizontal line segment to represent the policy space for a particular governance task. Draw the congressional ideal point somewhere in the left of the space, and label it "C" to represent the characteristic member of Congress. Draw the president's ideal point in the center, and label it "P." Now draw an agent called "A_I" somewhere to the right of the president. To understand outcome uncertainty in a simple way, suppose further that A_I directs an agency that has high capacity. Recall that the policy implementation process in the canonical model posits that when performing a governance task, the agency adjusts the policy enactment by the state of the world to produce the policy. In this example, the policy enactment is located at the agency's ideal point A_I. For present purposes, we take *administrative capacity* to mean the ability of the agency to precisely learn the state of the world. Because A_I has high capacity, this can be represented by shading a segment of the policy space that is centered at A_I and is not very large. Do that, and make sure that the shaded segment is not so large as to include C. The shaded area represents the possible outcomes that agency A_I will implement if it receives the delegation from Congress. Now consider a second agency called "A_2" that has an ideal point exactly at the same location as that of Congress. Represent this by writing $A_2 = C$. Although this agency is an ideological clone of Congress, it has low administrative capacity. For purposes of our example, this means that it is sufficiently ill equipped to learn the state of the world that it might implement a policy anywhere in the policy space. The essence of the Huber and McCarty (2004) logic becomes clear when comparing the outcomes that these two agencies can supply for Congress when implementing the delegated governance task. Although A_I is more conservative and will never give Congress exactly what it wants, namely, C, some of the outcomes that A_2 can possibly supply are much more conservative, and others may be far too liberal.[24] Although A_2 wants the same outcome as Congress, it simply cannot promise anything other than some outcome along the entire policy space. It should now be clear that Congress can prefer delegating to the more conservative A_2 over its perfect ideological ally due to the low administrative capacity of the latter.

Proposition 4.7 (Capacity Principle I). *Congress may delegate a governance task to an agency that prefers policies quite different than its own if its administrative capacity is higher than that of agencies aligned with its own policy views.*

---

[24] If this leads to some head scratching, recall that in the spatial model (Section 4.2), we assume that the actors have Euclidean preferences. That means that Congress is equally satisfied with a point to the left as with one to the right of C if those points are equidistant from C.

Can't A_2 do something about its low capacity? Under some conditions, it can acquire more and more expert staff, incorporate new technologies into its information-gathering processes, and so on. That may well have the effect of reducing its band of possible policy outcomes sufficiently to make it the optimal choice of Congress for performing the governance task under consideration. Ting (2011) revisits the question of whether high- or low-capacity agencies get more delegations by allowing administrative agencies to decide for themselves whether to develop a high or low capacity. Now, administrative capacity is *endogenous*, or determined within the model as a choice confronted by the agency. When the agency is allowed to choose, a contrasting prediction connecting capacity to delegation emerges.

Ting (2011) explicitly incorporates a trade-off between ideology on our spatial continuum and task quality in his model. The concept of task quality is simple to grasp: as it increases, an administrative agency improves its ability to perform a specific governance task. When an agency is delegated a governance task by Congress, the statute confronts the agency with this trade-off. Two types of agencies are considered in the model. A *generalist agency* cannot use investment in capacity to improve the quality of implementation for a specific governance task but can only improve its ability to perform all tasks for which it has responsibility. For instance, the U.S. Fish and Wildlife Service (FWS) is charged with implementing provisions of both the Endangered Species Act and the Estuary Protection Act. If FWS is a generalist agency, it can invest, say, in a new management information system that improves its general performance but does not make its role in protecting endangered species any more efficient than its estuary protection tasks. By contrast, a *specialist agency* can make investments in capacity that improve its ability to perform one governance task more than another. These types create different incentives for Congress in its delegation decisions.

A specialist agency is able to use superior task quality in one governance task to force Congress to make a difficult choice when delegating. Congress must choose between a poor quality implementation of its ideal policy and a high-quality implementation of a divergent policy more to the agency's liking. If a specialist FWS really wants to make a strong impact on endangered species protection, it can invest in capacity building that improves tasks related to that policy area rather than shoring up its estuary protection capabilities. A specialist agency's investment makes capacity increase with the policy conflict between the agency and Congress. This makes delegation of estuary-related governance tasks to FWS less attractive for Congress. By contrast, a generalist FWS cannot force these trade-offs for Congress because it is not able to improve endangered-species relative to estuary-task quality through capacity investment. As a result, Congress can appropriate the agency's capacity to help implement its own ideal policy per Capacity Principle I. Policies distant from congressional intent are not implemented by generalist agencies because the tasks that generate them are not delegated. This prediction can be stated more generally as follows.

Proposition 4.8 (Capacity Principle II). *Specialist agencies use capacity investments to create incentives for Congress to delegate governance tasks they prefer rather than those they dislike, but generalist agencies cannot create such incentives.*

Specialist agencies, thus, can move toward what is known in the bureaucratic politics literature as *bureaucratic autonomy*. Agencies having this quality are not entirely dominated by Congress and can work to shape public policy and even the congressional agenda. Carpenter (2001, 14) presents the characteristics of autonomous agencies in the following passage.

Bureaucratic autonomy requires the development of unique organizational capacities – capacities to analyze, to create new programs, to solve problems, to plan, to administer programs with efficiency, and to ward off corruption. Autonomous agencies must have the ability to act upon their unique preferences with efficiency and to innovate. They must have bureaucratic entrepreneurs.

Specialist agencies can be considered entrepreneurial because they are able to use investments in their capacity to make some governance tasks more appealing to Congress than they might otherwise have been. Generalist agencies are hamstrung in their entrepreneurial ability because of Capacity Principle II. Although Capacity Principle II tells us something very interesting about the acquisition of expertise by administrative agencies and its impact on delegation, it fails to answer a fundamental question: what is expertise in the first place?

The third and final extension of the canonical model that we consider addresses that question directly. In the canonical delegation model, expertise is "a single piece of information" about the state of the world that allows an expert agency to relate a congressional policy enactment to an implemented outcome (Callander, 2008, 124). When the agency was said to have a greater capacity to collect information about the state of the world than the congressional committee in Section 4.3, that meant it was able to learn more about that single piece of information. In other words, learning the state of the world fully reveals the process by which an actor can get what it wants. This fact about being informed about the state of the world also implies that any actor can become a specialist simply by learning the relevant piece of information. The specialist's expertise is said to be *invertible* when this is true.

Callander (2008) develops a richer, but still general, description of the policy implementation process. He models implementation as a mathematical process known as Brownian motion. We can intuitively understand such a process in the following way. Suppose that the EPA is charged with implementing a set of carbon emissions standards. This is not a straightforward thing to do, and local land and business owners and green groups, among others, have differing views of the level of carbon emissions that should be permitted under the standards. As before, envision the EPA's proposed policy as producing an outcome along a unidimensional policy space – the horizontal line segment from your previous pencil exercises. Interest groups, for instance, influence the policy at different times and in different directions, liberal or conservative, as the governance task is performed. The number of groups influencing the policy may change over the course of the deliberations. Ten liberal and five conservative groups at the outset of the debate may become five liberal and thirty conservative groups by the end. If these groups are equivalently powerful, the pressure they are bringing to bear on the EPA has moved from more liberal to more conservative. This is similar to the weight associated with the groups' influence strength in our discussion of implementation bargaining.

Group influence occurring in this way creates a sense of erratic movement of the EPA's policy in the outcome space. Nevertheless, such erratic movement is something that scholars of the policy process have long recognized. In one influential view of the policy process (Browne and Wildavsky, 1984, 208), implementation can be seen as a process of adaptation; it occurs "when a policy or program evolves in response to its environment as each alters the other." Incorporating Brownian motion into the canonical model improves the realism with which the model represents what policy process scholars know about the policy implementation process.

The Brownian motion also adds an important attribute to the policy implementation process; it is now not so easily invertible. Expertise is more nuanced and important to hold. When the erratic Brownian motion has a greater variance, policy implementation is more complex (Callander, 2008, 124). This means that the erratic movement described earlier moves the EPA's policy across greater ranges of the policy space. When policies are more complex in this way, expertise in implementation is less prone to inversion. A nonspecialist may uncover information that gives her more reliable expectations about where the outcome will lie in the policy space at a given time. Nevertheless, she cannot fully understand the rate at which outcomes change when a particular governance task is performed, and consequently, does not have the same level of knowledge as an honest-to-goodness expert who understands the implementation process. Like the autonomous agency at the end of the preceding section, the agency possessing noninvertible expertise can use it as leverage against Congress, which would like to appropriate it to move policy to its ideal point.

Congress can indeed appropriate invertible knowledge, but it does not have the chance. We have seen from our earlier discussion of menu laws that Congress has difficulty committing to its treatment of administrative agencies. Unless its commitment to the free exercise of policy-making discretion – exercise without appropriation – to a nonexpert agency is credible, the agency acquires no expertise. The agency knows that Congress has the incentive to appropriate the expertise it acquires. In this case, no delegation occurs (Callander, 2008, 135). Governance tasks will not be delegated if they are not sufficiently complex.

More interesting are cases in which expertise cannot be inverted.[25] Here the character of the agency's expertise is such that Congress cannot appropriate it in any event. Recall that the Brownian motion gives the policy implementation process an important time component. Policy bounces around erratically, creating a status quo described by the mean and variance of the process. This is important when revisiting the make-or-buy decision. When expertise is noninvertible, the expert administrative agency is charged with a governance task only when Congress prefers the status quo to incurring the cost of developing the expertise for itself, say, by creating and funding a competing agency. Because its expertise

[25] Callander (2008) also examines a scenario in which expertise is only partially invertible, but the result is not clear. The agency will keep the distributional and informational benefit, if possible; however, Congress faces a trade-off between lower uncertainty in implementing specific governance tasks and policy divergence from those policies drifting away from the congressional best outcome. Because mutual adjustment occurs, no equilibrium can be supported without additional institutions.

cannot be appropriated, the agency keeps both the informational and distributional benefits for itself when delegation does occur. This result presents reasons for the failure of Ally Principle II (Callander, 2008, 135). In the case of noninvertible expertise, an agency may receive a distributional benefit from implementing a governance task and also receive the discretion to perform it so as to realize that benefit. In this case, Congress delegates to a nonally agency because it can do no better without creating a new agency from whole cloth and will only do so if the status quo policy being implemented by the agency is bad enough to outweigh such startup costs. This violation can only occur in complex policy domains.

Proposition 4.9 (Inversion Principle). *Administrative agencies have no incentive to acquire invertible expertise, but they can get policies they prefer when their expertise is noninvertible, as long as their preferences are not so out of line with those of Congress that Congress prefers to create a brand-new agency to undertake a governance task.*

Each of the models described in this section suggests that the ally principle fails for a different reason. When thinking about the governance tasks you confront, one reason may be better than another. We will apply these and other principles from the last two chapters to some important contemporary public management phenomena in Part II of the book.

4.5. CONCLUSION

We have come to the end of our discussion of delegation. However, the literature that has been discussed in this chapter is only a sampling of a very large body of work on the subject. My intention has been to provide an introduction to the logic of delegation in public sector governance that builds on your knowledge of principal–agent relationships from Chapter 2 and ex post controls from Chapter 3. This will allow you to discover additional literature as your public management interests and challenges develop.

Delegation is the central problem of public administration in a democratic society. We began its discussion by enumerating its costs and benefits. Congress benefits from effort reduction, agency expertise, decreased outcome uncertainty, special interest protection, and blame shifting. Its costs came from policy conflict, information asymmetries, and monitoring technologies. Screening, it turns out, is not an efficient way for Congress to construct delegations because of the difficulty in policy commitment it faces because of the electoral connection. We introduced a spatial model for considering policy conflict and then proceeded to the canonical model of delegation and the Ally Principle. The failure of the Ally Principle empirically precipitated further theoretical examination. We examined interest group influence in as well as administrative capacity for performing particular government tasks as forces working against the Ally Principle.

This concludes our review of political–economic theories of public sector governance. We now turn to two applications of our framework: the first concerns delegating governance tasks through contracts and partnerships between government and private or nonprofit organizations; the second deals with the maintenance and monitoring of responsibility, a normative rationale for public management in the United States.

PART II

APPLICATIONS

O ur aim now is to apply the resource and monitoring incentives from Chapters 3 and 4. The material in Part II builds on the insights we have learned, stretching them into new territory. When empirical evaluation of the claims in these chapters is available, it is discussed. Yet the primary task here is to view public management problems through what can be a new lens. It is my hope that this exercise will inspire you to apply these theories to areas in your interest, to consult the literature more broadly, and even to consider contributing to it as you find opportunities for modification and extension. Before continuing, it would be helpful to review the propositions listed in Chapters 3 and 4 as they will be applied in subsequent discussions. These are also presented in Appendix A.

5

Contracts and Partnerships

[Public–private partnerships] do not emerge as a matter of whim or fancy. They are institutions rooted in a specific political and temporal milieu. At particular moments they seem to offer the solution to public policy problems.

– Chris Skelcher (2005, 349)

On October 1, 2010, the Los Angeles Gay and Lesbian Center announced that it had received a $13.3 million grant from the Department of Health and Human Services (HHS) to support a program for foster children, one of only six grants awarded. Other grants were provided to either government agencies or academic institutions. The executive director of the center announced the grant as follows: "This landmark grant will fund the development of a much-needed, model program to protect the health and well-being of [lesbian, gay, bisexual, transexual, and questioning] foster youth – a program that will save lives, save taxpayer dollars, and could be replicated in cities around the country" (St. John, 2010). Reductions in governance tasks performed through grants and contracts – a phenomenon known as contracting back in – are also common. In an effort to cut $100 billion from the Department of Defense budget, the Pentagon announced in 2009 that it would begin insourcing many previously contracted positions. Under the plan, the Pentagon would eliminate thirty-three thousand contractors and hire an additional thirty-nine thousand Department of Defense employees. However, the Pentagon abandoned the plan in summer 2010, with Secretary of Defense Robert Gates remarking, "As we were reducing contractors, we weren't seeing the savings we had hoped from insourcing" (Brodsky, 2010).

To provide more, and more efficient, services, governments at all levels have turned to cross-sectoral collaborations supported by contracts. Grants such as the HHS example are likewise supported by contracts. These represent delegations of governance tasks. Such arrangements bring together the resources of government and nongovernment actors and, like the delegations we discussed in the preceding chapter, shape policy. In the discussions that follow, we refer to the characteristic governmental actor as a *government principal* and to the agent as a contractor. Much contracting and partnership activity has been targeted toward improving the provision of public services that were once directly provided by government – from health care to defense, poverty and homeless intervention to trash collection. The impetus behind contracting is often to increase efficiency and effectiveness in service provisions, though such gains are not always realized. Insights about delegations of governance tasks from Chapters 3 and 4 can inform our understanding of the success and failure of contractual arrangements. Seen in this light, contracting provides public management practice and scholarship with a wide array of interesting questions. The theories we have covered focus our attention on the incomplete contracting problem. This focus can help to clarify analytic thinking about complex contracting and partnership arrangements.

This chapter tours the problems presented by public sector contracts and partnerships, giving significant attention to contracting with the non-profit sector. Our discussion integrates predictions from the political economy approach and engages a sampling of related literatures. We begin with the question of whether government should provide or contract a governance task. This is analogous to the make-or-buy choice that Congress faced in the preceding chapter. Much of the literature on this question employs transaction cost economic theories rather than the positive political theory of delegation from Chapter 4. While there are many similarities, the delegation approach reveals some nuances that are not often discussed in the public sector contracting literature.

The narrative then turns to what kinds of tasks are contractible or not contractible. Attributes of governance tasks such as the quality of services provided are considered. We then ask how contracts should best be enforced. The Monitoring Principle and a host of predictions from Chapter 3 provide insight. Finally, we address the concern over what type of organization makes the best contractor for a particular governance task. Agent selection returns us to the screening problem that Audrey faced in Chapter 2 and is informed by much of what we have learned.

5.1. MAKE OR BUY?

Why is our national defense not privately provided? Defense is a *public good*. Public goods or services benefit the public at large rather than some individual, and when one person consumes a public good, it is still available for others as well (Samuelson, 1954). They may also have the property that no one can easily be excluded from their use. If the air force intercepts an aircraft before it can attack the city of Pasadena, I benefit, along with all other residents. I cannot be easily left in harm's way if I do not buy some allotment of security. These properties make public goods and services unappealing to entrepreneurs because it is difficult to profit from a good or service prone to extensive free ridership. We call this situation a *market failure*.

Particularly in modern welfare states, government has often stepped in to perform governance tasks susceptible to market failure. As Weisbrod (1988, 20) put it, "government can finance, subsidize, mandate, or otherwise encourage the provision of goods and services that are inadequately provided by the private sector or that are not provided to particular groups in the population." Government is also called to action in cases of *voluntary failure*, which arise when the voluntary sector cannot provide a good or service. This may be because nonprofit organizations are unable to secure adequate and reliable funding or are interested only in serving a subgroup of the population. Government may step in to provide resources in this case as well. Voluntary failure can also arise when nonprofit organizations are paternalistic in defining the needs of the communities demanding the goods or services and when such organizations lack the capacity to provide services with sufficient quality or in sufficient quantity (Salamon, 1987).

A *government failure* occurs when individuals are not able to obtain a good or service at all, or rather, not at the level they desire. From our preceding discussions, you know quite well that the policy process does not supply all the outputs that citizens demand. The legislative and policy implementation processes change the character of proposals, and the Group Influence Principle (Proposition 4.6) reminds us that the pressure and influence does not stop when tasks are delegated by statute. Finally, *contract failure* exists where "ordinary contractual mechanisms do not provide consumers with adequate means to police producers" (Hansmann, 1987, 29–30). For instance, the right to sue for enforcement of a provision is not that easily exercised by poor clients of an agency. Given the particular nature of task environments and this hierarchy of failures, it is useful to examine contracting and partnership creation as delegations of specific governance tasks.

Delegation and transaction cost economic theories commonly used in public sector contracting studies share a focus on incomplete contracts. There is nothing inherently special about administrative agencies as agents. Grants and contracts can be viewed similarly as delegations when they lead to the performance of governance tasks by nongovernmental agents. As with delegations, contracts and partnerships can be terminated if agency loss is too great. Hefetz and Warner (2004) show evidence from a national survey that fully 81 percent of local governments between 1992 and 1997 moved from contractual to government provision of a service. Localities with less monitoring capacity were more likely to do so, they found, and drift from noncompliance was another factor making such moves more likely. The ideological aspect of spatial delegation theories is also useful for understanding this finding; task performance induces policy outcomes rather than simply nonperformance, as in the economics and legal literatures on contract.

Scholars have observed that administrative agencies strive to "at least give the appearance of fairness in resource distribution," yet they operate in the environment of budgetary politics and policy windows that we have described in the last two chapters (Lipsky and Smith, 1989, 631). If an agency did perform governance tasks according to a utilitarian distribution principle, creating, for instance, the widest possible reach for a service given the level at which it is resourced, problems would still result. Such an implementation strategy can create economic efficiencies and raise the ire of groups – including those for whom the legislative process has stacked the deck – who feel they deserve inequitably larger distributions than others. As we have seen, these groups can sound fire alarms to alert politicians about perceived undesirable results – what, in their view, is bad policy. The reality of the implementation process for contractors performing governance tasks is similar in important ways to that facing administrative agencies.

The delegation propositions in the preceding chapter provide several interesting predictions about the make-or-buy decision for governance tasks. The Uncertainty Principle (Proposition 4.4) states that more outcome uncertainty leads to increased discretion for contractors. Imprecise expectations about what policy is induced by task performance are clearly higher in human service provision than in trash collection. We should thus expect contracts between, say, a city government and a nonprofit staffed by social workers to provide wrap-around services to adolescents with disabilities to allow more discretion to the contractor. For any given child, the outcome of the service provider's interventions generates uncertainty, and characteristics of the child, local population, and so forth, systematically affect the probability of success or failure. Bad outcomes can generate very poor publicity for and even litigation against the city and contractor (depending on the default rules in the jurisdiction), reminding us of the risk that is distributed with contractual relationships and the blame-shifting rationale for delegations. Contracting and partnership creation can be used to shift blame from government principals.

An example of the Uncertainty Principle at work can be found in the U.S. Coast Guard Deepwater Project. Deepwater was the Coast Guard's largest-ever acquisition program, designed to replace an aging infrastructure of ships, aircraft, command-and-control communications, and intelligence and reconnaissance systems (Hutton, 2009). Rather than seeking contractors for each of the individual assets, the Coast Guard awarded a contract to Integrated Coast Guard Systems (ICGS), a joint venture between Lockheed Martin and Northrup Grumman to orchestrate the larger effort (Brown et al., 2009, 148). From the outset, both the Coast Guard and ICGS recognized the complexity of the project and its outcome uncertainty. The Coast Guard recognized its general needs but did not have clear specifications for desired outcomes. ICGS, for its part, had considerable uncertainty over its own cost of performing the complex set of governance tasks with which it was charged. This should sound to you like the expertise rationale for delegation. The resulting final contract left ICGS with high levels of discretion, as predicted by the Uncertainty Principle.[1] For instance, ICGS retained final decision-making authority over design specifications for the assets being produced in many cases (Brown et al., 2009). Broad delegations left the Coast Guard with difficulty in controlling its agent through budgetary means. By 2010, the project was expected to extend an additional ten years and cost an additional $10 billion. In 2007, the Coast Guard made significant management changes to the project in an attempt to regain control over key steps in the acquisition process (Hutton, 2009). The Coast Guard appeared to find the benefits of better monitoring worth its costs.

Expertise acquisition is important for public sector contracting, just as it was in the context of congressional delegations. We have seen that an administrative agency makes choices about acquiring expertise that

---

[1] It could be that the uncertainty in this scenario is so great that strategic agency choice under Capacity Principle I is of little use.

have impacts on the policy agenda. Public sector contractors face similar trade-offs. Capacity Principle II (Proposition 4.8) relies on the difference between specialist agencies, which can target their capacity-building investments to a particular governance task, and generalist agencies, which cannot. The essential insight here is that specialist agencies can create incentives for the government principal to perform certain tasks rather than others because they have developed the capacity to provide good outcomes by completing governance tasks they prefer. We shall call this process *strategic capacity building*. Government may consequently take on governance tasks that it might not have but for the capacity choices of contractors. Put differently, specialist agencies can strategically acquire expertise as a means of setting the policy agenda. This may be one reason for the cost overruns and delays in the partnership between ICGS and the Coast Guard.

Strategic capacity building implies, for instance, that the advocacy mission of nonprofit organizations and the contracting environment can work together. Our opening vignette regarding the Los Angeles Gay and Lesbian Center and the provision of foster care services provides an interesting example of this issue. The executive director's statement about the program's potential to be copied in other locations suggests an understanding of the role of strategic capacity building in policy advocacy. Advancing the mission in nonprofit organizations is an important undertaking (James, 1983); say Besley and Ghatak (2003, 237), "the notion of a mission replaces the conventional focus on profit." Capacity building and mission enhancement work hand in hand.

The Inversion Principle (Proposition 4.9) provides another aspect for strategic capacity building and a fuller logic connecting agenda setting to mission advocacy and expertise acquisition. Applying it to a contracting setting, we should expect that capacity acquired by contractors over time will be in complex tasks, such as the Deepwater Project, that make it noninvertible or especially difficult to learn. Such capacity cannot be easily appropriated by government principals to further their policy agenda even when functions are brought back into the government.

Strategic capacity building can, through the inversion principle, produce two interesting outcomes. First, the government principal will not face a true market for services when making contracting decisions. This happens because the services offered by potential contractors are defined, at least in part, by their strategic capacity-building choices. Contractors develop autonomy and agenda control just like administrative agencies in the preceding chapter. Second, noninvertible capacity for complex tasks permits contractors to achieve outcomes that they desire. Proposition 4.9 notes that this is possible unless the outcomes that the contractors prefer are very far from those envisioned by government principals or, in other words, because there is substantial policy conflict. For some groups, missions may drift closer to the preferences of the government principal but only as close as necessary given the size of the policy window.

Light (2004) has argued that organizations that engage in capacity building can enhance organizational effectiveness, which would in turn inspire donors and funders to provide additional support. This would have an important impact on the make-or-buy trade-off. In this sense, strategic capacity building, like bureaucratic autonomy, is an entrepreneurial pursuit in which contractors can help shape the menu of goods and services that government provides. In this environment, noninvertibility has an effect opposite to *asset specificity* in the transaction cost economics literature. Asset specificity refers to "the degree to which an asset can be redeployed to alternative uses and by alternative users without sacrifice of productive value" (Williamson, 1996, 59). Specific assets, such as vessels produced for the Coast Guard, cannot be employed elsewhere, creating a holdup scenario in which the government principal can extract distributional benefits from the contractor because the asset cannot be easily sold outside the contract. Strategic capacity building allows the contractor to get distributional benefits and potentially counteract this holdup problem.

Consider the following cases. At the height of the Cold War, the federal government was concerned about the vulnerability of ground missiles to attack. Responding to a request by the air force for a more robust missile navigation system, Raytheon Corporation developed the technology underpinning the now ubiquitous Global Positioning System (GPS). As the military began to understand the utility of satellites to coordinate navigation and communications, the government turned to engineers at academic institutions and to defense contractors for developing the system of interconnected satellites required for the technology to work (Getting, 1993). The first GPS experimental satellite – produced by Rockwell International, another contractor – was launched in 1978, and the developing system was used heavily during the 1991 Gulf War to coordinate the invasion of Iraq (Shaw et al., 1999). Innovations by private contractors in designing GPS technology uncovered a range of applications, and U.S. policy tracked these developments. President Reagan opened the system to civilian use in 1983, after the Soviet Union shot down a Korean Airlines passenger jet after its onboard navigation system failed (B. Smith, 2006). In 1996, the first year after the GPS system was fully operational for military use, President Clinton signed an executive order to encourage the development of civilian and space program applications. Four years later, the president ordered the military to stop degrading GPS signals used for commercial applications (B. Smith, 2006). If GPS could only be used by government, it would be characterized by asset specificity. However strategic capacity building created wider uses within and outside government, mitigating the holdup capability of the Department of Defense.

Nonprofit organizations, using government funds, have engaged in strategic capacity building. The Concord Consortium, a nonprofit dedicated to the use of technology in science, mathematics, and engineering education, won a $3 million grant from the National Science Foundation for an online education program in the mid-1990s. During the grant period, the director of the project recognized an opportunity to start a fully online school – a Virtual High School (VHS) – that yielded an additional $7.4 million grant from the Department of Education (Zucker, 2009, 40). Concord became responsible for developing the online infrastructure for the program, for designing its curriculum, and for training teachers in the new medium. Strategic capacity building had begun in earnest by 2001. VHS was spun off as its own nonprofit organization serving more than ten thousand students annually in thirty states and thirteen countries. Virtual schools like the VHSs assist governments in meeting their mission to provide educational opportunities to students with a broad range of needs and experiences. Initial innovations to develop this capacity came from nonprofit organizations like the Concord Consortium. Today, nearly half of all states offer their own online education program for high school students in addition to the nonprofit offerings (Zucker, 2009).

The lesson is straightforward. When governance tasks are complex, as in the case of social services, health care provision, or arts and cultural programming, contractors have the incentive to use expertise to shape those areas in their own image. This suggests that a politics – a process of determining who gets what, when, and how – develops between contractors and public officials about what kinds of governance tasks the public should have supplied and, through the agenda effects of strategic capacity building, demanded. That politics cannot be ignored by scholars and practitioners of public management.

5.2. CONTRACTIBLE ATTRIBUTES

Some economic arguments in favor of contracting with the private sector are based on market regulation of service attributes, such as quality, that present difficulties for contractual specification. Competition among service providers for government business will work to differentiate these firms and nonprofit agencies in ways that benefit service users to keep or acquire contracts. From this vantage, Shleifer (1998, 125) claims that "private ownership is the crucial source of incentives to innovate and become efficient." Because they operate through delegations of governance tasks, public managers are incentivized to reduce costs or improve quality only through provisions of incomplete contracts, namely, a variety of ex ante and ex post components of the incentive mechanism, as we have discussed in detail. By contrast, either a competitive bidding process for the contract or the adoption of a series of agreements with different contractors that offer choice to service users places these contractors in direct competition for profit from these services. While contract design presents a less efficient solution than well-functioning markets, simple comparisons between market and contractual outcomes tell only a rather naive political–economic story that is reiterated widely in the literature (e.g., Andrews and Entwistle, 2010; Bilodeau et al., 2006; Vining and Boardman, 1992). The political economy of public sector governance can add some nuance to the tale.

Consider the following case. In 1994, the British government integrated several preexisting urban development grant programs into a Single Regeneration Budget (SRB). It unified twenty existing funds and encouraged partnerships – including private companies, nonprofit organizations, chambers of commerce, educational institutions, and even local governments – to apply for the funds (John and Ward, 2005). The budget program lasted from 1995 to 2001 and disbursed over $5.7 billion. The stated goals of the new budget program were not only to create new government efficiencies in program management by incorporating a locally based approach to solving urban problems but also to increase the quality of projects through competition and to encourage innovation through proposal development and unique partnerships (John and Ward, 2005; Rhodes and Brennan, 2007). Successful partnerships had to implement programs that would meet at least one of the broad priorities of funding, including job training and skills development, particularly among young and disadvantaged communities; encouraging economic growth and wealth creation; improving local housing options; developing initiatives benefiting ethnic minorities; reducing crime; protecting the environment and infrastructure; and enhancing the general quality of life in the local community. Overall, more than one thousand proposals were accepted into the program, and the top ninety-nine most distressed communities received 80 percent of the available funding (Rhodes and Brennan, 2007).

John and Ward (2005) found that some goals of the project were met, slightly increasing the overall quality of proposals – particularly among the lower-tiered bidders. However, they also found that proposals tended to reflect the existing desires of the local governments and funding agencies rather than being truly innovative. In other words, bidders often tailored their approaches to what they believed the government wanted to see rather than being truly innovative. This is consistent with the delegation theories we reviewed. Missions and services may drift from their initial positions, but only so far as necessary given the dimensions of the policy window. Competition among bidders for a contract may help a government principal get its ideal point at the expense of service innovation. The reason is that competitive bidding is not a pure market mechanism but rather a market mechanism infused with key attributes of delegation problems.

Consider also consumer choice in health care. Many argue that allowing consumers to select from a wide range of options will drive down costs and increase quality of care. The Medicare Prescription Drug Improvement and Modernization Act of 2003 was an attempt by Congress to get the costs of prescription drugs under control, particularly for senior citizens. In fact, prescription drug costs are the most rapidly increasing component of health care in the United States, having grown from 5 percent of overall expenditures in 1990 to 10 percent in 2000 (Centers for Medicare and Medicaid Services, 2007). Rather than directly regulating prices, government turned to contracts with private health insurance companies to deliver the plans (Duggan and Morton, 2010). Under the plan, government would contract with private prescription drug plans, which would in turn negotiate prices with pharmaceutical companies. Beneficiaries of government funding under Medicare Part D would then have the option to select from a wide number of plans available in their areas, each offering different levels of benefits and covered drugs (Duggan and Morton, 2010). The intent of the legislation seems to have been met, with average out-of-pocket expenditures for prescription drugs falling (Duggan and Morton, 2010; Millet et al., 2010). As predicted by the Uncertainty Principle, high uncertainty leads to broad contractor discretion.

Scholars of public sector contracting have noted that many government agencies put an inappropriately low premium on the skills of effective contract design and management. But in the modern state, a lot of the work of delegating governance tasks is done through contracting and partnership formation. Cooper (2003, xi) expressed concern that "details about how to manage contracts are unimportant, to be left to third-level administrators to sort out." Monitoring is difficult just as it is in congressional delegations. Governments do construct monitoring institutions, which can be very costly as they require a great deal of expertise (Ferris and Graddy, 1994; Marvel and Marvel, 2007). As Prager (1994, 181) puts it, "anyone can tell if a bridge has been repainted ... but to determine whether the contractor used the proper consistency of paint rather than mixing in more thinner ... [a government needs] skilled technicians using sophisticated equipment." The theoretical claims that we have reviewed in Chapters 3 and 4 provide some insight into the design and monitoring of contracts for the performance of governance tasks. Incentives to increase the quality of information about the costs of service provision are essential to government principals that wish to accurately understand efficiencies from contracting. Our understanding of the political economy of public sector governance allows a fresh look at considerations of service quality and other attributes that have often been seen as noncontractible. They also serve to emphasize the importance of nuanced contract management.

Traditional discussions of contractible attributes in bureaucratic politics have focused on different agency types. Consistent with this practice, Chapter 3 made the distinction between project and task agencies. Project agencies performed governance tasks that could not be separated into easily measurable components. Social services organizations and providers of community cultural programs are placed in situations similar to project agencies inside government. Proposition 3.8 can be interpreted in our present context as asserting that contractors with nonseparable, complex tasks can be best incentivized by making their expectation of penalties for particular actions under the contract as unambiguous as possible. Clear penalties reduce the bias in their reports of the cost of performing the governance tasks for which they have contracted. This allows the government principal to better understand the cost of service provision. Expertise for performing these tasks is also unlikely to be invertible, so cost controls incentivized in this way can serve to counteract the agency loss associated with the Inversion Principle.

In the 1990s, information technology services for a large British government agency were contracted to a company called FutureTech, which developed and maintained the agency's computer systems and software. To begin the process, the agency conducted an internal audit to determine its needs and then sought proposals for the contract. Several hundred internal agency staff were transferred to a business office to develop and manage the contract. FutureTech was required to provide regular benchmarking of their costs against industry competitors. This served to "relay market signals on costs as well as reflect the difficulty of fixing prices in the context of fast-changing technologies" (Grimshaw and Willmott, 2002, 491).

As with many contracts with high levels of uncertainty, however, the government was challenged in providing the appropriate staffing levels and resources, leaving much of the project design to the contracting company. As Proposition 3.8 suggests, the contract between the government agency and FutureTech included explicit penalties if performance standards were not met. However, although FutureTech had publicly reported problems with other government contracts, and although the value of the contract nearly doubled during its implementation, no penalties were levied in this particular case. Discretion associated with the Uncertainty Principle made it difficult for the government principal to implement its reward and punishment scheme.

Task agencies, by contrast, perform governance tasks that can be easily subdivided. Certain contractual situations are analogous. For instance, trash collection involves expert logistic and technological considerations, but the process has easily measurable components, say, trucks are late or miss pickups. When these types of governance tasks are being considered, Proposition 3.8 suggests that contracts should create more uncertainty about penalties for noncompliance to reveal better cost information from the contractor.

In 2005, Hurricane Katrina slammed into Alabama, Louisiana, and Mississippi. In Mississippi alone, over 134,000 homes and ten thousand rental units were either damaged or destroyed, and tens of thousands of people were left homeless. Rushing to respond to the disaster, the Federal Emergency Management Agency (FEMA) sought to quickly secure temporary housing for displaced people, primarily through procurement of trailers and mobile homes (U.S. General Accounting Office, 2007). FEMA sought bids and awarded fifteen contracts for the maintenance of mobile homes. The work was invoiced and included routine trailer maintenance, emergency repairs, deactivation and removal of trailers, lawn care, and road and fence repair. Monitoring proved difficult; an audit by the Government Accountability Office (GAO) found that more than $30 million had been misspent through false invoices for work not completed, service overcharges, and poor selection of contractors (Hsu, 2007). As Senator Lieberman (I-VT), chair of the Senate Homeland Security Committee, put it, "The American taxpayer should be outraged – as I am – that in a six-month period FEMA managed to waste approximately half of the $60 million it spent" (Hsu, 2007). The GAO audit revealed an absence of penalties for contractual noncompliance. While FEMA sought to recover overpaid funds in some cases and alleged fraud against contractors in others, there was no systematic procedure in place to penalize companies who failed to perform appropriately under the terms of their contracts. While this penalty scheme was consistent with Proposition 3.8, the costs of monitoring worked against that incentive through the Monitoring Cost Principle, reducing information and ultimately costing taxpayers money. The example makes clear that it is very difficult to reach penalty-related incentives when high-quality monitoring is not in place – the lesson of Monitoring Accuracy Principle I.

Effective contract management depends on the complexity of the services being rendered to the public. Our observations suggest that one important tactic for contract managers is to communicate clearly with contractors performing complex governance tasks about when and how they will be sanctioned for nonperformance. With clearer expectations, contractors can provide credible information about potential pitfalls in performing the task. By contrast, when tasks can be subdivided into observable portions, better information about the costs of service provision can be elicited from contractors when noncompliance sanctions are less clearly defined. We shall refer to this two-part implication of Proposition 3.8 as the *penalty uncertainty principle.*

Adherence to the penalty uncertainty principle appropriately transfers the risk from the government principal to contractors of project- and task-oriented contractors. Project contractors are informed of both expectations and sanctions clearly. Task contractors are clearly informed about expectations but are kept uncertain about penalties. The rationale is that project contractors use many inputs to complete a governance task, whereas task agencies have few, so it is quite hard for the former type to decrease production in the case that penalties are put in place. These specialized contractors may lose key specialist personnel to other opportunities when resource flow from government contracts is uncertain. Project contractors thus protect their resources when they are uncertain by not fully revealing cost information.

Through the punishment uncertainty principle, a contract manager can learn more about the true cost of services and apply that knowledge toward achieving increased efficiency. Strikingly, the size of noncompliance penalties has far less impact on the quality of reported cost information than the penalty uncertainty principle. Proposition 3.7 claims that risk-neutral contractors provide better information regardless of their size. When contractors are risk averse, greater penalties are expected to make cost information even worse. Careful design of penalty structures can help to ensure that investments of resources targeted toward enhancing service quality are not lost to an information asymmetry about the cost of producing services. The forgoing examples provide an important cautionary note: incentives in each proposition that we have discussed do not work in isolation but are part of a system. The failure of one proposition can serve as a diagnostic for the performance of a broader mechanism, as it did in our discussion of the FutureTech and FEMA cases.

We should also recall some lessons from the preceding section when thinking about what is contractible. Strategic capacity building rests on credible representations by contractors to government principals that they are able to implement outcomes with reduced uncertainty about them. Contractors must take care to represent the governance tasks for which they are advocating credibly, say, by committing to specific quality metrics. Without credible statements about the impact of capacity building on the outcomes of governance tasks, contractors cannot engage the incentives embedded in the capacity and inversion principles to shape the range and character of government services. Credibility forges a contractor's reputation, which is important to the achievement of effective and efficient contractual governance.

5.3. ENFORCEMENT

Many governance tasks performed by public sector contractors involve services for which there is uncertain demand. This can have an important impact on the incentives facing contract managers when drafting and enforcing agreements. Proposition 3.1 implies that demand uncertainty for public services can increase the bias with which a contractor reveals information about its costs. Contract managers should have a clear understanding of demand for the service and provide that information to the contractor to gain true cost information and help to achieve more efficient cross-sectoral agreements.

When disasters strike, budgeting, tracking, and controlling costs are among the many challenges public managers face. Whether they are natural disasters like hurricanes, significant weather events or earthquakes, or man-made disasters from acts of terrorism, governments face significant costs that are not fully anticipated. Demand for the services provided by first responders as well as recovery and rebuilding expenses are variable by nature and can be either small or overwhelming, depending on the nature of the disaster. Governments often contract with private providers for emergency response services instead of directly providing the services themselves. Such contracts often cover volunteer fire departments and emergency medical services such as ambulances. In response to Hurricane Katrina, the Environmental Protection Agency (EPA) contracted with an Illinois-based firm to provide meals for their workers on site. That contract specified 150 meals three times a day and allowed for increased demand and additional payments. The EPA did not anticipate decreased demand for meals and was contractually required to pay for 450 meals a day when only 205 were served on average (Environmental Protection Agency, 2006).

Governments can contend with the variability of costs associated with disasters through several different mechanisms. Some government principals institute more flexible contracts; accumulate rainy-day funds; apply for federal grants to assist with preparedness; or absorb some of the planning, preparedness, and response expenditures into general operating funds (J. F. Smith, 2006). Some municipalities may contract for a period of time and pay regardless of whether the contractor's services are used (Flambard and Perrigne, 2006). However, increased discretion under the Uncertainty Principle is enhanced by the Inversion Principle in the case of complex governance tasks. This can make the strategies for dealing with uncertainty through contract quite difficult.

Monitoring is an important element of contractual enforcement, and we have seen several propositions that discuss the success and failure of monitoring schemes to reveal good information. Monitoring Accuracy Principle I can be read in the present context to mean that the contractor will seek to maximize the value of the contract unless the monitoring scheme provides good information about the costs of performing specific governance tasks in the contract. Outsourcing or partnerships will not be efficient in this case, as we saw in the example of FEMA and its trailer contracts. Better monitoring technology makes the value of deceiving the government principal about cost structure less profitable for the contractor, and this, in turn, makes such deception less likely under Monitoring Accuracy Principle II. Monitoring certainly is not costless to the government and places considerable pressure on contract managers.

The Monitoring Cost Principle suggests that higher monitoring costs can lead to poor-quality information. The Group Cohesion Principle holds that one way this can be mitigated is through the involvement of interested, say, community groups, who have their own incentives to monitor the performance of contractors. Parent groups who rely on, say, child care services provided through a contract can sound fire alarms about poor performance, reducing the costs of monitoring. Note, however, that the Group Cohesion Principle further requires that such groups be well organized. Less organized community groups will be less useful in monitoring contractual performance.

Pressure applied by citizen groups can provide additional impetus for government to identify and control costs and/or penalize contractors failing to meet performance standards. In Los Angeles, the Expo Line, an eight-and-a-half-mile light rail extension slated to run from downtown to Culver City, is facing $300 million in cost overruns and a delay of more than two years. Political pressure applied by citizens' groups opposed to the project lies at the heart of the delays (Tymon, 2008). Fix Expo and Neighbors for Smart Rail, two groups opposed to the Expo Line plan and strengthened by neighborhood associations in west Los Angeles, had particular concerns over the safety of the project, including at-grade crossings for trains located near schools, gridlock in communities with tracks and stations, and the crime rates in particular neighborhoods.[2] Santa Monica residents were troubled by attempts to locate the rail yard near Santa Monica College (Taborek, 2009). Citing citizen concerns over noise, the police refused to provide necessary permits, and round-the-clock construction was halted (Bloomekatz, 2010). In addition, the Los Angeles County School Board entered the debate by officially opposing at-grade crossings near two elementary schools, citing safety concerns for students (Weikel, 2009).

One primary contractor highlighted the trouble citizens groups created for providing on-time and on-budget services under their contract, going so far as to receive numerous stop and start orders over a two-year period from the Expo Authority for just one crossing near an elementary school. "There was also a lack of agreement between a number of third parties...and the [Expo] Authority as to what the final product should be.... Therefore, the design was constantly being revised due to the differing views of the authority and these third parties" (Maddaus, 2010). A fire alarm mechanism was at work, and the terms of the contract

[2] See http://www.smartrail.org/.

allowed for changes in the structure of crossings. The government principal did not seem to consider the consequences when stacking the deck, as in Section 3.4. Providing the opportunity for organized interests and stakeholders to influence the terms of the contract created a politics of executing the governance task that slowed completion and increased costs.

Chapter 3 provides some insights about the design of contractors in the event that contractors can be considered risk averse. There are a variety of contracting scenarios in which an assumption of risk aversion is warranted. Smaller contractors or those located far from the government principal, for example, may be unwilling to take the risks necessary for performing governance tasks. Nestled in the southwest corner of Arizona, near the borders of both California and Mexico, Yuma has a population of approximately one hundred thousand. When the city leaders attempted to give first priority to local businesses, they were unable to do so "because no local business responded to requests from the city to submit a bid" (Lobeck, 2011). Such preferences would make it relatively more difficult for remote communities to use contracting when compared to urban counterparts. Some governance tasks may be regulated by noncontractual legal provisions that open contractors up to additional concerns of financial liability.

In such situations, Proposition 3.3 states that when there is substantial uncertainty over the supply of a service – street-cleaning services in a particularly bad winter, for example – biased reporting of true cost structure is expected. The risk-averse contractor essentially protects its resources by inflating costs. Proposition 3.4 notes that this impact can be counteracted by increasing penalty uncertainty. As a consequence, good contract design in such cases should not create crystal clear expectations for a risk-averse contractor about punishment for nonperformance. This is one way that the city of Yuma, Arizona, can work to avoid overpaying for services.

Our insights from Chapter 3 are based on one-time agreements; the models are based on a single budget cycle. When governments have long-term partnerships with contractors, monitoring alone does not solve the incomplete contracting problem. In other words, Goldsmith and Eggers (2004, 121) observe that "an overreliance on box checking and rule compliance – in which government contract monitors focus on finding wrongdoing instead of making the partnership work – leads to an adversarial relationship with partners." An alternative to the type of contract design we have been discussing is known as *relational contracting*, in which managers work to nurture relationships beyond formal contracts (e.g., Sclar, 2000). The power of the relational contract is linked to the desire of both parties to continue the relationship. Motivation to renege on the contract in the short run is overpowered by potential future gains, and this changes some of the incentives that we have described. Relational contracts do not typically rely on third-party enforcement by the courts as a commitment device. Mutual benefits from the relationship make them self-enforcing. Put differently, such contracts are self-enforcing when the discounted present value to the agent from honoring the contract exceeds its immediate gratification from reneging (Kreps, 1990).

Contributions to the public management literature have uncovered important relational elements in various contractual settings. Van Slyke (2006) argues that relational contracts require the government principal to consider the preferences and knowledge of the agent, rendering the latter a steward, or caretaker, rather than a strategic actor. This suggests that the agent will take some distributional benefits from delegation, while providing the government principal with informational benefits. Fernandez (2007) presents evidence that contractual outcomes improve when the government principal and agent work together to solve problems that arise during the contract period. Gazely (2008) finds that a lack of formal contracting arrangements with nonprofit organizations does not displace a manager's authority as principal. Relationships can thus mitigate some of the problems we have been discussing. It is important to understand those problems rather than considering relationships to be a panacea for solving them.

Though outside our current scope, a lively formal literature on relational contracting has provided some very useful insights for scholars and practitioners alike. Bertelli and Smith (2010) review a number of influential pieces for a public management audience and show that the relational contracting literature also stresses the role that contract managers play in creating and nurturing relational contracts. One important insight is that contract managers are most effective in the relational setting if they can skillfully terminate some relationships without losing the credibility to develop and enhance others, even when these actions are being done simultaneously. With project contractors and areas such as human services, in which subjective performance assessments are prevalent, the threat of termination is essential to optimal performance of relational contracts. Like the mafioso described in Gambetta (1994), the contract manager must make the termination threat credible by choosing to terminate contracts when necessary. From the contractor's perspective, credibility is also important. The contractor – particularly in project rather than task scenarios – must also credibly threaten to end agreements to keep the state from appropriating excess benefits. This means that allowing bad relationships to fail will improve relational contracting for the government principal.

5.4. THE RIGHT CONTRACTOR

Free from the congressional commitment problem that affected delegations in Chapter 4, contract managers can use screening strategies, in the same way that Audrey did in Chapter 2, because commitment will lead contractors who are likely to incur losses due to their inefficient ways of performing a governance task not to contract to do so in the first place. The possibility of screening benefits is evident in the new public management (NPM), which, as we saw in Chapter 1, advocates for the use of contracting for the performance of a wide variety of governance tasks. For example, Boston et al. (1996, 137) note that applying NPM includes creating an environment in which "agencies would be required to compete for contracts to supply policy outputs (or output classes)...creating an open market in which public and private organizations would compete, on more or less equal terms, for contracts to supply policy outputs." Nonetheless, competitive bidding cannot work properly without the help of skilled contract managers. Such individuals play the crucial role of thinking through the incentives that their commitments impose on potential and actual bidders. The political economy of public sector governance provides some help for them in fulfilling that role.

When a government principal is selecting a contractor, it can select from a wide range of organizations. Advocates of market provision make the strongest case that government should choose the right contractor for a given governance task, and that contractor is revealed through competition with others. We have discussed the extent to which management reforms increased reliance on competing private firms to deliver public services, forming public–private partnerships (Young and Salamon, 2002). A government principal might also contract with a public agency, for example, from an adjoining state or locality, creating a public–public partnership. This form of contracting can produce consistent service delivery across jurisdictions, reduce transaction costs, or allow smaller governments to enjoy economies of scale through partnership with larger counterparts (Ferris and Graddy, 1986; Andrews and Entwistle, 2010; Marvel and Marvel, 2007, 2008). Government principals can also form public–nonprofit partnerships. The Great Society and Public Interest initiatives during the 1960s and 1970s generated a significant expansion of the nonprofit sector, which was hired to do the work of performing the many governance tasks authorized by statutes, and this continues to be true today (Gronbjerg and Salamon, 2002). Each type of partnership contributes to what is more generally called *collaborative governance*, and each has been used in examples throughout this chapter.

None of these three categories of agents is categorically superior to another. The answer to the question of which agent is the right agent depends, as you should know instinctively by this point in the book, on the specific task environment. Chapter 4 provided various insights into the selection of agents that are applicable in a public sector contracting environment. Most obvious among these are the incentives captured by the Ally Principle. Ally Principle I suggests that contractors who share values about outcomes with the government principal make the best contractors, whereas Ally Principle II predicts that a contractor's job will be more tightly cabined as the contractor and principal have greater goal conflict. In some cases, the primary consideration on the part of a government principal will be to conserve financial resources on performing the governance task. While competitive markets make private sector providers well suited to performing some governance tasks, others rely on contractual and organizational rather than market incentives. For example, Ferris and Graddy (1986) found that the use of volunteers in many nonprofit organizations may help to reduce costs overall. Understanding incentives is central to choosing the appropriate contractor.

As was true in the delegation context, the environment of contracting specific governance tasks can relax the power of the Ally Principle. When providing community oriented services, the Group Influence Principle suggests that given anticipated influence by organized community groups during the performance of a governance task, the government principal has the incentive to counteract them by choosing a contractor with divergent goals. Capacity Principle I implies that given exogenous capacity levels, the government principal may be willing to choose a contractor that prefers outcomes quite different than what the principal envisions. This can only occur under that claim if the nonally contractor has the capacity to reduce outcome uncertainty more than an organization that shares the government principal's vision.

In Section 5.1, we suggested that contractors can use capacity building to incentivize government to take on governance tasks through contracts that are consistent with their interests and missions. Such strategic capacity building may mitigate a phenomenon that sociologists call *goal displacement*, which occurs as organizations seek to grow their budgets by accepting government funding that is not congruent with the organization's mission (Suarez, 2010; Frumkin, 2002; Salamon, 1987). As organizations perform more governance tasks through contracts, they may experience a loss of flexibility in the types of programs they provide (Froelich, 1999; Rosenthal, 1996; Smith and Lipsky, 1993; Stone et al., 2001). This has an impact on those who work for nonprofits. One study of nonprofit service providers found that introducing market-based incentives saw "short-term gains in increased utilization of volunteers to meet contracted objectives, this risked a longer term disenchantment and erosion of volunteer contributions when they came to perceive that instead of adding value, they were substituting for government actions" (Francois, 2000, 294). Strategic capacity building and its impact on the policy agenda can help to renew the mission for these organizations. While this may help their membership retain motivation toward governance tasks with which they are charged, it may also lead the organization to a nonally contractor, providing agency loss for the government.

5.5. SOME NORMATIVE IMPLICATIONS

If contracting were to become ubiquitous, the government would rarely provide direct public services. Government would become the manager of networks of organizations contracted to provide the public services. Milward and Provan (2000, 362) call this scenario the *hollow state*: "carried to the extreme, it refers to a government that as a matter of public policy has chosen to contract out all its production capability to third parties, perhaps retaining [responsibility] for negotiating, monitoring, and evaluating contracts." Public management scholars have raised profound questions about what such a state would do for democratic governance. Can the political economy of public sector governance provide any further insight?

To be sure, some governments have operated as hollow states out of necessity for some time. For smaller government principals with limited budgets – like Yuma, Arizona – it can be cost prohibitive to hire, train, and manage a set of experts in a broad number of fields, from engineering to mental health to prison management. Local labor markets may also be limited in specialized fields, exacerbating the effect (Ferris and Graddy, 1986). Given the relatively small size of contracts with such communities, they are more likely to involve off-the-rack solutions, particularly from large contractors, than would more customized task provision for larger communities. Larger communities also have more contractors from which to choose, an observation made famous by Indianapolis mayor Goldsmith's "Yellow Pages rule," stating that more contractors listed in the Yellow Pages makes it more likely that a stable market for a governance task is existing or nascent (Super, 2008). In a study of trash collection in Columbus, Ohio, Brown and Potoski (2004) describe how city officials solicited bids from Cleveland and Cincinnati to improve competitiveness in the pool of potential agents. Limited agent choice suggests that government principals must have excellent contract managers to deal with the kinds of incentive problems that we have described in the preceding sections.

One of the most intriguing implications of our analysis is the notion of strategic capacity building. In the hollow state, that practice could severely tax the contract management function government performs. The logic of Capacity Principle II combined with the importance of the mission to nonprofit organizations can lead to a concern that is related to fears about public–private partnerships. Le Grand (1998, 418), for instance, argued that "the introduction of private provision and market mechanisms . . . would increase the rewards to self-interested behavior, thus encouraging it to develop at the expense of more altruistic concerns." It may be that mission-interested behavior in the form of strategic capacity building can create a form of bureaucratic autonomy for the contracting state, where mission-driven organizations incentivize the government to choose to engage in governance tasks their missions advocate. The hollow state could begin to lose control of its policy agenda.

The governance tasks produced by advocacy and strategic capacity building may have varying degrees of public support or opposition. Opposition to these services can create a form of *democratic deficit*, or lack of popular accountability. Sharing or transferring their legislatively mandated authority from government to contractor can blur the lines of legal responsibility, transparency, and accountability that these reforms were designed to support. With this increasing distance between the constitutional authority and the public, government is challenged with maintaining its legitimacy with the public it is designed to serve (Heinrich et al., 2010). While we have paid more attention to public–nonprofit partnerships, the argument, of course, also applies to public–private partnerships and the capacity building activities of private firms. The outcome in the latter case may be a relative of *bureaucratic capture*, where regulated interests receive the benefits of regulatory policy choices in part because of their substantial expertise (Peltzman, 1976, provides a general theory).

In either case, it is the democratic process of influencing which governance tasks should and should not be provided that suffers. This is not different from current conditions, but the incentives that create it are dissimilar in interesting ways and should be considered in scholarship and practice.

5.6. CONCLUSION

This chapter has been an exercise in extending the reach of theoretical implications. We applied lessons from the resource and delegation material we have reviewed to an area of growing and, some would say, already central importance to modern public management. Cross-sectoral partnerships are ubiquitous and, as the epigraph reminds us, are seen as ways to solve public policy problems.

Our application of political–economic delegation and resource theories led to two important implications. First, strategic capacity building has the ability to structure the public policy agenda, and mission-driven organizations as well as private firms have the incentive to engage it when they perform complex governance tasks through partnerships and contracts with government principals. Second, contract managers are very important figures, and the penalty uncertainty principle can help them gain better information about the true cost that contractors bear when performing governance tasks. That knowledge can make government contracts more efficient and effective, but no proposition in the political economy of public sector governance works in isolation.

Any discussion of contracting is a discussion of accountability also. Penalties, monitoring, and other contractual provisions are designed to produce accountable action by contractors for government. That is what solving principal–agent problems is all about. We now turn our attention to a broader and more normative discussion of accountability in American public management. What characteristics should public managers have in our constitutional system? We shall learn that being passionate about the governance task they are implementing is a very useful trait for public servants, either in agencies or contract agencies.

6

Responsibility and Good Governance

The very continuance of the democratic system depends on our ability to combine administrative responsibility with administrative discretion. Both are indispensable for the maintenance of a democratic service state.
– David Levitan (1946, 566)

Responsibility is central to public management; indeed, it is the purpose of public management in a democratic society (Bertelli and Lynn, 2006, 146). The concept is most commonly construed as synonymous with accountability in the way that the epigraph implies; the will of the people must be transformed into the governance tasks that government undertakes. A useful definition for our present purposes is to consider accountability as comprising "those methods, procedures, and forces that determine what values will be reflected in administrative decisions" (Simon et al., 1950, 513). Thinking of accountability in this way connects institutions, or rules and procedures, as discussed in Chapter 1, to values that are folded into ideology arrayed on a spatial dimension in Chapter 4. Responsible public managers maintain accountability when performing each governance task. This produces democratic governance.

Because of its importance, responsibility has been the subject of a very large literature. Most students of public management have probably read this book with some ideas from that literature in mind; that is a good thing. It is important to keep in mind that the political economy of public sector governance has core interests in common with traditional public administration literatures. In this chapter, we begin our discussion by thinking about responsibility in theory and then analyze examples of mechanisms that have been put in place to incentivize it in practice.

The next section explores a political–economic perspective on an essential normative debate in the public administration literature about how best to maintain responsibility among public managers. We then use our framework to understand two incentive mechanisms that have been used in the United States and United Kingdom respectively.

6.1. THE GOOD AGENT

One of the great debates in public management history took place between the New Deal and the beginning of World War II. It sought to identify the source of responsible public management. Does responsibility lie in the characteristics of statutory delegations or in the character of the people performing governance tasks? Beginning in the 1930s, Carl Friedrich and Herman Finer wrote a series of influential articles that would shape the way in which the field of public administration would think about this question. At the core of this debate was the extent to which public managers' own sense of duty could compel their performance of governance tasks in keeping with the interests of political principals. Finer (1941, 336) did not believe so, asserting that "the servants of the public are not to decide their own course; they are to be responsible to the elected representatives of the public, and these are to determine the course of action of the public servants to the most minute degree that is technically feasible." His is a belief in "the primacy of the people over officeholders," giving Congress "the authority and power to exercise an effect on the course which [officials] are to pursue, the power to exact obedience to orders" (Finer, 1941, 337). In other words, Finer believed that contracts for the delegation of governance tasks should be as complete as possible. He has no problem with the notion of delegation but fears that such things as strategic capacity building can render it undemocratic.

The reality of public management, wrote Friedrich (1940, 6), was quite different because "public policy, to put it flatly, is a continuous process, the formation of which is inseparable from its execution." In contrast to Finer's tight discretionary restrictions, Friedrich (1940, 12) offered a vision of managerial responsibility that welcomes the development of bureaucratic autonomy. Public managers, he continued, may consider

a policy irresponsible if it can be shown that it was adopted without proper regard to the existing sum of human knowledge concerning the technical issues involved [or] it was adopted without proper regard for existing preferences in the community.... The responsible administrator is one who is responsive to these two dominant factors: technical knowledge and popular sentiment.

Finer (1941, 335) interpreted Friedrich's position as "a sense of responsibility, largely unsanctioned, except by deference or loyalty to professional standards." That response fully reveals the conflict of ideas between these two scholars, and their debate remains active in public management scholarship today.

The debate begs a very important normative question for the field: is there such a thing as a good public manager? If so, what qualities might that ideal manager possess? Can public managers who have such qualities help politicians solve the agency problems we discussed in Part I? Friedrich believes that managers' responsibility should balance expertise with popular sentiment, whereas Finer and the literature we have reviewed finds the latter to be the province of Congress. Our discussions up to this point have made the general claim that managers with such broad discretion as to determine not just what Congress but also the public wants can seriously thwart the democratic foundation of governance. This is intolerable to Finer (1941, 335), who defines the job of a public manager as "working not for the good of the public in the sense of what the public needs, but of the wants of the public as expressed by the public." The public has a means of expression through its elected representatives, and these representatives build the enacting coalitions that give authority to public managers to perform governance tasks. Friedrich, he contends, has it the wrong way around. Friedrich would like to employ such things as professional identity to screen candidates for the good public service type, but we know Congress and other elected government principals face a commitment problem that makes doing this very difficult. We shall see, however, that it is useful to consider the result that might occur if a government principal were not to face a commitment problem as it tells us quite a lot about what the good agent looks like.

We spent considerable energy in Chapters 4 and 5 on understanding the growth of administrative autonomy through strategic capacity building. Combined with the Group Influence Principle, the strategic acquisition of expertise led to violations of the Ally Principle and a problem for Finerian control. This has led scholars to wonder whether there is a process that would select candidates for public service – a personnel mechanism – capable of selecting the kinds of public managers who would not drift so far from statutory authority as to sacrifice their responsibility. Bertelli and Lynn (2006, 130) argue that the constitutional position on public managers is that of Finer, whereas Friedrich's position establishes a foundation for how public managers should behave as they learn about the state of the world. They suggest that an ideal personnel mechanism might work like this. First, the candidate for a public management position must inform the personnel office about the preferences about the governance task she would perform if hired and what policy outcomes it would achieve. The government should then calculate a package of salary, benefits, and discretion for the candidate. The optimal remunerative package would offer a value equal to the expected change in social welfare that would occur if the candidate were to give false information about her preferences toward the task and act contrary to her statements.

Consider an example. If the position in question dealt with setting pollution standards in the Environmental Protection Agency, the candidate would be asked to provide information about his preferences over environmental outcomes and how he believes abatement programs and standards work to achieve those outcomes. Suppose that our candidate says that he is a strong environmentalist and believes that pollution standards are the perfect weapon in abating pollution. His reward package would be set according to the loss to society, say, a monetized pollution increase, that would accrue if the candidate in fact hated pollution standards and did everything in his power to undermine them. Such action could eliminate a governance task completely (through sabotage) and leave the public to experience the status quo prevailing before a democratically enacted policy change. In other words, the remuneration of a public manager depends on the amount of damage that her misrepresentations about policy preferences could inflict on the public. The social cost of irresponsible public management must be shifted to the public manager. The state must be able to commit to this cost-shifting mechanism as in any screening solution.

This personnel scheme relies on the representations of all applicants. Most important, each public manager shares the damage from each other's misrepresentations. When a candidate for a public management position provides this information, he is effectively asking the government to calculate a package of remuneration and discretion. This package depends on the views about the governance task held by all applicants and incumbent agency personnel. Taking the job under these conditions indicates the candidate's willingness to participate in public service, and that means sharing the costs and benefits imposed on everyone else implementing the governance task.

The Bertelli and Lynn (2006) mechanism is not practical to implement, but as a theoretical construction, it reveals two critical things about public management. Because the costs of a public manager's *maladministration*, or actions that cause harm to other people, spill over into the overall performance of governance tasks, they will be born by a broad range of public managers and, indeed, the public. Because these costs are incurred broadly by society, each public manager must accept the potential harms inflicted by each other's shortcomings in performing elements of governance tasks. When an individual official misuses authority in implementing one national security task, for instance, a wide range of officials who were behaving responsibly will find it difficult to carry out their contributions to the dispatch of other governance tasks. This interconnectedness of governance tasks lies at the heart of understanding responsibility in governance – indeed, our definition of governance is the aggregate of these interrelated tasks. If the Bertelli and Lynn (2006) cost and risk distribution mechanism is in place, individual public managers are incentivized against irresponsible behavior. Note, for instance, that it eliminates the credibility of the so-called Nuremberg Defense, or an excuse for irresponsible behavior on the grounds that superior officials ordered one's action. It is understanding and acceptance of the relationships among governance tasks that creates the right incentives for public managers to behave responsibly on behalf of the public and its elected representatives.

The key point is that public managers must understand that responsibility means the acceptance of risks from maladministration. Incentive mechanisms can help to do this. At times, such risk shifting is made clear at law. Because school attendance is compulsory for children of certain ages, school districts and certain employees – teachers, coaches, and so forth – in the state of California have the duty to take reasonable actions to ensure the safety of students.[1] As employees of a school district, individual teachers have a duty imposed by the legislature to "hold pupils to a strict account for their conduct on the way to and from school, on the playgrounds, or during recess" (California Education Code, Section 44807). Courts have interpreted this responsibility for the care of students as extending to potential, even unlikely, situations of harm. Specifically, teachers' responsibility attaches even when a particular danger has never occurred before or if the harms are merely threatened at a school that has never experienced such problems before.[2] Laws such as this shape incentives to achieve responsibility but do so by imposing risks from the

---

[1] *Rodriguez v. Inglewood Unified School Dist.*, 186 Cal. App. 3d 707, 714–715 (1986); *Leger v. Stockton Unified School Dist.*, 202 Cal. App. 3d 1448, 1458–1459 (1988).

[2] *Ziegler v. Santa Cruz City High Sch. Dist.*, 168 Cal. App. 2d 277, 284 (1959); *Leger v. Stockton Unified School Dist.*, 202 Cal. App. 3d 1448, 1460 (1988).

relationships among various elements of a governance task (providing public education) on all officials (teachers).

Proposition 4.1 suggests that government principals still have the incentive to delegate authority even without an expectation of governance tasks being performed by agents who fully accept the responsibility of public service. Regardless of these incentives, leading proposals to reform public sector employment have the aim of screening in candidates willing to share the costs and benefits of public service. This is because they make for better agents and reduce the costs of governance that we have described in forgoing chapters. For instance, Kettl (1996, 4) proposes reforms of the Office of Personnel Management that "promote the fundamental values of government service[,] promote high performance, collect critical data on how well the system works, and especially ensure adherence to the system's core objectives." This focus on core objectives might be read as a resort to *public service motivation* by readers familiar with the concept. Public service motivation is defined as a "general, altruistic motivation to serve the interests of a community of people, a state, a nation, or humankind" (Rainey and Steinbauer, 1999, 20). Note, however, that what public service motivation connotes is too general. What really matters is an acceptance of responsibility and motivation toward a particular governance task, not well meaning toward a broader humankind. We have just developed a rationale for the former. An important positive theory underscores the latter point.

Gailmard and Patty (2007) use a spatial delegation model to uncover a set of incentives for personnel selection and administrative discretion generated by the U.S. civil service system. The principal lesson from their theory for our present purpose is that, on one hand, the federal civil service system can benefit from the expert capacity of administrative agencies; on the other hand, it serves to create a bureaucratic politics. Like Audrey in Chapter 2, Gailmard and Patty (2007) must consider two types of public managers. A *policy-motivated* public manager is intrinsically concerned with the outcomes of governance tasks she implements or, in other words, enjoys increased utility from policies ever closer to her ideal point. This means that even if a policy-motivated individual was not performing the governance task – say, she was a private citizen – she would be worse off if it produced an outcome distant from her ideal point. By contrast, *policy-indifferent* public managers are not interested in policy outcomes directly – they draw utility from other things such as the salary, benefits, perquisites, and prestige of the job. Both types may draw intrinsic utility from other governance tasks as well as other things, but with regard to the particular task being delegated, the former cares about the policy it induces, and the latter does not.

Candidates for public management positions must choose to accept a position performing the governance task or a position with more salary and other benefits that is unrelated to the task under consideration. For instance, that outside option might be employment in the private sector. Gailmard and Patty (2007) show that policy-motivated agents are more likely to take the government job than their policy-indifferent counterparts. This happens because being a public manager gives policy-motivated individuals the opportunity to affect policies they care about. The more lucrative position elsewhere cannot do this. In the model, the public management position does not guarantee the policy-motivated person influence over the outcome she values, but the opportunity is enough to get her to sign on for the job. Once in the position, she is keen to engage, for example, in strategic capacity building. Gailmard and Patty (2007) then produce a result consistent with Capacity Principle II (Proposition 4.8) and the Uncertainty Principle (Proposition 4.4). They show that Congress provides greater discretion to agencies performing a governance task when they are staffed by policy-motivated agents. In other words, the good agent from a congressional – and Finerian – perspective is the policy-motivated agent. That motivation must be specific to the governance task, not general goodwill about serving the people. The policy window is a democratic constraint, which is an important part of what Finer had in mind for the promotion of responsible public management.

The implications of this theory are that the civil service system is operating in a way that invites policy-motivated agents to perform governance tasks. As Gailmard (2010, 38) puts it, "policy discretion conditioned on [public managers'] expertise development is a form of compensation. It is a compensation that is uniquely available in public service, and it is only policy-motivated agents who value it." Tenure in the job allows these public managers the time to engage in strategic capacity building, which provides an important commitment that this form of compensation can be realized. Congress does face a risk of policy drift from strategic capacity building under the Inversion Principle (Proposition 4.9). Note that a mechanism that draws in policy-motivated officials comes at a cost that is vocalized by some critics of civil service tenure. Cohen and Eimicke (1994, 11), for instance, argue that personnel rules "make it virtually impossible to hire the best people, reward top performers and terminate those who are unwilling or unable to do their jobs." Gailmard (2010) provides an argument for why Congress has the incentive to accept such consequences. A government principal gets agents who acquire the expertise to produce an informational benefit for it. That is what Bendor and Mierowitz (2004) identified as the key rationale for congressional delegations and is largely consistent with the canonical public administration literature.

Perhaps it is ironic that the very civil service system that brings policy-oriented individuals to public service and enhances the informational benefit from delegation also permits those same public managers to appropriate a distributional benefit that can make representative government less responsible to the public's expressed wants. We shall return to this problem momentarily, yet one thing should be very clear: policy-oriented individuals are clearly different than those with some broader sense of public spiritedness. These individuals' policy preferences drive their use of discretion when executing specific governance tasks.

Despite their benefits, a variety of reforms to state civil service laws have attacked existing civil service tenure systems. In 1996, the state of Georgia removed civil service protections for new hires, decentralized personnel authority, and established a new performance management system built largely on performance-based pay. To achieve this, the state filled vacant positions with "unclassified" titles over which the state personnel board had no jurisdiction. New employees were "at will," unable to attain tenure rights after serving the traditional one-year probationary period. Likewise, Florida legislation in 2001 replaced seniority with merit as a basis for promotion and required that open positions not be filled until at least two candidates from outside the public sector had been considered (Battaglio and Condrey, 2006). Hays and Sowa (2006) note that such reforms aim toward making government more efficient and responsive. However, they argue that the "due process rights of many civil servants are eroding," making public sector jobs less inviting to policy-oriented individuals (Hays and Sowa, 2006, 106). Research has also shown a motivation-crowding effect from one aspect of these reforms: performance-based pay. Weibel and Osterloh (2010, 397–398) show evidence that such schemes "affect a cognitive shift, which promotes two opposing motivational effects. On the one hand, performance-contingent rewards subdue the internalized meaning of the work itself. . . . On the other hand, [such a reward scheme] strengthens the meaning of external rewards, that is, boosts the power of external motivation for a particular activity." Without a civil service tenure system inducing the good agent into public management positions, we are compelled to unpack Friedrich's idea of professional responsibility.

The civil service system analyzed by Gailmard and Patty (2007) and the Bertelli and Lynn (2006) mechanism may invite the same types of individuals into public service, yet the latter seeks to incentivize policy-motivated individuals toward Finer's objective of administering to the public want. For instance, strategic capacity building may occur as a result of the expertise and actions of policy-motivated public managers, but those agents must be guided by the wants of the public as expressed through their elected representatives when doing so. Tenure in office only provides the security to engage in strategic capacity building. Accepting the risks and consequences of maladministration makes public managers focus on the democratic underpinnings of their roles. When agents behave responsibly, delegations work more efficiently as they come closer to being self-enforcing. It should not come as a surprise, then, that responsible public management behavior resolves the Friedrich–Finer debate.

As a framework for understanding responsibility, Bertelli and Lynn (2006) offer a *precept of managerial responsibility*. This normative principle centers on the judgment exercised by the public manager in performing a delegated governance task. Responsible judgment must be balanced, namely, "identifying and reconciling the inevitable conflicts among interests, mandates, and desires," and rational, emphasizing "the relationship between action and consequences to insure transparent justifications for managerial action" (Bertelli and Lynn, 2006, 147). Judgment that is balanced and rational is also accountable; "individual commitment to the exercise of judgment that is balanced and rational . . . , aggregated over all public managers, becomes the institutionalized acceptance of the authority" they hold under statutory delegations (Bertelli and Lynn, 2006, 147). Put differently, accountability ensures that public managers act as though they understand the size of the policy window for each governance task they perform; this means that they administer to the public's wants. In an ideal setting, the personnel screening mechanism described earlier would make this precept self-enforcing. Public management practice is not that ideal setting, and just as in Chapters 3 and 5 with regard to cost information, incentives must be designed to promote responsibility. In the next section, we examine monitoring mechanisms at the task rather than the individual level.

Ex ante controls and ex post incentives are designed to make irresponsible public management unattractive. Bertelli and Lynn (2006, 147) define this bad practice as "management that disavows accountability and that acts without authority or in an arbitrary, self-serving, ill-informed, or non-transparent fashion." Congress defined it in a very similar way when giving courts the power to review administrative actions in Section 706 of the Administrative Procedure Act of 1946 (60 Stat. 237):

> The reviewing court shall... hold unlawful and set aside agency action, findings, and conclusions found to be... arbitrary, capricious, an abuse of discretion, or otherwise not in accordance with the law... contrary to constitutional right, power, privilege or immunity... in excess of statutory jurisdiction, authority, or limitations, or short of statutory right... without observance of procedure required by law.

As in the case of private contracts between individuals, the courts provide one important mechanism for maintaining responsibility. Judicial review offers credibility for punishing. This credible commitment takes the form of a veto over a policy produced by public managers when they act irresponsibly. The courts are seen as a mechanism for maintaining managerial responsibility.

Judicial review provides government principals with a means of commitment to identifying and eliminating irresponsible public management. It transfers power to a third party, the courts, to enforce notions of responsibility. Because the courts are politically independent in their decision making, they provide credibility to the government principal's commitment to responsibility.[3] Historically, this was born of a fear of unchecked administration. Roscoe Pound, an advocate of judicial review of administrative action during the New Deal period, likened unchecked administration to totalitarianism: "in the soviet state... there were no laws but only administrative orders" (Pound 1940, 127). In remarks to a local bar association, Pound recanted the tale of Professor Evgeny Pashukanis, whose theory of law and Marxism provided that the state must disintegrate in the final state of communism (Pashukanis, 2002). Pound warned that unchecked administration sealed his fate in a purge: "The Professor is not with us now.... If there had been law instead of administrative orders, it might have been possible for him to lose his job without losing his life" (quoted in Bertelli and Lynn, 2006, 147). Clearly Pound believed that relying on professionalism in the sense of Friedrich was insufficient to solve the problem of responsibility and also that purges are a bad mechanism for doing so. Given that Finer's statutory detail inevitably leaves gaps

---

[3] It is easy to quibble with this point about political independence; students of judicial politics would certainly do so. Yet the notion behind judicial review draws on the role of the courts in deciding cases independently of political influence.

that create an incomplete contracting problem, as in Chapter 4, the courts provide information (through the pleadings of litigants) and the courts' enforcement powers to ensure adherence only to the powers delegated.

In the next section, we examine additional mechanisms for promoting responsibility at the governance task level and ask how the political economy of public sector governance can help explain, and improve, the role of these mechanisms in monitoring managerial responsibility. Behn (2001) argues that traditionally, the public sector has tried to increase responsibility by focusing on the areas of finance and fairness as these are often easier to measure than performance outcomes. What he calls an accountability dilemma arises when rules designed to increase accountability through finance and equity actually end up hampering performance. The next section considers mechanisms that attempt to extract government principals from that dilemma. Efforts toward enhancing the performance of the public sector have become one of the most popular subjects of contemporary public management research. They bring together the overarching normative concerns we have just described.

6.2. MONITORING RESPONSIBILITY

Policy windows (ex ante controls) combined with fire alarms, monitoring, and judicial review (ex post controls) compose a mechanism to ensure responsible governance that operates across policy domains in American governance. However, government principals commonly put additional incentives to work. The political–economic theories from Part I can help us to understand a set of important incentives that determine the effectiveness of these mechanisms. A recent federal assessment scheme that garnered substantial attention among public management scholars provides a fruitful example for applying what we have learned. The assessment of performance of local governments by the U.K. Parliament provides another. These examples differ on an important characteristic. In the first case, administrative agencies are being monitored. In the second, local governments that have been themselves elected are monitored by a sovereign government principal in those delegations. The latter setting is similar in an important way to American federalism, where the principal and agent in, for instance, federal block grants to the states are both elected by overlapping constituencies of voters. Each setting provides different manifestations of the politics we considered in Part I.

Performance incentives can be difficult to implement effectively because they require two things that we now know well. This is because they resemble a menu law, as discussed in Chapter 4. The government principal states the goal of a governance task and provides a menu of incentives for agencies or contractors given their performance in relation to that goal. Agent behavior is then observed, and rewards or punishments are meted out. As in the menu law case, this requires two things that can be difficult to achieve for an elected principal. First, it requires a government principal to clearly define goals at the level of the governance task so that performance can be assessed against them. Each of the benefits and costs of delegation is worthy of consideration here. Such action can, for instance, work against the possibility of blame shifting from the government principal to the agency or contractor. Second, the government principal must credibly commit to those goals as well as to a program of reward or punishment depending on whether agents meet them. The courts or other third parties are often not present in these schemes to enhance credibility. We have seen that government principals have the incentive to undermine policy commitments in pursuit of reelection and that incentive remains in place in the performance context. It is important to keep these issues in mind as we discuss the following example mechanisms, the first of which has the president as principal.

6.2.1. Monitoring Agency Responsibility

In August 2001, President George W. Bush released the President's Management Agenda, which established five areas of managerial focus for his administration: (1) strategic management of human capital, (2) competitive sourcing, (3) improving financial performance, (4) expanded electronic government, and (5) budget and performance integration (Breul, 2007). Consistent with these goals, the administration sought to implement a performance-based budgeting system called the Performance Assessment Rating Tool (PART). PART questionnaires were completed by Office of Management and Budget (OMB) officials (Gueorguieva et al., 2009), and the scheme measured the effectiveness of government programs using twenty-five questions along four dimensions on a scale of 0 to 100: clear purpose and objectives; strategic planning of the agency; rating of management; and results.[4] PART is a particularly interesting example from our perspective because it operates at the same unit of analysis that we have employed. PART seeks to measure success or failure in achieving goals when administrative agencies perform particular

---

[4] Information about PART is available at http://ExpectMore.gov/.

governance tasks. Also, it intends to measure policy outcomes rather than outputs (Gilmour, 2007). By September 2010, OMB had assessed 1,015 programs; among those, 19 percent were found effective, 61 percent moderately effective or adequate, and only 2.5 percent ineffective.

Drawing back from the larger normative questions we have been considering, we now ask the question of what makes programs successful in achieving higher PART scores. As a threshold matter, it is necessary to understand what the goals of a program really are. Reviewing briefly, we said in Chapter 4 that the goals of a program could be identified by the location of a policy enactment in a unidimensional policy space and that a policy window provided a range of outcomes that would be consistent with those goals. Proposition 4.3 states that the enacted policy is set at the ideal point of the congressional median. This means that the policy window is constructed around congressional preferences at the time a delegation is made. This allows an administrative agency to learn about the state of the world and to use that knowledge when performing the governance task but maintain accountability to the will of the people as expressed through their congressional representatives. Ally Principle II (Proposition 4.5) holds that the size of that policy window decreases as policy conflict between the enacting Congress and the administrative agency implementing the task increases. Thus we expect that if the statute is passed in an era of divided party government – when spatial distances between the policy preferences of Congress and the president are large – the amount of discretion granted for implementing the task is likely to be smaller than if the president and congressional majority were to share a partisan affiliation.

An administrative agency produces a policy outcome by performing a governance task. In the canonical model of delegation, the policy implementation process was such that the ultimate policy outcome was simply an additive adjustment to the enacted policy dictated by the state of the world the agency observes. In Chapter 4, we noted that the agency would choose a policy that was both within the discretion afforded to it by the policy window and as close to its own ideal outcome as possible. Administrative action can be considered responsible here because it induces a policy that falls within the policy window established in the statute enabling the agency to perform the governance task. Policy-motivated agents enjoy it because it allows for policy drift toward their ideal points when dispatching governance tasks.

Because the president has the authority to appoint agency heads consistent with Ally Principle I (Proposition 4.2) or the Group Influence

Principle (Proposition 4.6), we should expect that, for instance, programs implemented by a Republican presidential appointee are likely to more closely resemble their goals when the program was established by legislation in a Republican-controlled Congress. Groups exerting considerable influence may have been part of a deck-stacking arrangement by the enacting coalition. As we have discussed, appointment power can be more frequently used in executive agencies. The *politicization* of agencies – or their staffing with appointees at lower levels of the internal hierarchy – can also allow the president to use his appointment power to influence policy.

Did the politics just described emerge in PART outcomes? Lewis (2008) examined the influence of politicization on PART scores, finding that program implementation teams led by political appointees are more politicized than those led by career civil servants. On average, he found that appointee-directed programs scored lower on PART than careerist-directed programs. Policy-motivated agents are doing what the theory in Section 6.1 expected of them; they are changing policy based on their preferences. He also found evidence that programs created under unified government had higher average PART scores than those created under divided government. More homogeneous enacting coalitions, clearer policy windows, and stronger deck-stacking arrangements seem to be important factors motivating the unified government effect.

Complex programs implemented by specialist administrative agencies may achieve success even when the president and Congress disagree on policy. This is due to their expertise or their ability to strategically acquire it under the capacity and inversion principles. The Uncertainty Principle (Proposition 4.4) implies that programs having greater outcome uncertainty are implemented with greater discretion by the administrative agencies to which they have been delegated. This allows for the application of expertise but also the possibility that programmatic outcomes could drift farther from the enacted policy, making the program appear unsuccessful. Gilmour and Lewis (2006b) identified problems consistent with strategic capacity building. PART included a rating called "results not demonstrated," indicating a difficulty in developing appropriate measurements for its assessment. In scores collected for fiscal year 2004, 51 percent of programs were so rated, with still 41 percent having that designation in the following year. There is some evidence of agency bias consistent with the Uncertainty Principle and strategic capacity building.

Gilmour and Lewis (2006b) also point out that measurements for purpose, planning, and management do not measure outcomes but instead may simply capture the strength of program staff in constructing a paper trail. Finding accurate information in so many programs reminds us that the costs of monitoring differ by governance task. The Monitoring Cost Principle (Proposition 3.13) holds that higher costs reduce the quality of information. Cohesive interest groups, for instance, in areas such as environmental and business regulation can drive these costs down according to the Group Cohesion Principle.

The resource literature from Chapter 3 also sheds important light on performance audits such as PART. In particular, it helps to understand how such a mechanism incentivizes agencies to provide information. Proposition 3.2 states that as PART creates greater penalty uncertainty, reporting will be less reliable. Mullen (2006) argues that PART must serve the president's interest but that the actors making budgetary decisions, notably Congress, are not likely to utilize the information if they do not feel that PART is credible. Even without commitment, Monitoring Accuracy Principle II (Proposition 3.10) claims that better monitoring through PART will lead to better information. Taken together, these propositions suggest that if PART represents a credible commitment to budgetary penalties through presidential budget requests, it can help the president better understand the cost of service provision to facilitate "making budget decisions based on results" (Office of Management and Budget, 2003, 9). That said, president must actually ask for fewer resources for agencies that do not score highly.

Empirical studies shed some light on aspects of the credibility question. Gilmour and Lewis (2006a, 2006b) showed evidence that PART scores have an impact on 2004 budget allocations, Olsen and Levy (2004) find an even larger effect. Gilmour and Lewis (2006a, 180) noted with some surprise that regarding PART scores generated under Republican president George W. Bush, "programs housed in Democratic departments or created under unified Democratic Party control are no more likely than other programs to get budget increases or decreases." This evidence suggests that PART represents a credible commitment to imposing budgetary penalties.

The president also seems to be responding to the incentives described by the Penalty Uncertainty Principle. Our theories suggest that PART should represent as strong a commitment as possible to a punishment scheme for unsuccessful programs, but not for every program. Frisco and Stalebrink (2008) examined subcommittee and committee reports from the 109th Congress, finding limited mention of PART scores equally dispersed between the House of Representatives and the Senate. A handful of committees discussed the scores most, including Appropriations, Budgeting, and Government Affairs. The Penalty Uncertainty Principle states that certainty about penalties would only work for governance tasks that can easily be subdivided and are likely candidates for outsourcing, but not in complex projects that cannot be subdivided in a straightforward way. Stalebrink (2009) finds that block grant programs score lower on PART evaluations than programs less reliant on intergovernmental collaboration.

To better assign a value to the efficiency of a particular program, agencies were encouraged to develop better measures. The budgeting process provided the incentive to accomplish this task (Gilmour, 2007). The Strategic Budget Uncertainty Principle (Proposition 3.9) states that penalty uncertainty for those agencies making large budgetary requests can incentivize more truthful reporting; actual budget reductions can have the same impact. This holds regardless of whether the agency is of program or task type. Gilmour and Lewis (2006b, 2006a) find strong average patterns that lower PART scores are associated with budget cuts but are not distinguished by agency type. Moreover, the Task-Type Uncertainty Principle (Proposition 3.5) suggests that agencies spending more resources on perquisites will get more scrutiny than constituency service agencies, with program agencies getting less still. This provides an incentive for program-related expenditures to increase that has not been examined in the literature.

Performance measurement through PART scores is politicized. Posner and Fantone (2007, 365) observe that "far from removing politics from budgeting, the linkage of performance to budgeting raises the stakes associated with performance goals and measures. As such, the performance analysis marshaled to support budget decisions may be more vulnerable to political debate and conflict." However, PART appears to maintain credibility in a way that makes it effective in this politics. Our theories provide a useful way of thinking about the PART experience. Public managers must understand these political incentives to understand PART. In the next section, we examine a scenario in which politics plays a different and equally important role.

6.2.2. Monitoring Government Responsibility

Strategic capacity building or the Group Influence Principle can lead to the failure of the Ally Principle regarding agent selection. However, in some cases, the agent has its own electoral connection, and elections, not appointments, allow the voters to directly create nonally agents. Bertelli and John (2010) refer to this situation, in which a principal monitors an agent and both actors are elected by overlapping constituencies, as *government checking government*. Incentives in these situations are much simpler and straightforwardly political. Principals are expected to use or create mechanisms, including monitors, to drive out policy conflict by keeping nonally agents from being elected. This is driven simply by the incentives described by Ally Principle I (Proposition 4.2).

While government checking government occurs in various settings, including many federal assessments of state or local programs, such as the No Child Left Behind scheme of high-stakes testing, one widely studied example comes from the United Kingdom. Local government in the United Kingdom comprises a series of organizations performing a range of governance tasks, including education, environmental protection, and public safety. Local politicians are elected but implement governance tasks subject to policy windows and budgetary appropriations established by Parliament. This leads to a monitoring problem of the type we have been considering, in which the central government in Westminster monitors local government responsibility in governance (Broad et al., 2007, 124). Local election outcomes are related to parliamentary electoral prospects. Because local contests occur more frequently than national elections, they are seen widely as referenda on the national government's policy agenda (Miller, 1988). Local political outcomes, then, matter to the central government in its ambition to be reelected. Relationships with copartisans in local government may also make governance easier for Parliament for a variety of reasons that go beyond a spatial model and politics such as better information transmission through established personal networks. The value of party ties underlies the government-checking-government problem.

Assessments of the responsibility of local authorities started in the 1990s with measures developed by an independent agency within the central government called the Audit Commission. In 2002, the Audit Commission created the Comprehensive Performance Assessment (CPA), a rating – poor, weak, fair, good, and excellent – that was conducted through 2006. These scores were based on more specific functional monitoring. For instance, a "use of resources" assessment incorporates information about internal management and efficiency in the use of financial services. The Audit Commission used national performance comparisons in concert with judgments made by its own inspectors (Audit Commission, 2005). Five-point CPA scores were developed by six-member inspection teams to "simplif[y] the complex, doing so in a way that aligned many of the other activities and motivated councils to take action. For the first time it made credible, explicit comparisons of performance between whole councils, and not just individual services" (Audit Commission, 2009, 6).

Crucial to our present purposes, a poor score was publicized and also lowered electoral prospects for incumbent local politicians. Local news media may be interested only in specific aspects of performance, but the free availability of summary performance ratings creates a headline, particularly when the scores are extreme in one direction or the other. When they can be transmitted to voters by third parties, their publication provides a form of commitment to performance goals that helps make the scheme credible. Voters appear to have responded as well. James and John (2006) found that incumbent elected officials in communities with a rank of poor saw a 6 percent decrease in support at the ballot box. Interestingly, they found that only the negative rankings seemed to have an impact on voter choices; good or excellent scores were not rewarded by voters. Additionally, a negative CPA score resulted in a loss of some incumbents, and all had other major local changes in the year following the election, including a change of party leadership. This result was supported by Boyne et al. (2009) in a study following elections over multiple years. Revelli (2008) also found that CPA scores could lead to a change of partisan control in local government.

If lower publicized evaluations could yield electoral problems for incumbents, a commitment by the central government to use poor ratings for actual punishment is not required to reduce policy conflict. The punishment and change of agent comes from the electorate through voting, not through an appointment by the parliamentary principal in Westminster. That lack of commitment can, of course, lead to penalty uncertainty, which in turn can lead to poor information quality (Proposition 3.2) unless the local authority can be considered risk averse (Proposition 3.4). Rewards and punishments did occur. Localities with strong scores were granted additional autonomy, while weaker-performing governments endured more invasive monitoring. According to Game (2006, 467–468), "excellent authorities are trusted a little more, given a little more discretion in spending their pocket money, and suffer a little less constant pestering," and because weaker scores resulted in varying forms of "ministerial and external oversight, [poor-performing authorities] would be 'assisted' in drawing up and implementing recovery plans." Boyne et al. (2010) find that higher performance on the CPA is associated with lower senior management turnover in the local authorities. This is consistent with interests of policy-motivated bureaucrats. As we have seen, Gailmard and Patty (2007) show that when a public management position does not offer policy influence, outside options can become more appealing. Credibility, then, was established by actions of Parliament in response to the ratings and not simply through the independence of the Audit Commission. It permits application of the Penalty Uncertainty Principle from Chapter 5 to the CPA.

The technocratic credibility of the scheme was not absolute. Andrews et al. (2005) argue that the performance measurements used in the CPA can be partially attributable to difficult circumstances rather than poor management decisions by local policy makers. They find that CPA scores are influenced by circumstances beyond the policy maker's control such as social diversity, discretionary resources, the prevalence of single-parent households, and economic prosperity. Yet there was also a purely political aspect. Bertelli and John (2010) showed evidence that throughout the entire period of the CPA, local authorities controlled by Labour Party politicians – the incumbent party in national government – received more favorable ratings than those under opposition party control. Boosts to CPA scores for Labour-controlled authorities and corresponding drops for opposition authorities were particularly likely in swing areas, where members of Parliament were vulnerable. What is more, Bertelli and John (2010) also found evidence that scores were influenced by the presence of current or former local government officials from an area now employed by the Audit Commission. These effects were observed when controlling for the difficult circumstances that Andrews et al. (2005) observed. Bertelli and John (2010) provide some evidence that the incentives of Ally Principle I in the government-checking-government context yield credibility problems for monitoring the responsibility of agents. An intriguing facet of this scheme is that credible commitments to objective ratings are not strictly required of the principal because agents are chosen by the voters. The central government's problem is to use the CPA to convince voters to elect the local councilors it wants them to elect. It would be useful to examine federal, state, and local arrangements in the United States with these incentives in mind.

6.3. CONCLUSION

We began this chapter by examining an essential normative question in public management through the lens we crafted in Part I of this book.

That analysis led us to understand the importance of policy-motivated public managers to the effectiveness of delegated governance tasks. Policy motivation was distinguished from a broader notion of public service motivation, with the latter concept being far more general than what is contemplated by the political economy of public sector governance. We saw the role of personnel systems in screening such individuals into public service and described a normative principle that defines responsible public management.

Although the U.S. civil service system does incentivize the successful hiring of policy-motivated public managers, that characteristic does not solve all the incentive design problems we have discussed. It does not produce responsibility on its own, as the normative precept of managerial responsibility and its corresponding incentive mechanism suggested. Our attention then turned to efforts by government principals to monitor the responsibility of the performance of governance tasks they delegate. Albeit on a grander scale, these efforts are comparable to contractual monitoring provisions in Chapter 5. The federal PART scheme provided an example of monitoring agencies and the British CPA an instance of monitoring in a scenario where both principal and agent are elected governments. Many of the same concerns of contractual monitoring were present in each of these examples, but important differences were presented.

Our applications for the political–economic framework we have considered in this book are now complete. All that remains is a conclusion that briefly reviews all that we have considered.

Conclusion

We began our exploration of the political economics of public sector governance by emphasizing the connection between the actions of government and the will of the people as expressed through their elected representatives. This link was the linchpin of democratic governance through responsible public management in the preceding chapter. Responsibility represents the paramount and constant demand of the democratic setting in which public management operates. Because politicians represent citizens and public managers are authorized to perform governance tasks by politicians, this democratic relationship was present in all the theories we covered in this book. Those theories provide a set of propositions that, when taken together, create a framework for thinking about governance. Though the literature we covered was selected from a vast collection of contributions, it reveals the heart of our approach.

That approach requires institutions, the rules and norms that shape behavior. In Chapter 1, we distinguished institutions from organizations, or collections of institutions that enable their members to engage in collective behavior. Mixtures of institutions and organizations create incentive mechanisms – an agreement with your doctor, a job advertisement from the Department of Social Services (DSS), a budgetary appropriation to the Department of Defense, a delegation to the Environmental Protection Agency to establish pollution abatement standards, a contract between the city of Los Angeles and a nonprofit to provide low-income child care, professional ethics, the Program Assessment Rating Tool (PART), or the Comprehensive Performance Assessment (CPA). Incentive mechanisms propelled our analytic strategy throughout the book.

Institutions depend on each other, and these mechanisms do not operate in a political vacuum. History helps to determine the current institutional environment, as discussions ranging from new public management to bureaucratic autonomy suggested. Incentive mechanisms are meant to affect behavior, and they do so by making it costly. Yet the costs of these mechanisms can make them less effective, as we saw in various discussions and examples of monitoring.

The basic unit of analysis, or observational focus, in the book has been the governance task. Governance, then, is a collection of tasks that government has chosen to perform. While this is far simpler than the way that governance is defined in a burgeoning literature within public administration, it serves to focus our attention on particular programs and services in which government is involved. Such is the concern of a practicing public manager. We noted that each governance task has information and enforcement components that are important to understanding incentive mechanisms in both theory and application. Designing governance tasks by skillfully weaving institutions into incentive mechanisms is the central problem of public sector governance. It is a pivotal role for the contemporary public manager.

Chapter 2 briefly introduced the reader to rational choice theory, focusing our attention on individuals – later, organizations through characteristic actors – having preferences over alternatives such as the policy outcomes produced by performing governance tasks. We first turned to the standard principal–agent model, the workhorse of this literature, which provided a way of thinking about designing incentives in situations analogous to the incomplete contracting problem. We then wondered whether we could choose an appropriate agent who would not take advantage of the informational problems uncovered in your doctor's office. Screening agents required commitments, which some government principals in Chapter 5 may have been able to make but with which Congress in Chapters 3 and 4 had considerable difficulty. We also learned that screening and signaling are two sides of the same problem of choosing the right agent. This set the stage for our review of an important selection of theories in Part I.

Because the political–economic theories we review have been developed largely in the context of American political institutions, our discussion remained in the United States and at the federal level throughout Part I. This does not mean that such incentives are unique to the American context. Chapter 3 considered on the congressional power of the purse granted by the Constitution. The budgetary process is of interest to us as a tool for the political control of the bureaucracy, in which use it is a double-edged sword. We learned about conflicts of interest that are created by the constitutional separation of powers. These conflicts are created by design and provide incentives that shape the way in which American government, like any organization, works. We learned that a characteristic actor in Congress, just like Audrey at the DSS, could elicit excellent information about the cost of performing governance tasks if she could commit to a budgetary reward-and-punishment schedule for particular agency actions.

When Congress could not make such a commitment, monitoring provided less accurate information. Interest groups monitoring agencies on their own time and with their own resources could report information about agency behavior to Congress through a mechanism known as fire alarm oversight. This could lower the costs and improve the quality of monitoring information but required cohesive interest groups to clarify the information being reported to Congress. While our discussion centered on the role of monitoring in yielding information about the cost of performing governance tasks, these propositions presented in Chapter 3 prove useful in thinking about the monitoring of many aspects of agency performance. They proved helpful in the perspective on contracting and partnerships we developed in Chapter 5.

In Chapter 4, we considered the preeminent problem of public management in a democratic society, namely, the delegation of legitimate policy-making authority. To understand the centrality of delegation, we depicted a variety of agency problems arising among various institutions of government, the voters, and the regulated entities and interest groups in American politics. Executive and independent agencies were distinguished in terms of presidential control over them. The president's appointment power was introduced. Our discussion of delegation itself began with its costs and benefits. The benefits to Congress include effort reduction, the development of expertise by administrative agencies, the reduction of outcome uncertainty from the performance of governance tasks, the protection of special interests, and the relocation of blame to administrative agencies for making unpopular policy. Agency costs, introduced in Chapter 2, accrue in delegation settings as well and are due in important part to policy conflict, which we treated as ideological. Other costs were generated by information asymmetries and monitoring. We noted that screening through the use of menu laws was not an efficient way for Congress to approach the delegation of authority. This was due to what we called the congressional commitment problem – the difficulty

Congress faces in committing to a particular policy because of the electoral connection and reelection schedules of its members.

To represent the policy conflict present in delegation models, we introduced the spatial model by thinking about buying a churro on a day at the beach. Spatial models power theories of delegation in the political economy literature. The canonical model produces an important result known as the Ally Principle that proves, with apologies to Shakespeare, more honored in the breach than the observance. The failure of the Ally Principle is in part tied up with a realistic representation of the policy implementation process. We examined the impact of interest groups in that process as well as the building of capacity by administrative agencies for performing particular government tasks. These aspects of policy making lead to agents with divergent policy preferences performing governance tasks on behalf of principals. When the implementation process is complex, a result we called the Inversion Principle likewise generates a failure of the Ally Principle.

Part II of this book began by applying the political economy of public sector governance to contracts and partnerships between government principals and private or nonprofit organizations. A large component of governance has in recent years been delegated to nongovernmental organizations. We saw that many of the same incentives in resource monitoring and delegation decisions are at work in the contracting setting. Those incentives had an interesting impact on the way we think about contracts and partnerships. Strategic capacity building facilitated by the Capacity and Inversion principles from Chapter 4 suggested a way in which nongovernmental contractors can influence the policy agenda. These incentives carry the potential for mission-driven contractors to fulfill their advocacy missions through partnerships with government rather than displacing their goals. The penalty uncertainty principle suggests that the expectations about earnings through contracts should be strategically defined, depending on the type of governance task that a contractor performs. Both these principles advise that the role of contract manager in the contemporary state – as in the hollow state – is exceptionally important. We discussed maintaining and terminating relationships with contractors as an important aspect of contemporary public management.

Chapter 6 was framed by a classic debate in the traditional literature of public administration. That debate centered on the question of whether a public manager's sense of duty as a servant of the public is enough to maintain her responsibility when performing a governance task or whether tight controls over her discretion are necessary. This led us to a normative view of responsible public management. A key quality for public managers also emerged from a positive analysis of the American civil service system through a delegation model. A good agent is motivated toward the performance of the particular governance task with which she is charged. This also means that the individual is motivated to use her position to produce a particular policy outcome. As such, the good agent could also induce a failure of the Ally Principle and engage in strategic capacity building. We discussed a normative precept for maintaining responsibility that would ensure that such action serves the interests of the people, as articulated by their elected representatives.

We then examined incentive mechanisms for monitoring responsibility at the governance task level. The federal PART scheme exemplified an overarching responsibility assessment for administrative agencies, while the CPA program in the United Kingdom exemplified government at one level monitoring tasks performed by government at another. The latter scenario introduced a raw form of partisan politics in which a principal has incentives to use the assessment mechanism to influence the electoral prospects of the agent.

Our approach in this book has been different than in many other public policy texts in one very important way: it takes administrative agencies and nongovernmental contractors seriously in their role in governance. These organizations provide public services and create and implement the regulations that affect our daily lives. They are also the places where public managers work. It is critical to consider their role in the policy process and our study of public policy and management has been integrated as a result. That said, it is vitally important to understand the limitations of this book. The preceding chapters are introductory and exclude a great many elements of real public management that can be incorporated into models. They provide a flavor for a political–economic approach to governance but do not represent in any sense a definitive statement of the field. Moreover, the book has focused on the American context, while the capability of this approach is much broader. Yet it is not constructive to apply these chapters to other political jurisdictions without careful consideration of the institutional environments therein.

Perhaps most important among these concluding caveats is this: Chapter 1 made the point that the approach to explaining and designing institutions in this book is not uniquely suited to addressing the questions of contemporary public management. It is one of many tools and helps more in some contexts and less in others. With more traditional approaches to public management, it shares a central focus on the representation of the people throughout the administrative process. The book makes that connection explicit at various points, and it underscores the commonalities in research programs in public sector governance. Public management is a complex and varied practice, and it requires a host of complementary approaches to its research questions if it is to be relevant. While we made several comparisons, a clear point emerges. No single view of public sector governance is sufficient. This book introduces one, and readers are encouraged to consider how it relates to other ways of thinking.

We have come to the end of our introductory study. If the ideas in this book were provocative, exciting, confirmatory, annoying, or repulsive in some way, I hope that you will explore them further. Chapters 5 and 6 represent my own thinking about the topics covered through the lens established in Part I. If those ideas seem either right or wrong, they can be tested with data, quantitative or qualitative. If you think that they do not follow from the literature, argue why that is so. All fields at all times benefit from the vigorous exchange of ideas, and public management deserves that kind of intellectual engagement. With colleagues in the practice and study of governance engaged in these issues in a lively matter, both the literature and the practice of public management will improve. That is the goal of knowledge building, and I hope you will join the enterprise.

Appendix A: Propositions from Chapters 3 and 4

3.1 Increases in demand uncertainty yield decreases in agency bias.

3.2 Increases in penalty uncertainty yield decreases in agency bias.

3.3 In risk-averse agencies, increases in supply uncertainty yield increases in agency bias.

3.4 In risk-seeking agencies, increases in penalty uncertainty yield decreases in agency bias.

3.5 **Task-Type Monitoring Principle.** Congress monitors agencies with a penchant for perquisites more than those oriented toward constituency service; the least monitored agencies are those that expend additional resources performing more of the governance tasks they were created to perform.

3.6 **Monitoring Accuracy Principle I.** When monitoring provides accurate information for Congress, the agency provides accurate information about its cost of performing a governance task. However, if monitoring provides inaccurate information, the agency provides a cost estimate consistent with budget maximization.

3.7 When the agency is risk neutral, its bias in reporting costs decreases regardless of the penalty that Congress will impose. When the agency is risk averse, its bias increases.

3.8 When they become more uncertain about the budgetary penalty that Congress will impose, project agencies increase their bias, while task agencies reduce it.

3.9 **Strategic Budget Uncertainty Principle.** If Congress can increase uncertainty over reward or penalty budgets only when agencies request large (not small) budgets, then the agency always reduces its bias. When Congress does impose budget cuts, both project and task agencies are always less likely to bias its cost information.

3.10 **Monitoring Accuracy Principle II.** Improvements in monitoring technologies always lower the value of deception for the agency, producing truthful cost information.

3.11 Under a closed rule and as long as monitoring costs are not excessively high, the agency signals its true cost type in making its budgetary request. The agency types separate through the budgets each type request.

3.12 When Congress is permitted to make a counterproposal under an open rule and monitoring costs are not excessively high, the agency's budget request reveals no information about its true cost type in this scenario.

3.13 **Monitoring Cost Principle.** As monitoring costs rise, Congress uncovers less information about the agency's cost of performing a governance task.

3.14 **Group Cohesion Principle.** Given the difficulty of monitoring the actions of an administrative agency, greater interest group cohesion in the governance task environment decreases the costs of monitoring.

4.1 Congressional utility is greater when it uses a policy window delegation than under a menu law, regardless of the degree of policy conflict with the agency performing the governance task.

4.2 **Ally Principle I.** The president will choose an agent who precisely shares his ideology to implement a delegated governance task.

4.3 **Uncertainty Principle.** The floor median sets its ideal point as the enacted policy when delegating a governance task.

4.4 **Uncertainty Principle.** As outcome uncertainty increases, the amount of discretion an agency is granted by Congress to perform a governance task likewise increases.

4.5 **Ally Principle II.** As the preferred policies of the legislature and administrative agency diverge, statutory discretion for performing a governance task is restricted.

4.6 **Group Influence Principle.** The president appoints agency heads strategically and, to the extent permitted by the confirmation process, chooses them to offset the influence of interest groups in the implementation process.

4.7 **Capacity Principle I.** Congress may delegate a governance task to an agency that prefers policies quite different than its own if its administrative capacity is higher than that of agencies aligned with its own policy views.

4.8 **Capacity Principle II.** Specialist agencies use capacity investments to create incentives for Congress to delegate governance tasks they prefer rather than those they dislike, but generalist agencies cannot create such incentives.

4.9 **Inversion Principle.** Administrative agencies have no incentive to acquire invertible expertise, but they can get policies they prefer when their expertise is noninvertible as long as their preferences are not so out of line with those of Congress that it prefers to create a brand-new agency to undertake a governance task.

Appendix B: Recommended Readings

This appendix includes a selection of additional sources that readers may wish to consult. These references provide an indication of the variety present in the political economy of public sector governance literature. In many cases, the referenced articles speak to multiple themes in the text, but they are categorized by at least one major focus.

CHAPTER I

Institutions and Organizations

Bernstein, L. (2001). Private commercial law in the cotton industry: Creating cooperation through rules, norms, and institutions. *Michigan Law Review*, 99:1724–1790.

Milgrom, P., North, D. C., and Weingast, B. R. (1990). The role of institutions in the revival of trade: The medieval law merchant, private judges, and the champagne fairs. *Economics and Politics*, 1:1–23.

Moe, T. M. (1984). The new economics of organization. *American Journal of Political Science*, 28:739–777.

North, D. C. (1990). *Institutions, institutional change, and economic performance*. Cambridge University Press, Cambridge, U.K.

Weingast, B., and Marshall, W. (1988). The industrial-organization of Congress: or, why legislatures, like firms, are not organized as markets. *Journal of Political Economy*, 96:132–163.

Williamson, O. E. (1985). *The economic institutions of capitalism: Firms, markets, relational contracting*. Free Press, New York.

Williamson, O. E. (1996). *The mechanisms of governance*. Oxford University Press, New York.

Policy Expertise

Bertelli, A. M., and Wenger, J. B. (2009). Demanding information: Think tanks and the US congress. *British Journal of Political Science*, 39:225–242.
Esterling, K. M. (2001). *The political economy of expertise*. University of Michigan Press, Ann Arbor.

New Public Management

Horn, M. J. (1995). *The political economy of public administration: Institutional choice in the public sector*. Cambridge University Press, Cambridge, U.K.
Lynn, L. (1998). The new public management: How to transform a theme into a legacy. *Public Administration Review*, 58:231–237.

Governance and Public Management

Lynn, L. E. Jr. (2006). *Public management old and new*. Routledge, New York.
Pierre, J., and Peters, B. G. (2000). *Governance, politics, and the state*. St. Martin's Press, New York.
Rhodes, R. A. W. (1997). *Understanding governance: Policy networks, governance, reflexivity, and accountability*. Open University Press, Buckingham, U.K.
Riccucci, N. M. (2010). *Public administration: Traditions of inquiry and philosophies of knowledge*. Georgetown University Press, Washington, D.C.

CHAPTER 2

Principal–Agent Models

Brehm, J., and Gates, S. (1997). *Working, shirking, and sabotage: Bureaucratic response to a democratic public*. University of Michigan Press, Ann Arbor.
Laffont, J.-J., and Tirole, J. (1993). *A theory of incentives in procurement and regulation*. MIT Press, Cambridge, Mass.
Macho-Stadler, I., and Pérez-Castrillo, J. D. (2001). *An introduction to the economics of information: Incentives and contracts*, 2nd ed. Oxford University Press, Oxford, U.K.
Miller, G. (2005). The political evolution of principal–agent models. *Annual Review of Political Science*, 8:203–225.

CHAPTER 3

Budgetary Politics

Baumgartner, F. R., and Jones, B. D. (2002). *Policy dynamics*. University of Chicago Press, Chicago, Ill.

Carpenter, D. (1996). Adaptive signal processing, hierarchy, and budgetary control in federal regulation. *American Political Science Review*, 90:283–302.

Ferejohn, J., and Krehbiel, K. (1987). The budget process and the size of the budget. *American Journal of Political Science*, 31:296–320.

Padgett, J. (1980). Bounded rationality in budgetary research. *American Political Science Review*, 74:354–372.

Padgett, J. (1981). Hierarchy and ecological control in federal budgetary decision-making. *American Journal of Sociology*, 87:75–129.

Pollack, H., and Zeckhauser, R. (1996). Budgets as dynamic gatekeepers. *Management Science*, 42:642–658.

Wildavsky, A. B. (1984). *The politics of the budgetary process*, 4th ed. Little, Brown, Boston, Mass.

Wood, B. D., and Waterman, R. W. (1994). *Bureaucratic dynamics: The role of bureaucracy in a democracy*. Westview Press, Boulder, Col.

Monitoring and Procedures

Bertelli, A. (2006). Governing the quango: An auditing and cheating model of quasi-governmental authorities. *Journal of Public Administration Research and Theory*, 16:239–261.

Bertelli, A. (2008). Credible Governance? Transparency, Political control, the personal vote, and British Quangos. *Political Studies*, 56:807–829.

de Figueiredo, R., Spiller, P., and Urbiztondo, S. (1999). An informational perspective on administrative procedures. *Journal of Law, Economics, and Organization*, 15:283–305.

Krause, G. (2003). Coping with uncertainty: Analyzing risk propensities of SEC budgetary decisions, 1949–97. *American Political Science Review*, 97:171–188.

Krause, G. A., and Corder, J. K. (2007). Explaining bureaucratic optimism: Theory and evidence from US executive agency macroeconomic forecasts. *American Political Science Review*, 101:129–142.

Krause, G. A., and Douglas, J. W. (2005). Institutional design versus reputational effects on bureaucratic performance: Evidence from U.S. government macroeconomic and fiscal projection. *Journal of Public Administration, Research, and Theory*, 15:263–280.

Krause, G., and Douglas, J. (2006). Does agency competition improve the quality of policy analysis? Evidence from OMB and CBO fiscal projections. *Journal of Policy Analysis and Management*, 25:53–74.

Krause, G., Lewis, D., and Douglas, J. (2006). Political appointments, civil service systems, and bureaucratic competence: Organizational balancing and executive branch revenue forecasts in the American states. *American Journal of Political Science*, 50:770–787.

Shipan, C. (2004). Regulatory regimes, agency actions, and the conditional nature of congressional influence. *American Political Science Review*, 98:467–480.

Weingast, B. (1984). The congressional-bureaucratic system: A principal agent perspective (with applications to the SEC). *Public Choice*, 44:147–191.

Weingast, B., and Moran, M. (1983). Bureaucratic discretion or congressional control: Regulatory policy-making by the Federal Trade Commission. *Journal of Political Economy*, 91:765–800.

Whitford, A. B. (2003). Adapting agencies: Competition, imitation, and punishment in the design of bureaucratic performance. In Krause, G. A., and Meier, K. J., eds., *Politics, policy, and organizations: Frontiers in the scientific study of public bureaucracy*, pages 160–183. University of Michigan Press, Ann Arbor.

Deck Stacking and Group Influence

Balla, S. (1998). Administrative procedures and political control of the bureaucracy. *American Political Science Review*, 92:663–673.

Becker, G. (1983). A theory of competition among pressure groups for political influence. *Quarterly Journal of Economics*, 98:371–400.

Carpenter, D. (2002). Groups, the media, agency waiting costs, and FDA drug approval. *American Journal of Political Science*, 46:490–505.

Carpenter, D. (2004). Protection without capture: Product approval by a politically responsive, learning regulator. *American Political Science Review*, 98:613–631.

Peltzman, S. (1976). Toward a more general theory of regulation. *Journal of Law and Economics*, 19:211–240.

Stigler, G. J. (1971). The theory of economic regulation. *The Bell Journal of Economics and Management Science*, 2:3–21.

CHAPTER 4

Delegation

Bawn, K. (1995). Political control versus expertise: Congressional choices about administrative procedures. *American Political Science Review*, 89:62–73.

Bennedsen, M., and Feldmann, S. (2006). Lobbying bureaucrats. *Scandinavian Journal of Economics*, 108:643–668.

Bertelli, A. M., and Whitford, A. B. (2009). Perceiving credible commitments: How independent regulators shape elite perceptions of regulatory quality. *British Journal of Political Science*, 39:517–537.

Callander, Steven (2011). Searching for good policies. *American Political Science Review*, 105:643–662.

Dewatripont, M., and Tirole, J. (1999). Advocates. *Journal of Political Economy*, 107:1–39.

Ferejohn, J., and Shipan, C. (1990). Congressional influence on bureaucracy. *Journal of Law, Economics, and Organization*, 6:1–20.

Holmström, B., and Milgrom, P. (1991). Multitask principal agent analyses: Incentive contracts, asset ownership, and job design. *Journal of Law, Economics, and Organization*, 7:24–52.

Volden, C. (2002). Delegating power to bureaucracies: Evidence from the states. *Journal of Law, Economics, and Organization*, 18:187–220.

Volden, C. (2002). A formal model of the politics of delegation in a separation of powers system. *American Journal of Political Science*, 46:111–133.

Wiseman, A. E. (2009). Delegation and positive-sum bureaucracies. *Journal of Politics*, 71:998–1014.

Multiple Principals

Cameron, C. M. (2000). *Veto bargaining: Presidents and the politics of negative power.* Cambridge University Press, New York.

Canes-Wrone, B. (2003). Bureaucratic decisions and the composition of the lower courts. *American Journal of Political Science*, 47:205–214.

Huber, J. D., and Shipan, C. R. (2002). *Deliberate discretion?* Cambridge University Press, New York.

Huber, J., Shipan, C., and Pfahler, M. (2001). Legislatures and statutory control of bureaucracy. *American Journal of Political Science*, 45:330–345.

Kiewiet, D., and McCubbins, M. (1988). Presidential influence on congressional appropriations decisions. *American Journal of Political Science*, 32:713–736.

Spiller, P. (1990). Politicians, interest-groups, and regulators: A multiple-principals agency theory of regulation, or let them be bribed. *Journal of Law and Economics*, 33:65–101.

Whitford, A. B. (2002). Decentralization and political control of the bureaucracy. *Journal of Theoretical Politics*, 14:167–193.

Whitford, A. B. (2005). The pursuit of political control by multiple principals. *Journal of Politics*, 67:29–49.

Whitford, A. B. (2007). Decentralized policy implementation. *Political Research Quarterly*, 60:17–30.

Bureaucratic Decision Making

Bertelli, A. M., and Grose, C. R. (2009). Secretaries of pork? A new theory of distributive public policy. *Journal of Politics*, 71:926–945.

Carpenter, D. (2000). State building through reputation building: Coalitions of esteem and program innovation in the national postal system, 1883–1913. *Studies in American Political Development*, 14:121–155.

Hammond, T. (1986). Agenda control, organizational-structure, and bureaucratic politics. *American Journal of Political Science*, 30:379–420.

Huber, G. A. (2007). *The craft of bureaucratic neutrality: Interests and influence in governmental regulation of occupational safety.* Cambridge University Press, Cambridge.

Kernell, S., and McDonald, M. (1999). Congress and America's political development: The transformation of the Post Office from patronage to service. *American Journal of Political Science*, 43:792–811.

Miller, G. J. (1992). *Managerial dilemmas: The political economy of hierarchy.* Cambridge University Press, Cambridge.

Miller, G. J., and Whitford, A. B. (2007). The principal's moral hazard: Constraints on the use of incentives in hierarchy. *Journal of Public Administration Research and Theory*, 17:213–233.

Moe, T. M. (1995). The politics of structural choice: Toward a theory of public bureaucracy. In Williamson, O., ed., *Organizational theory: From Chester Barnard to the present and beyond*, pages 166–183. Oxford University Press, Oxford, U.K.

Prendergast, C. (2003). The limits of bureaucratic efficiency. *Journal of Political Economy*, 111:929–958.

Prendergast, C. (2007). The motivation and bias of bureaucrats. *American Economic Review*, 97:180–196.

Scholz, J., and Wood, B. (1999). Efficiency, equity, and politics: Democratic controls over the tax collector. *American Journal of Political Science*, 43:1166–1188.

Scholz, J., Twombly, J., and Headrick, B. (1991). Street-level political controls over federal bureaucracy. *American Political Science Review*, 85:829–850.

Ting, M. (2002). A theory of jurisdictional assignments in bureaucracies. *American Journal of Political Science*, 46:364–378.

Ting, M. (2003). A strategic theory of bureaucratic redundancy. *American Journal of Political Science*, 47:274–292.

Appointments

Bertelli, A. M., and Grose, C. R. (2011). The Lengthened Shadow of Another Institution? Ideal Point Estimates for the Executive Branch and Congress. *American Journal of Political Science*, 55:767–781.

Clinton, J. D., Bertelli, A. M., Grose, C. R., Lewis, D. E., and Nixon, D. C. (2011). Separated Powers in the United States: The Ideology of Agencies, Presidents, and Congress. *American Journal of Political Science*, forthcoming.

Indridason, I. H., and Kam, C. (2008). Cabinet reshuffles and ministerial drift. *British Journal of Political Science*, 38:621–656.

Lewis, D. E. (2008). *The politics of presidential appointments: Political control and bureaucratic performance*. Princeton University Press, Princeton, NJ.

Warren, P. (2011). Allies and adversaries: The roles of appointees in administrative policymaking in a separation of powers system. *Journal of Law, Economics, and Organization*.

Non-U.S. Institutions

Levy, B., and Spiller, P. T., eds. (1996). *Regulations, institutions, and commitment: Comparative studies of telecommunications*. Cambridge University Press, New York.

Saiegh, S. M. (2011). *Ruling by statute: How uncertainty and vote buying shape lawmaking*. Cambridge University Press, New York.

Strøm, K. (2000). Delegation and accountability in parliamentary democracies. *European Journal of Political Research*, 37:261–290.

CHAPTER 5

Mission-Driven Organizations

Besley, T., and Ghatak, M. (2003). Incentives, choice and accountability in the provision of public services. *Oxford Review of Economic Policy*, 19:235–249.
Besley, T., and Ghatak, M. (2005). Competition and incentives with motivated agents. *American Economic Review*, 95:616–636.

CHAPTER 6

Performance Measurement

Courty, P., and Marschke, G. (2003). Dynamics of performance measurement systems. *Oxford Review of Economic Policy*, 19:268–284.
Heinrich, C. J., and Marschke, G. (2010). Incentives and their dynamics in public sector performance management systems. *Journal of Policy Analysis and Management*, 29:183–208.
Meier, K. J., and O'Toole, L. J. (2006). *Bureaucracy in a democratic state: A governance perspective*. Johns Hopkins University Press, Baltimore, Md.
Moinyhan, D. M. (2008). *The dynamics of performance management: Constructing information and reform*. Georgetown University Press, Washington, D.C.

Normative Conceptions of Public Management

Dubnick, M., and Romzek, B. S. (1987). Accountability in the public sector: Lessons from the Challenger Tragedy. *Public Administration Review*, 47:227–238.
Frederickson, H. G. (1997). *The spirit of public administration*. Jossey-Bass, San Francisco, Calif.
Rohr, J. (1986). *To run a constitution: The legitimacy of the administrative state*. University Press of Kansas, Lawrence.

Judicial Review

McCubbins, M., Noll, R., and Weingast, B. (1989). Administrative procedures as instruments of political control. *Journal of Law, Economics, and Organization* 3:243–277.
McCubbins, M., Noll, R., and Weingast, B. (1989). Structure and process, politics and policy: Administrative arrangements and the political control of agencies. *Virginia Law Review*, 75:431–482.

Shipan, C. (2000). The legislative design of judicial review – a formal analysis. *Journal of Theoretical Politics*, 12:269–304.

Stephenson, M. (2006). Legislative allocation of delegated power: Uncertainty, risk, and the choice between agencies and courts. *Harvard Law Review*, 119:1035–1070.

References

Ackerman, B. A. (1998). *We the people.* Belknap Press of Harvard University Press, Cambridge, Mass.

Andrews, R., and Entwistle, T. (2010). Does cross-sectoral partnership deliver? An empirical exploration of public service effectiveness, efficiency, and equity. *Journal of Public Administration Research and Theory,* 20:679–701.

Andrews, R., Boyne, G., Law, J., and Walker, R. (2005). External constraints on local service standards: The case of comprehensive performance assessment in English local government. *Public Administration,* 83:639–656.

Arrow, K. J. (1963). *Social choice and individual values,* 2nd ed. John Wiley, New York.

Audit Commission (2005). *CPA – the harder test.* Audit Commission, London.

Audit Commission (2009). *Final score: The impact of the comprehensive performance assessment of local government 2002–2008.* Audit Commission, London.

Banks, J. (1989). Agency budgets, cost information, and auditing. *American Journal of Political Science,* 33:670–699.

Banks, J., and Weingast, B. (1992). The political control of bureaucracies under asymmetric information. *American Journal of Political Science,* 36:509–524.

Barnard, C. I. (1938). *The functions of the executive.* Harvard University Press, Cambridge, Mass.

Battaglio, R. P., and Condrey, S. E. (2006). Civil service reform: Examining state and local government cases. *Review of Public Personnel Administration,* 26(2):118–138.

Behn, R. (2001). *Rethinking democratic accountability.* Brookings Institution Press, Washington, D.C.

Beik, M. (2005). *Labor relations.* Greenwood Press, Westport, Conn.

Bendor, J., and Mierowitz, A. (2004). Spatial models of delegation. *American Political Science Review,* 98:293–310.

Bendor, J., Taylor, S., and VanGaalen, R. (1985). Bureaucratic expertise versus legislative authority: A model of deception and monitoring in budgeting. *American Political Science Review*, 79:1041–1060.

Bendor, J., Taylor, S., and VanGaalen, R. (1987). Politicians, bureaucrats, and asymmetric information. *American Journal of Political Science*, 31:796–828.

Bertelli, A., and Feldmann, S. E. (2007). Strategic appointments. *Journal of Public Administration Research and Theory*, 17:19–38.

Bertelli, A., and John, P. (2010). Government checking government: How performance measures expand distributive politics. *Journal of Politics*, 72:545–558.

Bertelli, A. M., and Grose, C. R. (2009). Secretaries of pork? A new theory of distributive public policy. *Journal of Politics*, 71:926–945.

Bertelli, A. M., and Grose, C. R. (2011). The lengthened shadow of another institution: Ideal point estimates for the executive branch and congress. *American Journal of Political Science*, 55:767–786.

Bertelli, A. M., and Lynn, L. E. Jr. (2004). Policymaking in the parallelogram of forces: Common agency and human service provision. *Policy Studies Journal*, 32:297–315.

Bertelli, A. M., and Lynn, L. E. (2006). *Madison's managers: Public administration and the Constitution*. Johns Hopkins University Press, Baltimore, Md.

Bertelli, A. M., and Smith, C. R. (2010). Relational contracting and network management. *Journal of Public Administration Research and Theory*, 20:i21–i40.

Besley, T., and Ghatak, M. (2003). Incentives, choice, and accountability in the provision of public services. *Oxford Review of Economic Policy*, 19:235–249.

Bilodeau, N., Lauria, C., and Vining, A. (2006). Choice of organizational form makes a real difference: The impact of corporatization on government agencies in Canada. *Journal of Public Administration Research and Theory*, 17:119–147.

Black, D. (1958). *The theory of committees and elections*. Cambridge University Press, New York.

Bloomekatz, A. (2010). Following noise complaints, LAPD halts 24-hour construction of Westside rail line. *Los Angeles Times LA Now*. http://latimesblogs.latimes.com/lanow/2010/01/lapd-halts-24-hour-construction-of-westside-rail-line-noise-complaints.html

Boston, J., Martin, J., Pallot, J., and Walsh, P. (1996). *Public management: The New Zealand model*. Oxford University Press, Auckland, New Zealand.

Boyne, G. A., James, O., John, P., and Petrovsky, N. (2009). Democracy and government performance: Holding incumbents accountable in English local governments. *Journal of Politics*, 71:1273–1284.

Boyne, G. A., James, O., John, P., and Petrovsky, N. (2010). Does public service performance affect top management turnover? *Journal of Public Administration Research and Theory*, 20(Suppl. 2):i261–i279.

Bozeman, B. (1987). *All organizations are public: Bridging public and private organizational theories*, 1st ed. Jossey-Bass, San Francisco, Calif.

Breton, A., and Wintrobe, R. (1975). Equilibrium size of a budget-maximizing bureau: Note on Niskanen's theory of bureaucracy. *Journal of Political Economy*, 83:195–207.

Breul, J. (2007). Three Bush administration management reform initiatives: The president's management agenda, freedom to manage legislative proposals, and the program assessment rating tool. *Public Administration Review*, 67:21–26.

Broad, M., Goddard, A., and Alberti, L. V. (2007). Performance, strategy and accounting in local government and higher education in the UK. *Public Money and Management*, 27:119–126.

Brodsky, R. (2010). Pentagon abandons insourcing effort. *Government Executive*, August 10.

Brown, R. E. (1970). *The GAO: Untapped source of Congressional power*. University of Tennessee Press, Knoxville.

Brown, T. L., and Potoski, M. (2004). Managing the public service market. *Public Administration Review*, 64:656–668.

Brown, T. L., Potoski, M., and Van Slyke, D. M. (2009). Contracting for complex products. *Journal of Public Administration Research and Theory*, 20:141–158.

Browne, A., and Wildavsky, A. B. (1984). *Implementation as adaptation*. Berkeley, University of California Press.

Cain, B. E., Ferejohn, J. A., and Fiorina, M. P. (1987). *The personal vote: Constituency service and electoral independence*. Harvard University Press, Cambridge, Mass.

Callander, S. (2008). A theory of policy expertise. *Quarterly Journal of Political Science*, 3:123–140.

Carpenter, D. P. (2001). *The forging of bureaucratic autonomy: Reputations, networks, and policy innovation in executive agencies, 1862–1928*. Princeton University Press, Princeton, N.J.

Centers for Medicare and Medicaid Services (2007). Strong competition and beneficiary choices contribute to medicare drug coverage with lower costs than predicted. *CMS Fact Sheet*, August 13.

Clinton, J., Jackman, S., and Rivers, D. (2004). The statistical analysis of roll call data. *American Political Science Review*, 98:355–370.

Coase, R. H. (1937). The nature of the firm. *Economica*, 4:386–405.

Cohen, S., and Eimicke, W. (1994). The overregulated civil service: The case of New York City's personnel system. *Review of Public Personnel Administration*, 14:11–27.

Committee on the Budget, U.S. Senate (1998). *The congressional budget process: An explanation*, vol. 104-70. Government Printing Office, Washington, D.C.

Conybeare, J. (1984). Bureaucracy, monopoly, and competition – a critical analysis of the budget-maximizing model of bureaucracy. *American Journal of Political Science*, 28:479–502.

Cooper, P. J. (2003). *Governing by contract: Challenges and opportunities for public managers*. CQ Press, Washington, D.C.

Cremer, J., and Palfrey, T. (2000). Federal mandates by popular demand. *Journal of Political Economy*, 108:905–927.

Dahl, R. A. (1964). *Modern political analysis*. Prentice Hall, Englewood Cliffs, N.J.

Dahl, R. A., and Lindblom, C. E. (1953). *Politics, economics, and welfare: Planning and politico-economic systems resolved into basic social processes*. Harper, New York.

Davey, M. (2007). A bridge's private ownership raises concerns on security. *New York Times*, October 12.

de Tocqueville, A. ([1835] 2000). *Democracy in America*, 1st perennial classics ed. Perennial Classics, New York.

Dixit, A. K. (1996). *The making of economic policy: A transaction-cost politics perspective*. MIT Press, Cambridge, Mass.

Dixit, A. K. (2004). *Lawlessness and economics: Alternative modes of governance*. Princeton University Press, Princeton, N.J.

Downs, A. (1957). *An economic theory of democracy*. Harper, New York.

Downs, A. (1967). *Inside bureaucracy*. Little, Brown, Boston, Mass.

Duggan, M., and Morton, F. S. (2010). The effect of Medicare Part D on pharmaceutical prices and utilization. *American Economic Review*, 100:590–607.

Dupuit, J. (1853). On utility and its value. *Journal des Économistes*, 35:1–27.

Elster, J. (1986). *Rational choice*. New York University Press, New York.

Environmental Protection Agency (2006). *Existing contracts enabled EPA to quickly respond to Hurricane Katrina; future improvement opportunities exist*, Report No. 2006-P-00038. Washington, D.C.

Epstein, D., and O'Halloran, S. (1999). *Delegating powers: A transaction cost politics approach to policy making under separate powers*. Cambridge University Press, Cambridge, U.K.

Fenno, R. F. (1978). *Home style: House members in their districts*. HarperCollins, New York.

Ferejohn, J., and Krehbiel, K. (1987). The budget process and the size of the budget. *American Journal of Political Science*, 31:296–320.

Fernandez, S. (2007). What works best when contracting for services? An analysis of contracting performance at the local level in the U.S. *Public Administration*, 85:1119–1141.

Ferris, J., and Graddy, E. (1986). Contracting out: For what? With whom? *Public Administration Review*, 46:332–344.

Ferris, J., and Graddy, E. (1994). Organizational choices for public service supply. *Journal of Law, Economics, and Organization*, 10:126–141.

Finer, H. J. (1941). Administrative responsibility in democratic government. *Public Administration Review*, 1:335–350.

Flambard, V., and Perrigne, I. (2006). Asymmetry in procurement auctions: Evidence from snow removal contracts. *Economic Journal*, 116:1014–1036.

Francois, P. (2000). 'Public Service Motivation' as an argument for government provision. *Journal of Public Economics*, 78:275–299.

Friedrich, C. J. (1940). *Public policy and the nature of administrative responsibility*. Harvard University Press, Cambridge, Mass.

Frisco, V., and Stalebrink, O. J. (2008). Congressional use of the program assessment rating tool. *Public Budgeting and Finance*, 28:1–19.

Froelich, K. A. (1999). Diversification of revenue strategies: Evolving resource dependence in nonprofit organizations. *Nonprofit and Voluntary Sector Quarterly Report*, 28:246–286.

Frumkin, P. (2002). *On being nonprofit*. Harvard University Press, Cambridge, Mass.

Gailmard, S. (2009). Discretion rather than rules: Choice of instruments to control bureaucratic policy making. *Political Analysis*, 17:25–44.

Gailmard, S. (2010). Politics, principal–agent problems, and public service motivation. *International Public Management Journal*, 13:35–45.

Gailmard, S., and Patty, J. W. (2007). Slackers and zealots: Civil service, policy discretion, and bureaucratic expertise. *American Journal of Political Science*, 51:873–889.

Gambetta, D. (1994). Inscrutable markets. *Rationality and Society*, 6:353–368.

Game, C. (2006). Comprehensive performance assessment in English local government. *International Journal of Productivity and Performance Management*, 55:466–479.

Gazely, B. (2008). Beyond the contract: The scope and nature of informal government-nonprofit partnerships. *Public Administration Review*, 68:141–154.

Getting, I. (1993). Perspective/navigation: The global positioning system. *Spectrum, IEEE*, 30:36–38, 43–47.

Gilmour, J. B. (2007). Implementing OMB's Public Assessment Rating Tool (PART): Meeting the challenges of integrating budget and performance. *OECD Journal on Budgeting*, 7:1–40.

Gilmour, J. B., and Lewis, D. E. (2006a). Assessing performance budgeting at OMB: The influence of politics, performance, and program size. *Journal of Public Administration Research and Theory*, 16:169–186.

Gilmour, J. B., and Lewis, D. E. (2006b). Does performance budgeting work? An examination of the Office of Management and Budget's PART scores. *Public Administration Review*, 66:742–752.

Goldsmith, S., and Eggers, W. D. (2004). *Governing by network: The new shape of the public sector*. Brookings Institution Press, Washington, D.C.

Goodnow, F. J. (1900). *Politics and administration: A study in government*. Macmillan, New York.

Gosling, J. J. (2006). *Budgetary politics in American governments*, 4th ed. Routledge, New York.

Grimshaw, D., Vincent, S., and Willmott, H. (2002). Going privately: Partnership and outsourcing in UK public services. *Public Administration*, 80:475–502.

Gronbjerg, K. A., and Salamon, L. M. (2002). Devolution, marketization, and the changing shape of government–nonprofit relations. In Salamon, L., ed., *The state of nonprofit America*. Brookings Institution Press, Washington, D.C., 447–470.

Grossman, G. M., and Helpman, E. (2000). *Special interest politics*. MIT Press, Cambridge, Mass.

Grossman, G. M., and Helpman, E. (2008). Separation of powers and the budget process. *Journal of Public Economics*, 92:407–425.

Gueorguieva, V., Accius, J., Apaza, C., Bennett, L., Brownley, C., Cronin, S., and Preechyanud, P. (2009). The program assessment rating tool and the government performance and results act: Evaluating conflicts and disconnections. *American Review of Public Administration*, 39:225–245.

Hamilton, A., Madison, J., and Jay, J. (1982). *The Federalist papers*. New York: Bantam Books.

Hamman, J. R., Loewenstein, G., and Weber, R. A. (2010). Self-interest through delegation: An additional rationale for the principal–agent relationship. *American Economic Review*, 100:1826–1846.

Hammond, T. H., and Thomas, P. A. (1989). The impossibility of a neutral hierarchy. *Journal of Law, Economics, and Organization*, 5:155–184.

Hansmann, H. (1987). Economic theories of nonprofit organization. In Powell, W. W., ed., *The nonprofit sector: A research handbook*, pages 27–42. Yale University Press, New Haven, Conn.

Hays, S., and Sowa, J. (2006). A broader look at the "accountability" movement: Some grim realities in state civil service systems. *Review of Public Personnel Administration*, 26:102–117.

Hefetz, A., and Warner, M. (2004). Privatization and its reverse: Explaining the dynamics of the government contracting process. *Journal of Public Administration Research and Theory*, 14:171–190.

Heinrich, C. J., L. E., Lynn, Jr., and Milward, H. B. (2010). A state of agents? Sharpening the debate and evidence over the extent and impact of the transformation of governance. *Journal of Public Administration Research and Theory*, 20(Suppl. 1):i113–i19.

Hood, C. (1983). *The tools of government*. Macmillan, New York.

Hotelling, H. (1929). Stability in competition. *Economic Journal*, 39(153):41–57.

Hsu, S. S. (2007). FEMA accused of wasting more Katrina funding: $30 million misspent last year on trailers in Miss., GAO says. *Washington Post*, November 16.

Huber, J., and McCarty, N. (2004). Bureaucratic capacity, delegation, and political reform. *American Political Science Review*, 98:481–494.

Huber, J. D., and Shipan, C. R. (2002). *Deliberate discretion: The institutional foundations of bureaucratic autonomy*. Cambridge University Press, Cambridge, U.K.

Hutton, J. (2009). *Report to congressional committees. Coast Guard: Change in course improves deepwater management and overights, but outcome still uncertain*. General Accounting Office, Washington, D.C.

Indridason, I. H., and Kam, C. (2008). Cabinet reshuffles and ministerial drift. *British Journal of Political Science*, 38:621–656.

James, E. (1983). How nonprofits grow: A model. *Journal of Policy Analysis and Management*, 2:350–365.

James, O., and John, P. (2006). Public management at the ballot box: Performance information and electoral support for incumbent English local governments. *Journal of Public Administration Research and Theory*, 17:567–580.

John, P., and Ward, H. (2005). How competitive is competitive bidding? The case of the single regeneration budget program. *Journal of Public Administration Research and Theory*, 15:71–87.

Jones, B. D., and Baumgartner, F. R. (2005). *The politics of attention: How government prioritizes problems*. University of Chicago Press, Chicago, Ill.

Kettl, D. F. (1996). *Civil service reform: Building a government that works*. Brookings Institution Press, Washington, D.C.

Kooiman, J. (1993). *Modern governance: New government–society interactions*. Sage, London.

Krause, G. A. (2003). Coping with uncertainty: Analyzing risk propensities of SEC budgetary decisions, 1949–97. *American Political Science Review*, 97:171–188.

Krause, G. A., and Douglas, J. W. (2005). Institutional design versus reputational effects on bureaucratic performance: Evidence from U.S. government macroeconomic and fiscal projection. *Journal of Public Administration Research and Theory*, 15:263–280.

Krehbiel, K. (1991). *Information and legislative organization*. University of Michigan Press, Ann Arbor.

Krehbiel, K. (1998). *Pivotal politics: A theory of U.S. lawmaking*. University of Chicago Press, Chicago, Ill.

Kreps, D. M. (1990). Corporate culture and economic theory. In Alt, J. E., and Shepsle, K. A., eds., *Perspectives on positive political theory*, pages 90–144. Cambridge University Press, New York.

Kydland, F., and Prescott, E. (1977). Rules rather than discretion – inconsistency of optimal plans. *Journal of Political Economy*, 85:473–491.

Laffont, J.-J., and Tirole, J. (1993). *A theory of incentives in procurement and regulation*. MIT Press, Cambridge, Mass.

Le Grand, J. (1998). Ownership and social policy. *Political Quarterly*, 69:415–422.

Leibenstein, H. (1966). Allocative efficiency vs x-efficiency. *American Economic Review*, 56:392–415.

Leibenstein, H. (1987). *Inside the firm: The inefficiencies of hierarchy*. Harvard University Press, Cambridge, Mass.

Levitan, D. (1946). The responsibility of administrative officials in a democratic society. *Political Science Quarterly*, 61:562–598.

Lewis, D. E. (2008). *The politics of presidential appointments: Political control and bureaucratic performance*. Princeton University Press, Princeton, N.J.

Light, P. C. (2004). *Sustaining nonprofit performance: The case for capacity building and the evidence to support it*. Brookings Institution Press, Washington, D.C.

Lindblom, C. E. (1968). *The policy-making process*. Foundations of modern political science series. Prentice Hall, Englewood Cliffs, N.J.

Lipsky, M. (1980). *Street-level bureaucracy: Dilemmas of the individual in public services*. Russell Sage Foundation, New York.

Lipsky, M., and Smith, S. R. (1989). Nonprofit organizations, government and the welfare state. *Political Science Quarterly*, 104:625–648.

Lobeck, J. (2011). City making effort to support local businesses. *Yuma Sun*, January 5.

Lynn, L. E. (2010). Adaptation? Transformation? Both? Neither? The many faces of governance. In *Jerusalem Papers in Regulation and Governance*. Jerusalem: Hebrew University.

Lynn, L. E., Heinrich, C. J., and Hill, C. J. (2001). *Improving governance: A new logic for empirical research*. Georgetown University Press, Washington, D.C.

Maddaus, G. (2010). L.A.'s light rail fiasco: How rail service to the westside jumped the track. *LA Weekly*, December 2.

Maltese, G., ed. (2000). *The U.S. federal budget process*. Nova Scientific Publishers, Huntington, N.Y.

Marvel, M. K., and Marvel, H. P. (2007). Outsourcing oversight: A comparison for in-house and contracted services. *Public Administration Review*, 67:521–530.

Marvel, M. K., and Marvel, H. P. (2008). Government-to-government contracting: Stewardship, agency and substitution. *International Public Management Journal*, 11:171–192.

McCarty, N., and Poole, K. T. (1995). Veto power and legislation: An empirical analysis of executive and legislative bargaining from 1961–1986. *Journal of Law, Economics, and Organization*, 11:282–312.

McCubbins, M., and Schwartz, T. (1984). Congressional oversight overlooked – police patrols versus fire alarms. *American Journal of Political Science*, 28:165–179.

McCubbins, M., Noll, R., and Weingast, B. (1989). Structure and process, politics and policy – administrative arrangements and the political control of agencies. *Virginia Law Review*, 75:431–482.

McLean, B., and Elkind, P. (2003). *The smartest guys in the room: The amazing rise and scandalous fall of Enron*. Portfolio, New York.

Migué, J.-L., and Bélanger, G. (1974). Towards a general theory of management discretion. *Public Choice*, 17:27–43.

Mikesell, J. L. (2007). *Fiscal administration: Analysis and applications for the public sector*, 11th ed. Wadsworth, Belmont, Calif.

Miller, G., and Moe, T. (1983). Bureaucrats, legislators, and the size of government. *American Political Science Review*, 77:297–322.

Miller, H., and Simmons, J. (1998). The irony of privatization. *Administration and Society*, 30:513–532.

Miller, W. L. (1988). *Irrelevant elections? The quality of local democracy in Britain*. Clarendon Press, Oxford, U.K.

Millet, C., Everett, C. J., Matheson, E. M., Bindman, A. B., and Mainous, A. G. (2010). Impact of Medicare Part D on seniors' out-of-pocket expenditures on medications. *Archives of Internal Medicine*, 170:1325–1330.

Milward, B., and Provan, K. (2000). Governing the hollow state. *Journal of Public Administration Research and Theory*, 10:359–380.

Moe, T. M. (1995). *The politics of structural choice: Toward a theory of public bureaucracy*. Oxford University Press, New York.

Mosher, F. C. (1984). *A tale of two agencies: A comparative analysis of the General Accounting Office and the Office of Management and Budget*. Louisiana State University Press, Baton Rouge.

Mueller, D. C. (2003). *Public choice III*. Cambridge University Press, Cambridge, U.K.

Mullen, P. (2006). Performance-based budgeting: The contribution of the program assessment rating tool. *Public Budgeting and Finance*, 26:79–88.

Nagy, D. M. (2005). Playing peekaboo with constitutional law: The PCAOB and its public/private status. *Notre Dame Law Review*, 80:975–1071.

Niskanen, W. A. (1971). *Bureaucracy and representative government*. Aldine, Atherton, Chicago, Ill.

Niskanen, W. A. (1975). Bureaucrats and politicians. *Journal of Law and Economics*, 18:617–643.

Niskanen, W. A. (1991). *The budget-maximizing bureaucrat: Appraisals and evidence.* University of Pittsburgh Press, Pittsburgh, Pa.

North, D. C. (1990). *Institutions, institutional change, and economic performance.* Cambridge University Press, Cambridge, U.K.

Office of Management and Budget (2003). *Performance and management assessments, budget of the United States government, fiscal year 2004.* Government Printing Office, Washington, D.C.

Olsen, R., and Levy, D. (2004). Mathematica policy research. http://www.mathematica-mpr.com/publications/PDFs/OMBbudgeting.pdf.

Osborne, D. (1993). Reinventing government. *Public Productivity and Management Review*, 16:349–356.

Osborne, D., and Gaebler, T. (1992). *Reinventing government: How the entrepreneurial spirit is transforming the public sector.* Addison-Wesley, Reading, Mass.

Parker, F. (1931). Constructing and financing toll bridges. *Journal of Land and Public Utility Economics*, 7:127–137.

Pashukanis, E. B. (2002). *The general theory of law and Marxism.* Law and society series. Transaction, New Brunswick, N.J.

Pauly, M. V. (1974). Overinsurance and public provision of insurance – roles of moral hazard and adverse selection. *Quarterly Journal of Economics*, 88:44–62.

Peltzman, S. (1976). Toward a more general theory of regulation. *Journal of Law and Economics*, 19:211–240.

Pierre, J., and Peters, B. G. (2000). *Governance, politics, and the state.* St. Martin's Press, New York.

Pollack, H., and Zeckhauser, R. (1996). Budgets as dynamic gatekeepers. *Management Science*, 42:642–658.

Pollitt, C., and Bouckaert, G. (2004). *Public management reform: A comparative analysis*, 2nd ed. Oxford University Press, Oxford, U.K.

Poole, K. T., and Rosenthal, H. (1997). *Congress: A political–economic history of roll call voting.* Oxford University Press, New York.

Poole, K. T., and Rosenthal, H. (2007). *Ideology and Congress*, 2nd rev. ed. Transaction, New Brunswick, N.J.

Posner, P., and Fantone, D. (2007). Performance budgeting: Improving prospects for sustainability. *Public Performance and Management Review*, 30:351–368.

Pound, R. (1940). Administrative law: Its growth, procedures, and significance. Pittsburgh: University of Pittsburgh Press.

Prager, J. (1994). Contracting out government services: Lessons from the private sector. *Public Administration Review*, 54:176–184.

Pugh, D., Hickson, D., and Hinings, C. (1969). Empirical taxonomy of structures of work organizations. *Administrative Science Quarterly*, 14:115–126.

Putnam, R. D. (1995). Tuning in, tuning out: The strange disappearance of social capital in America. *PS: Political Science and Politics*, 28:664–683.

Ragavan, S., Partlow, J., and DeYoung, K. (2007). Blackwater faulted in military reports from the shooting scene. *Washington Post*, October 5.

Rainey, H. G., and Steinbauer, P. (1999). Galloping elephants: Developing elements of a theory of effective government organizations. *Journal of Public Administration Research and Theory*, 9:1–32.

Revelli, F. (2008). Performance competition in local media markets. *Journal of Public Economics*, 92:1585–1594.

Rhodes, J., Tyler, P., and Brennan, A. (2007). *The single regeneration budget: Final evaluation*. Department of Land Economy, Cambridge University, Cambridge, U.K.

Rhodes, R. A. W. (1997). *Understanding governance: Policy networks, governance, reflexivity, and accountability*. Open University Press, Buckingham, U.K.

Riker, W. H. (1993). The experience of creating institutions: The framing of the United States Constitution. In Sened, I., and Knight, J. H., eds., *Explaining social institutions*, pages 121–144. University of Michigan Press, Ann Arbor.

Rosenthal, D. (1996). Who "owns" aids service organizations? *Polity*, 29:97–118.

Sabatier, P. A. (2007). *Theories of the policy process*, 2nd ed. Westview Press, Boulder, Colo.

Salamon, L. (1987). Partners in public service: The scope and theory of government–nonprofit relations. In Powell, W., ed., *The nonprofit sector*, pages 99–117. Yale University Press, New Haven, Conn.

Salamon, L. M., and Elliott, O. V. (2002). *The tools of government: A guide to the new governance*. Oxford University Press, Oxford, U.K.

Samuelson, P. A. (1954). The pure theory of expenditure. *Review of Economics and Statistics*, 36:387–389.

Saturno, J. (2000). *The congressional budget process*. Washington, DC: Congressional Research Service.

Sclar, E. (2000). *You don't always get what you pay for: The economics of privatization*. Cornell University Press, Ithaca, N.Y.

Shaw, M., Levin, P., and Martel, J. (1999). The DOD: Stewards of a global information resource, the Navstar Global Positioning System. *Proceedings of the IEEE*, 87:16–23.

Shipan, C. (2000). The legislative design of judicial review – a formal analysis. *Journal of Theoretical Politics*, 12:269–304.

Shleifer, A. (1998). State versus private ownership. *Journal of Economic Perspectives*, 12:133–150.

Shuman, H. E. (1992). *Politics and the budget: The struggle between the president and Congress*. Prentice Hall, Armonk, N.Y.

Simon, H. A., Smithburg, D. W., and Thompson, V. A. (1950). *Public administration*. Knopf, New Brunswick, N.J.

Singer, P. (2003). *Corporate warriors: The rise of the privatized military industry*. Cornell University Press, Ithaca, N.Y.

Singer, P. (2007). Sure he's got guns for hire, but they're just not worth it. *Washington Post*, Opinions Section, October 7.

Skelcher, C. (2005). Public–private partnerships and hybridity. In Ferlie, E., Lynn, L. E., Jr., and Pollitt, C. eds., *Oxford Handbook of Public Management*, pp. 347–370. Oxford University Press, New York.

Skinner, Q. (1989). The state. In Ball, T., Farr, J., and Hanson, R. L., eds., *Political innovation and conceptual change*, pages 90–131. Cambridge University Press, Cambridge, U.K.

Smith, B. (2006). *Space-based positioning, navigation and timing police: The tension between military and civil requirements.* U.S. Army War College, Carlisle Barracks, Pa.

Smith, J. F. (2006). Budgeting for disasters: Part I. Overview of the problem. *Public Manager*, 35:11–19.

Smith, S. R., and Lipsky, M. (1993). *Nonprofits for hire: The welfare state in the age of contracting.* Harvard University Press, Cambridge, Mass.

Stalebrink, O. (2009). National performance mandates and intergovernmental collaboration: An examination of the Program Assessment Rating Tool (PART). *American Review of Public Administration*, 39:619–639.

Stephenson, M. (2006). Legislative allocation of delegated power: Uncertainty, risk, and the choice between agencies and courts. *Harvard Law Review*, 119:1035–1070.

St. John, S. (2010). Landmark $13.3 million grant to fund L.A. gay and lesbian center's development of model program to serve LGBTQ foster youth. Press release, Los Angeles Gay and Lesbian Center.

Stone, G. R. (1991). *Constitutional law*, 2nd ed. Little, Brown, Boston, Mass.

Stone, M., Hager, M., and Griffin, J. (2001). Nonprofit organizational characteristics and funding environments: A study of a population of United Way–affiliated nonprofits. *Public Administration Review*, 61:276–289.

Suarez, D. F. (2010). Collaboration and professionalization: The contours of public sector funding for nonprofit organizations. *Journal of Public Administration Research and Theory*, Advance Access, September 3.

Super, D. A. (2008). Privatization, policy paralysis and the poor. *California Law Review*, 96:393–469.

Taborek, N. (2009). Delays won't derail expo project. *Santa Monica Daily Press*, December 19.

Templar, R. (2005). *The rules of management.* Upper Saddle River, NJ: Pearson Education.

Ting, M. (2001). The "power of the purse" and its implications for bureaucratic policy-making. *Public Choice*, 106:243–274.

Ting, M. (2011). Organizational capacity. *Journal of Law Economics and Organization*, 27:245–271.

Tomkin, S. L. (1998). *Inside OMB: Politics and process in the President's Budget Office.* M. E. Sharpe, Armonk, N.Y.

Tullock, G. (1965). *The politics of bureaucracy.* Public Affairs Press, Washington, D.C.

Tymon, S. (2008). Panel takes up rail safety: The PUC will decide whether planners have taken steps to protect students at 2 campuses along L.A.'s expo line. *Los Angeles Times*, November 28.

U.S. General Accounting Office (2007). *Government auditing standards*, rev. July 2007 ed. U.S. General Accounting Office, Washington, D.C.

U.S. House of Representatives (2007). *Memorandum: Additional information about Blackwater USA*. Committee on Oversight and Government Reform, Washington, D.C.

Van Slyke, D. M. (2006). Agents or stewards: Using theory to understand the government–nonprofit social service contracting relationship. *Journal of Public Administration Research and Theory*, 17:157–187.

Vining, A. R., and Boardman, A. F. (1992). Ownership versus competition: Efficiency in public enterprise. *Public Choice*, 73:205–239.

Volden, C. (2002). A formal model of the politics of delegation in a separation of powers system. *American Journal of Political Science*, 46:111–133.

Volden, C. (2005). Intergovernmental political competition in American federalism. *American Journal of Political Science*, 49:327–342.

Warren, P. (2011). Allies and adversaries: The roles of appointees in administrative policymaking in a separation of powers system. *Journal of Law, Economics, and Organization*, forthcoming.

Weber, M. (1964). *The theory of social and economic organization*. Free Press, New York.

Weibel, A., Rost, K., and Osterloh, M. (2010). Pay for performance in the public sector – benefits in (hidden) costs. *Journal of Public Administration Research and Theory*, 20:387–412.

Weikel, D. (2009). Citing student safety, school board opposes expo line rail route. *Los Angeles Times*, June 24.

Weimer, D. L., and Vining, A. R. (2005). *Policy analysis: Concepts and practice*, 4th ed. Pearson Prentice Hall, Upper Saddle River, N.J.

Weingast, B., and Marshall, W. (1988). The industrial-organization of Congress – or, why legislatures, like firms, are not organized as markets. *Journal of Political Economy*, 96:132–163.

Weisbrod, B. A. (1988). *The nonprofit economy*. Harvard University Press, Cambridge, Mass.

Whitford, A. B. (2003). *Adapting agencies: Competition, imitation, and punishment in the design of bureaucratic performance*. University of Michigan Press, Ann Arbor.

Wildavsky, A. B. (1984). *The politics of the budgetary process*, 4th ed. Little, Brown, Boston, Mass.

Williamson, O. E. (1985). *The economic institutions of capitalism: Firms, markets, relational contracting*. Free Press, New York.

Williamson, O. E. (1996). *The mechanisms of governance*. Oxford University Press, New York.

Willoughby, W. (1913). Allotment of funds by executive officials, an essential feature of any correct budgetary system. *American Political Science Review*, 7:78–87.

Wilson, J. Q. (1989). *Bureaucracy: What government agencies do and why they do it*. Basic Books, New York.

Wittwer, J., and Renkl, A. (2010). How effective are instructional explanations in example-based learning? A meta-analytic review. *Educational Psychology Review*, 22:393–409.

Young, D. R., and Salamon, L. M. (2002). Commercialization, social ventures, and for-profit competition. In Salamon, L., ed., *The state of nonprofit America*. Brookings Institution Press, Washington, D.C., 423–446.

Zacharias, P. (2007). The building of the ambassador bridge. *The Detroit News*, http://info.detnews.com/.

Zucker, A. (2009). The role of nonprofits in educational technology innovation. *Journal of Science Education and Technology*, 18:37–47.

Index